Agatha Christie
Under the
Magnifying Glass

ALSO BY NICHOLAS BIRNS
AND FROM MCFARLAND

Anthony Trollope: A Companion
(by Nicholas Birns and John F. Wirenius, 2021)

Agatha Christie Under the Magnifying Glass
Close Readings of 12 Novels

Margaret Boe Birns
and Nicholas Birns

McFarland & Company, Inc., Publishers
Jefferson, North Carolina

LIBRARY OF CONGRESS CATALOGING-IN-PUBLICATION DATA

Names: Birns, Margaret Boe, 1940– author | Birns, Nicholas author
Title: Agatha Christie under the magnifying glass : close readings of 12 novels / Margaret Boe Birns and Nicholas Birns.
Description: Jefferson, North Carolina : McFarland & Company, Inc, 2026 | Includes bibliographical references and index.
Identifiers: LCCN 2025042736 | ISBN 9781476698373 paperback ∞
    ISBN 9781476656359 ebook
Subjects: LCSH: Christie, Agatha, 1890-1976—Criticism and interpretation | Detective and mystery stories, English—History and criticism | BISAC: LITERARY CRITICISM / Mystery & Detective | LITERARY CRITICISM / Women Authors | LCGFT: Literary criticism
Classification: LCC PR6005.H66 Z5626 2025
LC record available at https://lccn.loc.gov/2025042736

ISBN (print) 978-1-4766-9837-3
ISBN (ebook) 978-1-4766-5635-9

© 2026 Margaret Boe Birns and Nicholas Birns. All rights reserved

No part of this book may be reproduced or transmitted in any form or by any means, electronic or mechanical, including photocopying or recording, or by any information storage and retrieval system, without permission in writing from the publisher.

Front cover image: © Cristina Conti/Shutterstock.

Printed in the United States of America

McFarland & Company, Inc., Publishers
  Box 611, Jefferson, North Carolina 28640
    www.mcfarlandpub.com

To our friend and neighbor
Riecelle Dubitsky Schecter

Acknowledgments

Margaret Boe Birns—Adam Sexton, my dean at New York University, who gave me the green light to change his proposed course on Sherlock Holmes to my inaugural class on Agatha Christie way back in the 20th century; Helen Wells; Dilys Winn; all my warm, witty, wise, wonderful Agatha Christie students at New York University and The New School past and present; the late John Dobby Boe and the late Herb Foerstel, the best brothers a girl could have.

Nicholas Birns—The late John Dobby Boe and the late Herb Foerstel, the best uncles a boy could have. My beautiful wife, Isabella Smalera-Birns; Batman, Emerson, and the groundhog; the Metuchen Public Library for being a great place to research detective fiction; and in recognition of, as my mother once put it, "the essential mysteriousness of things."

We both thank Elizabeth Foxwell and the team at McFarland for their help in bringing this book about.

Table of Contents

Acknowledgments — vi
Preface — 1
Introduction: Closely Reading Agatha Christie — 3

1. The Innocence Project: *The Murder of Roger Ackroyd* — 19
2. The Guilty Vicarage: *The Murder at the Vicarage* — 37
3. Rough Justice: *Murder on the Orient Express* — 55
4. The Wheel of Fortune: *The ABC Murders* — 70
5. Patriots and Traitors: *N or M?* — 86
6. Deep Egypt: *Death Comes as the End* — 101
7. Flight from the Enchanter: *Towards Zero* — 117
8. The Artist Is Present: *The Hollow* — 131
9. The Murder Game: *A Murder Is Announced* — 151
10. Time Shelter: *At Bertram's Hotel* — 165
11. Peacocks and Pretenders: *Third Girl* — 178
12. No More Murders: *Curtain* — 196

Bibliography — 213
Index — 217

Preface

Our analyses within the work before you will examine how particular characters, phrases, contexts, and plot lines contribute to the success of Agatha Christie's authorial compositions. But we will also look at them as they tear against the seams and beg for the scrutiny that goes outside the text as traditionally conceived. Rather than concentrating exclusively on overall themes, tropes, and effects in her oeuvre (as in Tison Pugh's 2023 *Understanding Agatha Christie*), our emphasis on the uncertainties of particularity leads us to also concentrate on individual works by Christie.

This book includes an introduction and 12 chapters devoted to reading Christie's novels, featuring 12 specific books. We start with the 1920s in *The Murder of Roger Ackroyd*, go through the 1930s with *The Murder at the Vicarage, Murder on the Orient Express*, and *The ABC Murders* to the 1940s with *N or M?, Death Comes as the End, Towards Zero*, and *The Hollow*, to the 1950s with *A Murder Is Announced*, to the 1960s with *At Bertram's Hotel* and *Third Girl*, and finally to a book published in the 1970s though written decades earlier, *Curtain*.

The number of books covered both gives a representative sample of Christie's astoundingly prolific oeuvre and allows for enough variety in genres, modes, and decades to show the diversity of Christie's corpus. The number of articles and book chapters published this century that have concentrated on just one novel of Christie's show that, despite a prejudicial presumption that her work is sufficiently formulaic to make many of her books similar to each other, Christie's novels, as with those of Anthony Trollope or James Fenimore Cooper, feature sufficient differences thematically, structurally, and historically.

Even if the author's overall oeuvre has a tighter set of defining characteristic than is the case of other authors, Christie's novels possess enough integrity in themselves to be considered on their own.

Though we have not explored the short stories or the Mary Westmacott novels, instead concentrating exclusively on Christie as the author of detective and crime novels, we wish to convey both how various her fictional practice is and the different reading strategies they necessitate. Understanding the diversity of Christie's oeuvre also means situating her work in history, especially given that her career spans more than half the 20th century. Christie's novels are never static; they always depict change not just in individual and social terms. Even in *Death Comes as the End*, her historical mystery set in ancient Egypt, is positioned at a hinge of crisis and revival for that society. Christie's oeuvre, indeed, is well positioned to show that close reading does not and cannot operate to the exclusion of historical or social contexts.

With the publication of Gill Plain's *Agatha Christie: A Very Short Introduction* by Oxford University Press in 2025, the years 2020–2025 will have seen a flourishing of commentary on Christie's work that is unprecedented, with contributions by J.C. Bernthal, Mark Aldridge, Jessica Gildersleeve, Alistair Rolls, and many others, including scholars working outside the English-speaking world. Our hope is to contribute to this renaissance in Christie studies by focusing on the dynamics and architectonics of what make her individual novels so distinctive and how those novels underscore traits operative in her entire oeuvre.

Introduction

Closely Reading Agatha Christie

Originally Agatha Christie was known almost exclusively for her ingenious puzzles. Even though no more than three-fifths of her literary oeuvre is devoted to puzzle-oriented novels, she is still often associated only with her brilliant plots and narrative strategies. There was little recognition of her as a novelist concerned with character, motive, setting, and society. Since 1990, awareness of Christie's literary importance has increased. She has been the focus of a small if articulate body of critical work, even as continued strong book sales and media adaptations have made her corpus a part of the 21st-century cultural landscape, where she is recognized, in J.C. Bernthal's phrase, as "a significant historical figure and a genre innovator" (Bernthal, *Ageless*, 4–5).

Later, she came to be recognized as a thriller writer; her safe, cozy settings were dismantled, exposing a dark underworld that fed fear and anxiety. Even her ingenious narratives could cause discomfort, with her surprise endings trending into shock, and her twists of plot humbling many a proud mind. As Raymond Chandler noted in his *The Simple Art of Murder*, which did so much to derogate Christie's reputation and raise that of Chandler's own hardboiled method in literary-critical esteem, Christie's *Murder on the Orient Express* did indeed "knock the keenest mind for a loop," a comment followed by a face-saving, defensive quip that waves the flag of surrender even as it suggests "only a halfwit could guess it" (Chandler 9).

Even her puzzles, then, are provocative and complicated and lead us into a fertile darkness that is the foundation of Christie's work. There is uncertainty and disorder underneath her cozy worlds, which, far from remaining conservative enclaves, address modern times; modern problems; and the realities of war, social change, unraveling traditions, and emerging and multiple modernities.

But although Christie's work features consistent themes and patterns, our examination of 12 important mysteries by Agatha Christie will address each mystery novel as specifically itself. Each novel will bring its own literary references, historical background, psychology of character, narrative strategies, its own often untidy moral and ethical explorations of the mysteries and surprises that belong to life and which are there to remind us of the continued existence of the vast and unknowable.

We assume that Christie, however popular and commercially successful were her mysteries, and however less-than-highbrow her reputation in her lifetime, has entered the high-literary canon of the 21st century, just as musicals like *Show Boat* and *Carousel* are now in opera houses, performed in the same context as Massenet or Gluck. One of the messages conveyed by the operatic canon's absorption of these once merely popular forms is that they can now be experienced and analyzed as operas; another is that there was always *sub rosa*, an operatic influence on the 20th-century musical theater. Equally, Christie's mysteries can now, under the aegis of a more heterodox approach to canons and literariness, be interpreted as high literature in another sense: the ghosts of high-literary forms haunt Christie's oeuvre, complicating her reputation as simply a writer of "whodunits." That Christie wrote several "straight" novels under the pseudonym of Mary Westmacott, and that these coincided with arguably her deepest and most moving literary period, including novels such as *Towards Zero*, *The Hollow*, and *A Murder Is Announced*, argues for permeability between her stories and a broader variety of novelistic forms.

Christie has not often been closely read. There have been exceptions—the commentary of Julian Maclaren-Ross in British newspapers of the 1950s comes to mind, the final chapter of Richard York's *Power and Illusion*—but these have been rare. Even those who have appreciated Christie's artistry and craft have tended to admire her in thematic ways, and not through scrupulous attention to a specific text. Part of this insufficiency is that it was not until 1990 or so that Christie was taken seriously in literary terms. Critics such as Gillian Gill, R.A. York, and, more recently, J.C. Bernthal, Merja Makinen, Gill Plain, and Tison Pugh have written about Christie in modes and styles analogous to the way other important 20th-century British writers are addressed. She is no longer placed within a popular culture that can sharply be distinguished from high culture. Bernthal, Nicola Humble, and Alison Light have all positioned Christie as a writer to be understood via middlebrow reading habits and cultural forms.

But surely Christie's continued success in the 21st century has put her in a different category from writers such as Jan Struther (whose *Mrs. Miniver* no longer possesses a wide public) or E.M. Delafield (whose stories of a "Provincial Lady" owe their 21st-century canonicity to feminist presses and readers reviving her in a primarily academic context) or writers such as Taylor Caldwell and R.F. Delderfield, with whom Christie shared space on bestseller lists in the 1960s and early 1970s, but whose cultural impact has now ceased.

Christie's multimedia popularity continues as evidenced by Kenneth Branagh's cycle of adaptations and her mysteries are still prominent in public libraries and bookstores. Even the controversy over publishers changing her words to exclude racist or other outdated attitudes indicates Christie's continued importance; there is no need to update or sugarcoat something archival that merely catered to a particular age's consumer preference. After a certain point, a literary classic is a book that lasts—that is, a book that can travel through time and land in a completely different era. In the 19th century, Dickens might have seemed a much more popular writer than Thackeray or George Eliot, but now all three are on the Victorian literature syllabus together.

Indeed, Christie's French reception, as evidenced by Pierre Bayard and Michel Houellebecq's praise of Christie and Pascal Thomas's adaptation of *Towards Zero*, is already evaluating her as a highbrow writer to be scrutinized in ways usually afforded to highbrow writers. The same may ensue, *mutatis mutandis*, in the Anglosphere.

Christie was situated in a middlebrow context in her day, but writers of the 20th century are still culturally viable in the 21st and have undergone an alchemy of survival that has transmuted them into something at least classic enough to outlive all their original readers.

In addition, as productive as middlebrow studies have been in rehabilitating the importance of previously critically slighted early- and mid-20th century writers, there remains an element of aesthetic condescension to them. Humble, for instance, in her online essay "The Pleasures of Reading: Camp and the Middlebrow," characterized Nancy Mitford's novels as "brittle comedies of social snobbery," but an aesthetic assessment of Mitford's work has to contend with the fact not only were Mitford's politics, as Laura Thompson (also Christie's biographer) notes, "more to the left" (Thompson, *The Six*, 178), brittle as Mitford may be, her work is read and discussed in the 21st century in a way that is not true of more robust novelists such as Harvey Swados or Stanley Middleton.

This development is discernible in the case of Christie as well. Part of aesthetic distinction is simply remaining in the public taste even as the very nature (and, particularly, demographic profile) of "the public" has changed over a century's time. It would do well to bear in mind Frank Kermode's definition of the classic as those texts that succeed in "working through time, across generations" (Kermode 43), and that Christie, even if not receiving aesthetic kudos in her day, is becoming a classic in what Kermode calls a "humbler" (43) way, having not been originally received in a middlebrow context of taste.

That Christie has been read frequently in more thematic ways and under the aegis of popular culture and cultural studies, does, though, mean that she has been addressed through techniques of what Franco Moretti has termed "distant reading"—reading in terms of sales, the aggregate number and composition of her audience, library holdings, and as a literary phenomenon of print culture. This emphasis on reception and publication contexts means that close reading, when it occurs, is not and cannot be hermetically sealed off from "distant reading," the social/historical context. The configuration that close reading assumed in the New Criticism of the 1950s insisted on severing the aesthetic from social, cultural, and affective determinants. But we do not have to do this, nor does the practice of close reading have to do this in general. Close reading pays heed to what the text is in itself, even as it acknowledges there are inevitably supplementary interpretive and contextual factors. Thus, our close readings will reveal subtexts of which Christie might not have either intended or approved; as Dougal McNeill advises, close reading should sometimes be "too close for comfort" (McNeill 22).

There is also the possibility of what might be called a "middle-distance reading" that keeps the text in view but not as the exclusive focus; when our argument dilates the texts under scrutiny to reflect wider social and cultural horizons, it solicits this interpretive middle distance. "Middle distance," a term from early modern landscape painting, emerges most fruitfully for the current conversation in Frances Ferguson's 1993 book *Solitude and the Sublime*. Here, Ferguson speaks of nature as adept at producing "striking particulars" yet has a problem with "organizing particulars within harmonious relationships." Composition, Ferguson says, involves the observer "supplying a middle distance" (138). The host of particulars in Christie's novel are even more numerous than in a standard realistic fiction because of the way most particulars function as clues or are situated within the guiding frameworks of her plots, often in tantalizingly mysterious ways.

In general, we follow what Stephen Knight, in his 2014 book *Secrets of Crime Fiction Classics*, calls the need to "pay attention to the voices of the texts themselves" (Knight 4). We also agree with Knight that "to make the text speak it is first necessary to give an account of it" (14).

Such a particular-focused account might seem like a mere synopsis. But here we need to take stock of the major use of the word "synopsis" in English—the three synoptic Gospels (see Dungan), whose agreement on the essential facts of Jesus' ministry is remarkable in the light of the

Introduction

mystery and controversy surrounding that figure. Though the stakes are, to put it mildly, not entirely as high in the case of the detective genre, both the customary highbrow condemnation of that genre and the way that basic facts of the situation are in question in detective stories, means that what might seem to be synopsis has a more strategic and interpretive direction.

A 21st-century critical paradigm for reading Christie that counters Knight's approach might be the "irreverent reading" (Rolls and Gulddal 8) called for by Alistair Rolls and Jesper Gulddal, as in Gulddal's demonstrating (addressed in Chapter 3) the limitations of Poirot's ratiocinative authority in *Murder on the Orient Express*. These irreverent rereadings trespass the assumed contours of the text, especially in refusing the determinate solutions proffered by the plots and exploring alternate narratological and discursive scenarios. Rolls' and Gulddal's approaches are generally although not exclusively inspired by Pierre Bayard, whose reading of *The Murder of Roger Ackroyd* will be addressed in Chapter 1. Bayard's "counterinvestigative" reading of Ackroyd turns the text's procedural logic against itself and shows how, despite that novel's radical narrative procedure, that procedure can, in turn, be subject to interpretive question.

"Irreverent reading" (Rolls and Gulddal 8) is an effective close reading strategy of Christie because, as Rolls and Gulddal state, Christie criticism has been encumbered both by stereotypes of her work and conventional expectations of the detective story itself. We propose a mode of reading that is irreverent enough not to transcend the literal level of the text, yet not so irreverent as to fail to respect the text's primary intelligence, as in Wayne Booth's model of an implied author, with whom the reader can engage in a mutually responsive dialogue. In other words, a rewarding close reading of Christie is not mandated as simply a one-sided readerly jouissance, even if the narrative strategies at work are not always consciously intended.

One rejoinder to this technique vis-à-vis Christie would be that however bracing the critical legerdemain and however impressive the interpretive bravura of such an approach, Christie's texts have not really received adequate recognition on their own terms. Indeed, even in the 2020s, it is podcasts such as Kemper Donovan and the late Catherine Brobeck's "All About Agatha" and Caroline Crampton's "Shedunnit" that take a painstaking exegetical approach to her texts. And there certainly have been some strong recent readings of individual novels, such as Sylvia A. Pamboukian's 2024 reading of Christie's neglected *The Pale Horse* which takes the novel "beyond the puzzle plot and into the seemingly marginal details" (Pamboukian 75). Though we do not abandon the puzzle plot entirely, our approach to reading Agatha Christie tracks that of Pamboukian, which in turn is a viable alternative to the more radical approach of Bayard, Rolls, and Gulddal.

On one level, we are, as Peter Brooks put it, "reading for the plot," and since her narratives are themselves so highly dependent on the plot, this kind of surface reading is required. Colleen Ruth Rosenfeld has also spoken of "metaphrasis," a mode of paraphrase that also elucidates and pluralizes interpretive meaning. In our case, paying close attention to plot turns and minor characters highlights details that an exclusively whodunnit-oriented reading of the book might obscure.

There are many ways in which close reading, as a practice, is relevant to Christie. One is that the timespan of her literary production, from the 1920s to the 1970s, is exactly the period in which close reading comes into play in literary practice. Whether through the New Critics, the Russian Formalists, or critics of fiction such as Percy Lubbock and Mark Schorer, this is the era in which close reading becomes the model par excellence of literary criticism.

Furthermore, even though Christie's novels emphasize elements—an exciting plot, a clear easy-to-read style, an avoidance of explicitly edgy locales, subjects, or techniques—that are not in synch with literary modernism, her novels do include certain elements that would gain the approval of close readers of high literary fiction. These include the brevity of Christie's novels; their status as closely integrated, autotelic units rather than loose, baggy monsters. Her work conforms more to the modern short form than to the novel in the way we feel a rapid rearrangement of our perceptions, introducing a sense of unexpected revelation. There is modernity, too, in the way that narrative point-of-view, or "consciousness" matters; that, by the very mission of keeping a narrative secret, her narratives dispose of the omniscient narrators so often favored by the 19th-century novel; and the way so much of each novel's meaning is disclosed between the lines or in dialogue.

Thus, Christie writes the same sort of novel that is approved for close-reading practice. We are now able to recognize this because there is no longer the 20th-century practice of separating literary modernism from other texts of the time deemed insufficiently modern. By emphasizing the modern period rather than a modernism as such, what was a small and exclusive 20th-century British canon has diversified, particularly, as Alison Light has argued, by the inclusion of women writers once thought to be too conservative, traditionalist, or referential. As Elizabeth Pender has recently pointed out, newly canonical modern-period writers have not received the benefits of the close reading applied in their reception history to well-ensconced modernists. Closely reading Christie is part of this project of critical reclamation, inclusion, and diversification.

Introduction

The second way close reading is particularly present in Christie is through the concept of what Sharon Marcus and Stephen Best have termed "surface reading." By this, they mean looking at what is there in the text rather than leaping off the page to do suspicious, symptomatic readings, guided by Freudianism and Marxism, readings that scant what is present in the book in favor of what is absent or in favor of what can be read ideologically or theoretically. This might be particularly apt for Christie, who, as J.C. Bernthal puts it, "positively dwells on surfaces" (Bernthal, *Queering Agatha Christie* 103).

In Christie's *A Murder Is Announced*, there is an obvious example of this. Miss Hinchcliffe and Miss Murgatroyd are presented as a lesbian couple, although established so with considerable reticence on Christie's part. For all that *A Murder Is Announced* tries to keep up with the changed, postwar conditions of Labour England, the most radical move made by Christie in the book is right on the surface—to simply include Murgatroyd and Hinchcliffe in the community. The surface consideration of this relationship is as much a part of the novel's portrayal of a changed, postwar rural England as its other representations of diversity. Indeed, as so often in Christie, details included in the puzzle enrich the literary texture as well. In *A Murder Is Announced*, one of the clues to the identity of the murderer is a pet cat who also doubles as a witty historical reference. Without closely attending to what is on the page, we will not adequately register the very carefully arranged stage set Christie has prepared for us.

Furthermore, what might be called the minor characters in Christie's novels—characters who might be suspects—are given greater consideration through the practice of close reading. Critics have often scanted these characters because, if one assumes the centrality of the whodunit mode to Christie's fictions, the minor characters are there as red herrings to swell the plot or to start a scene or two as reshufflings of stock stereotypes. But these characters often supply the novelistic base that gives ballast to the book's manifest puzzles or work out larger social and representational issues that are important to the concerns of the novel beyond the plot.

As we shall see in Charles Kent and Ursula Bourne in *The Murder of Roger Ackroyd*, Gladys Cram and Mr. Stone in *The Murder at the Vicarage*, Megan Barnard in *The ABC Murders*, and Thomas Royde and Ted Latimer in *Towards Zero*, these characters can be elucidated and analyzed in ways like characters in 19th-century realistic fiction. They may have specific role in Christie's novels as false leads to keep our attention away from the actual murderer, but this does not mean they do not matter in other narrative terms.

Furthermore, Christie's use of names is key not only to her criminals but also to the subordinate characters. Many of her character names comment on class, ethnic, regional, or attitudinal divisions within England. Thus, paying attention to the grammar of her *dramatis personae* is to understand the nuances of her social representation.

A close reading of Christie will show us that her narrative strategies establish her as a novelist of consciousness. The ingenuity of her puzzles, the teasing relationship she constructs with her readers, her pacing and capacity to control her narrative through what she chooses to conceal or reveal, and especially the activation of free cognitive play are examples of how Christie will alter the consciousness of her readers. All mystery writers use a variation of these strategies, but it is Christie who is particularly adept at keeping control of the mind of the reader, guiding the reader to construct a perspective in which the truth is no longer self-evident, but concealed and must be discovered—it is a truth we must find.

As Richard York in *Power and Illusion* notes, what you see may be not all there is; or, far more likely, all there is may be unavailable simply because we have the wrong perspective. We have been invited inside the limited box Christie has created for us, and we will find it difficult to think outside it. She has closed us off from a solution that will be disclosed only after we have developed a more open and questioning sensibility. Her introduction of an element of play can produce a state of trance in which the reader can consider and imagine options and alternatives and develop a readiness to consent to the ingenious solution Christie finally supplies. As Marcel Danesi notes in "The Puzzle Instinct," a positive mood is the best requirement for new insights, the acceptance of new information, or the use of the imagination.

One layer of Christie's narratives centers on constructing that light-hearted, high-spirited, open, and receptive mode of consciousness associated with the playing of a game—a mood that will enhance the reader's ability to cognitively reappraise a narrative thread or a character. A sense of humor is part of this: as the philosophical team of Matthew M. Hurley, Daniel C. Dennett, and Reginald B. Adams, Jr., note in their book on humor, humor is linked to thinking, to human cognition. The humor we will find in Christie's mysteries provide us with an agility that can look beyond our assumptions or first impressions. And, as Hurley suggests, may be the way the brain rewards itself for being mistaken—if we can sustain a large comic perspective, we can self-correct with surprising agility. It is only if we are put in a dark place psychologically that we will double down on our previous, false narrative and resist coming to understand what it is we did not know, but what we somehow could have or should have known.

But since Christie's narrative strategies elevate the idea of comic play, we are more likely to tolerate our numerous mistakes or misreadings or misdirections. The great lesson of her game is one of the basic tenets of her mysteries: the player must never assume. She is also reminding us that in our daily lives we think our assumptions are correct—as Kathryn Schulz notes in *Being Wrong*, we generally feel we are "basically right, basically all the time, about basically everything" (Schulz 4). When reading a Christie novel, however, the rules of her game mean we can never be sure about our readings. The reader's task is to reconsider, rethink and even reread to discover the true, hidden story. This deliberate disorientation leads to a useful recognition that what we know, or think we know is always open to discussion, to question: in novelist Zia Haider Rahman's words, "Everything new is on the rim of our view, in the darkness, below the horizon, so that nothing new is visible but in the light of what we know" (Rahman 290).

Hercule Poirot, like Sherlock Holmes before him, promises us that he will always be right. He assures the characters and the reader that he will solve the mystery. But is Poirot always right? Certainly, he always is right about who it is that committed the crime. But a close reading of Christie will show that Poirot can come to controversial conclusions concerning crime, punishment, justice. Theoretically a detective in a mystery story is impartial, "scientific." Poirot's identity as a Belgian suggests this—a stranger on English ground, he would have no interest in any particular outcome, other than that it be fair and accurate. And there is a suggestion that Poirot is not only detached from English soil, at times he even does not seem to be from planet earth.

As Marysa Demoor has argued, Poirot is always "the other." That he is Belgian has to do with the Belgian refugees encountered by Christie in World War I, who are conveniently "othered" in terms of language (Francophone at least in the case of Poirot's Walloon community), religion (Catholic) and, more generally, the enigmatically continental. On a geopolitical level, England was also deeply invested in Belgium's independence to preserve a balance of power on the continent—the very reason England had sanctioned and encouraged Belgian independence in 1830. It was to come to the defense of Belgium that England declared war on Germany, which had in October 1914 occupied nearly all that country.

Belgium has been of strategic importance to England since Sir Philip Sidney died at Zutphen, in defense of the Low Countries against the Spanish. That, indeed, Hercule Poirot is a Belgian at all, that there is a "Belgium," is owed to specifically English valuation of Belgium as a crucial ally. Belgium was also admired by the English as gallant in their opposition to the invading Germans, lending Poirot a certain automatic heroic status. Christie took this self/other ambiguity regarding the Belgians, and apply it to Poirot, providing him with the sense of mystery necessary to all truly great detectives. Poirot is the subject of a paradoxical and simultaneous othering that provides him with a numinous unknowability.

It is that sense of trust/distrust that Christie deploys beyond Poirot's identity as a Belgian. For instance, while Christie never permits us to second-guess Poirot's solution to the mystery—these we must always trust—there is more ambiguity introduced in the way the reader is consistently asked to evaluate Poirot's moral choices. In a mystery as early as *The Murder of Roger Ackroyd*, for instance, Poirot makes choices that require him to deceive an entire community and evade an entire system of justice that required exposure and penance. And in her official last Poirot mystery, *Curtain*, Poirot himself questions not the cognitive processes by which he has identified the criminal, but the moral choices made in consequence of this identification. It is here that the never-wrong Poirot confesses to Arthur Hastings, "I don't know." Perhaps, Christie, suggests, Poirot is not always right—this means a close reading of her work will then require a step into the slow time of reflection.

Poirot's own soul-searching in his last mystery speaks to the way everything ultimately is not quite made right in Christie's work. The conventional wisdom is that her work is a gradual or, quite often, a sudden correction or the reader's various misinterpretations and that, in the end, we have all the answers to all the problems, returning this society to a state of grace. But a close reading of Christie will show us that she often wounds her stories so that there are questions left over, even after all has been said and done. Her stories are not airtight and hermetically sealed; her mysteries are allowed to breathe and grow and change.

There are moments in a Christie novel when she will become unpredictably loose and undisciplined, as opposed to the carefully planned plot she has executed elsewhere in the narrative—less obvious than her "surprise endings," there are disorderly, untidy, or dubious layers to her outcomes that disarm or even possibly alarm us. Christie will also complicate or undermine the seemingly untouchable ratiocinative aspects of her novels through her introduction of the uncanny or the mystical, introducing a narrative thread that is an alternative to the ratiocinative one. The introduction of such ideas as the wheel of fortune, the phenomenon of second sight, or the vengeful spirits of the dead, establishes an argument with the dominant spirit of ratiocination.

One of the basic paradoxes of Christie's oeuvre, one that comes up in initial reviews and in every companion or compendium devoted to her work, is that famous as she might be for unfolding puzzles, she was far less consistently a puzzle-writer than the popular imagination would have us believe. From *The Man in the Brown Suit*, her fourth novel, forward to *Passenger to Frankfurt*, her fourth-to-last novel, Christie produced thrillers, adventure stories, stories without a series detective, stories without a particularly challenging puzzle. These novels are routinely put at the bottom of the pile of her work in terms of assessment even as the same commentators castigate Christie for being a mere puzzle-writer. Christie clearly never saw herself as just this, yet she was often expected to keep within that format. An example of this is the response to *The Secret of Chimneys* (1925) and *The Seven Dials Mystery* (1929). These two novels are both parodies—the first of Anthony Hope's *The Prisoner of Zenda* (1894), the second of G.K. Chesterton's *The Man Who Was Thursday* (1908). They also are both "capers" in which a certain fundamental unseriousness coincides with plots that are in places too obvious for a puzzle and in other places too preposterous for ratiocinative processes to even apply. Although successful in terms of their own purposes (*Chimneys* especially), what explains the reserved response is that they do not conform to the genre expectations we have of Christie's work.

Furthermore, Christie consistently tried to infuse the puzzle mystery with elements of more novelistic genres. These can include the thriller, the adventure story, the spy story, and, in *Death Comes as the End*, the historical novel. But her body of work can also include the conventional psychological novel. Christie's fiction of the 1940s is often evaluated as the richest period of her work in terms of literary quality. Novels such as *Towards Zero*, *The Hollow*, and *Five Little Pigs* have an emotional depth, psychological subtlety, and a sense of aesthetic craft far more redolent of the high-literary 20th century novel than of puzzle-oriented tales such as *Murder on the Orient Express*.

It has long been noted that this was about the point at which Christie started to publish "straight" psychologically attuned romance novels under the pseudonym of Mary Westmacott. Writing these novels undeniably enriched Christie's detective stories, giving them a sense of psychological intricacy and emotional nuance. *Absent in the Spring* (1944), for instance, has concerns that directly flow into those of *The Hollow*; there are similarities between Joan Scudamore, the protagonist of that novel, and Henrietta Savernake in *The Hollow*. Yet Christie's Mary Westmacott novels, as such, have received little critical attention or esteem. *Unfinished Portrait* is mined for details of Christie's marriage, but there have been few appreciations of the Westmacott novels on their own terms.

Thus, we have a paradox: Christie's detective stories are at their best when they are closest to the Westmacott novels. But the Westmacott novels themselves are no one's idea of "best." In other words, one genre is at its best when it asymptotically converges on another genre; but that other genre is not in itself of supreme value. If, e.g., George Eliot's novels are at their best when most proximate to the essayistic, this does not mean that

George Eliot herself is outstandingly valued as an essayist or, certainly, that her essays are better than her novels. Similarly, Christie's fiction is at its best when it converges upon the Westmacottian; but this does not mean the Westmacottian, without the "pressure" exerted by the contact with the detective genre, is of any great value.

This model can help us understand the relation of the detective story to other genres in Christie's work. In every decade of her career, not only does she produce thrillers or adventure stories, many of her more conventional mysteries—certainly, the Tommy and Tuppence books—are informed by those sorts of genres. For instance, Christie wrote three books entirely set in Mesopotamia—*Murder in Mesopotamia*, *They Came to Baghdad*, and the "Westmacott" *Absent in the Spring*. Of these, it is the detective story—*Murder in Mesopotamia*—that is the best. But the character of Amy Leatheran in that mystery, so important as the narrative point-of-view, comes from the world of Westmacott—the woman past her first youth who still has meaningful choices to make, who is required to assess and judge her relationships. Even the Miss Marple stories are not quite cozy mysteries, in the sense recently detailed by the critical work of Phyllis M. Betz on the cozy form. For one thing the criminals in them—certainly in the three novels covered in this book, but also in *Nemesis* and *The Body in the Library*—are simply too diabolical for the novels to be cozy.

Additionally, the genres in which Christie was less successful—thriller, spy novel, romance novel—haunt the one in which she was spectacularly successful: the detective story. Much of the aesthetic depth in her detective stories comes from this haunting, even if it is still her detective genre where she flourished most as a writer.

Christie's spirit of ratiocination is enriched by a bevy of masterminds or artists of crime, or wizards or Svengalis. But some murderers are more guilty than others. Whether guilty, or not, however, Christie will draw the reader at some point into the murderer's mind, usually through the uncanny sympathetic imagination of her detective. And her detectives on occasion will openly admire their murderers. Even the evilest of Christie's murderers will possess the virtues of ingenuity, tenacity, daring—like Christie, her murderers possess what Robert Barnard described as "a talent to deceive." She might also agree with G.K. Chesterton, who noted that "the criminal is the creative artist; the detective only the critic." But Christie also asks us to regard each of her criminals individually—some will secure a certain victim status; others will elicit a certain admiration; still others will emerge as essentially demonic.

Who, exactly, are the guilty and who are the innocent is the central source of mystery in Christie's novels. But while the criminal is always identified in the end, issues of guilt and innocence may remain uncertain. This issue of innocence includes Poirot himself. In *Murder on the Orient Express*, for instance, not only is Poirot complicit with the guilty murderers, we as readers are also invited to take their side. In the final Poirot mystery, *Curtain*, Poirot declares himself guilty, and there have been other cases, such as *The Hollow*, in which Poirot's conduct is hardly perfectly innocent. And in choosing Hercule Poirot as her detective, Christie deliberately selected someone that, as Alison Light has noted, a British readership would perceive as "the other," and it is that "otherness" that allows Poirot to often construct a special relationship with the guilty in his mysteries.

Like the villains in his mysteries, however Poirot, performs his "otherness" in a deceptive way. His presentation of self as that of a comical stage Frenchman, or even more accurately a stage Walloon who is more likely to inspire laughter than fear, is a tactic, not a reality. As is true of so many wrongdoers in Christie's novel, Poirot himself is in disguise. Much in a Christie novel is staged: so many characters are delivering a performance, creating illusions about who they are. As Christie has famously said, "Very few of us are what we seem" (Christie, "Agatha Christie Quotes") but even more her characters often are playing parts, even those who are not under any suspicion. There is always a gap between surface and depth, role and role-distance, illusion and reality. Christie herself will remind us of the performative nature of her characters, sometimes even presenting them at the beginning of her mystery as dramatis personae.

Christie takes conventional appearances and plays them off against what each character conceals; appearances conceal reality, rather than express it. The familiarity of ordinary appearance in her work lulls us into a false sense of security. In so doing, Christie loads our minds and dulls the edge of our discrimination, encouraging us to settle characters into stereotypes; she will play to the prejudices and blindnesses of her British audience, but not to flatter their preconceptions. Instead, she is negotiating us into a more mindless version of ourselves, so that she can successfully prove us wrong.

The most dangerous of these performative figures in Christie's mysteries is the murderer who has doubled his identity by splitting into a false, trusted self, and a true treacherous one. Some of these perpetrators know very well the pretense they are sustaining; others may have undergone a process of genuine dissociation. In each case, the model is dramaturgical—the role you are playing is at a significant remove or distance from the self that is performing the part. The sense of a performative self may be, as Erving Goffman has suggested, intrinsic to the psychology of the self. Or, as Judith Butler suggests, the social construction and expression of a performative self is an ongoing existential project. But in Christie's work, those who undergo the most powerful sense of dissociation from their social constructions are those most likely to deceive or betray.

Christie also finds highly suspect those who, in their modernity, neither remember, nor consult the dimension of the past. On the other hand, Elvira Blake in *At Bertram's Hotel*, a child of privilege, has become twisted by her very careful, insulated upbringing which is a perfect imitation of an Edwardian childhood—a good example of the way Christie's work will tell us that there is no bringing back the past, and if one attempts to do so, what you will produce instead is a dangerously wishful false reality. Indeed, Christie deploys the character of Miss Marple to make the point that times have changed, and if, as Marion Shaw and Sabine Vanacker argue (64), she is "an intellectual force" it is a force often directed towards change.

Since Christie's work documents so many decades of the 20th century, her stories address many historical upheavals, including the profound effects of World Wars I and II, the dissolution of Edwardian England, the rise of Hitler, and the establishment of modernity. In some of Christie's novels history is indeed crucial—there are mysteries of hers that can be considered in a way "condition of England" novels. A close reading of Christie will show that it is wrong to assume her work is not contemporary with modernism, the modern period, or modernity.

Christie's stories feature change problems—the problems that accompany historical change. As British journalist Johann Hari notes, Christie will especially support the social changes that come about through the operation of the wheels of justice, social or cosmic, that are set in motion once there is a mystery to be investigated. Change is brought about through the solution of the mystery and both Marple and Poirot are there to guide especially the younger generation, through passage into a new world. Hercule Poirot especially feels summoned to this task, as if his presence was the fulfillment of a mission, including clearing the crime away to make space for the future, activating generational changes that are as if written in the stars, a very nearly transcendental mandate.

There is perhaps something occult and hermetic in this layer of Poirot's identity—it has been pointed out many times that, like the trickster-god Hermes, Poirot acts as a psychopomp, or "soul guide" or sounder of hearts. Or, as Elizabeth Michaelson Monaghan suggests, a figure who connects the conscious with the hidden truths of the unconscious. Poirot, like a psychopomp, can move as if between the world of the human and the divine—most notably when he prefers to set aside the workings of society's justice system and resolves his mystery by choosing a poetic, celestial or "higher" law of Justice, something outside the present social circumstances, something outside the world.

One can even conclude that Poirot in each mystery is summoned by its murder victim, as in Eleanor Catton's long mystery novel, *The Luminaries*, which suggests that the victim cannot complete his or her journey into the afterlife until the detective reveals the identity of the murderer. Once the identity of the murderer is discovered, the victim can begin to turn towards whatever is awaiting him in the next life, or the afterlife; those in the land of the living can now get on with their new lives. Although hardly ratiocinative or even a correct feature of what is considered the detective genre, a close reading of Christie will add hints or indications of this hermetic layer to her narratives, suggesting deeper spiritual tasks, purposes, and intentions that, as it were, open the door, as Christie herself would put it, to the postern of fate.

Chapter References

Barnard, Robert. *A Talent to Deceive: An Appreciation of Agatha Christie* (London: Collins, 1980).
Bernthal, J.C. *The Ageless Agatha Christie* (Jefferson: McFarland, 2016).
Best, Stephen, and Sharon Marcus. "Surface Reading: An Introduction." *Representations*, vol. 108, no. 1, 2009, pp. 1–21.
Birns, Nicholas, and Margaret Boe Birns. "Agatha Christie: Modern and Modernist," in *The Cunning Craft: Original Essays on Detective Fiction and Contemporary Literary Theory*, eds. Ronald G. Walker and June Frazer (Macomb: Western Illinois University, 1990).
Brooks, Peter. *Reading for the Plot* (New York Knopf, 1984).
Catton, Eleanor. *The Luminaries* (New York: Back Bay Books, 2014).
Chandler, Raymond. *The Simple Art of Murder*. 1944. (New York: Knopf Doubleday Publishing Group, 2002).
Chesterton, G.K. "The Blue Cross." 1910. https://www.eastoftheweb.com/short-stories/UBooks/BlueCros919.shtml/.
Christie, Agatha. "Agatha Christie Quotes." Goodreads.com.
Conan Doyle, Arthur. "A Scandal in Bohemia." https://etc.usf.edu/lit2go/32/the-adventures-of-sherlock-holmes/345/adventure-1-a-scandal-in-bohemia/.
Danesi, Marcel. *The Puzzle Instinct: The Meaning of Puzzles in Human Life* (Bloomington: Indiana University Press, 2004).
Demoor, Marysa. *A Cross-Cultural History of Britain and Belgium, 1815–1918: Mudscapes and Artistic Entanglements* (Britain and the World) (New York: Palgrave Macmillan, 2023).
Dungan, David L. "Theory of Synopsis Construction." *Biblica*, vol. 61, no. 3, 1980, pp. 305–29.
Ferguson, Frances. *Solitude and the Sublime: The Romantic Aesthetics of Individuation* (London: Routledge, 1992).
Goffman, Erving. *The Presentation of Self in Everyday Life* (New York: Overlook Books, 1974).
Hari, Johann. "Agatha Christie: A Radical Conservative Thinker.'" *Independent on Sunday*, October 5, 2003. Accessed March 20, 2023, http://johannhari.com/2003/10/04/agatha-christie-radical-conservative-thinker/.
Humble, Nicola. "The Queer Pleasures of Reading: Camp and the Middlebrow." Working Papers on the Web. Accessed August 1, 2024, https://extra.shu.ac.uk/wpw/middlebrow/Humble.html#.
Hurley, Matthew M., Daniel C. Dennett, and Reginald B. Adams, Jr. *Inside Jokes: Using Humor to Reverse-Engineer the Mind* (Cambridge: MIT Press, 2013).
Kermode, Frank. *The Classic* (New York: Viking, 1975).

Knight, Stephen. *Secrets of Crime Fiction Classics: Detecting the Delights of 21 Enduring Stories* (Jefferson, NC: McFarland, 2014).
Light, Alison. *Forever England: Femininity, Literature and Conservatism Between the Wars* (London: Routledge, 1991).
McNeill, Dougal. *Forms of Freedom: Marxist Essays in New Zealand and Australian Literature* (Dunedin: Otago University Press, 2024).
Monaghan, Elizabeth Michaelson. "The Allure of Mysteries: Elizabeth Michaelson Monaghan Meets Researchers to Look Behind the Painting…" *The Psychologist*, British Psychological Society, November 2, 2020. Accessed July 10, 2023, https://thepsychologist.bps.org.uk/volume-33/december-2020/allure-mysteries.
Pamboukian, Sylvia A. "Witches and Pharmacists in Agatha Christie's *The Pale Horse*." *Clues: A Journal of Detection*, vol. 42, no. 1, Spring 2024, pp. 75–87.
Paulhus, D.L., and K.M. Williams. "The Dark Triad of Personality: Narcissism, Machiavellianism and Psychopathy." *Journal of Research in Personality*, vol. 36, no. 6, 2002, pp. 556–563. Accessed February 12, 2024, https://doi.org/10.1016/S0092-6566(02)00505-6.
Pender, Elizabeth. *The New Modernist Novel: Literary Criticism and the Task of Reading*. (Edinburgh: Edinburgh University Press, 2024).
Pugh, Tison. *Understanding Agatha Christie* (Columbia: University of South Carolina Press, 2023).
Rahman, Zia Haider. *In the Light of What We Know* (New York: Farrar, Straus & Giroux, 2014).
Rolls, Alistair, and Jesper Gulddal. "Reappropriating Agatha Christie." *Clues: A Journal of Detection*, vol. 34, no. 1, 2016, pp. 5–10.
Rosenfeld, Colleen Ruth. "The Contingency of Form in Renaissance Poetics." *PMLA*, vol. 138, no. 5, 2023, pp. 1094–1109. doi:10.1632/S0030812923000962.
Schulz, Kathryn. *Being Wrong: Adventures in the Margin of Error* (New York: HarperCollins, 2011).
Thompson, Laura. *The Six: The Lives of the Mitford Sisters* (New York: St. Martin's, 2015).
Tregillis, Ian. *The Allure of Mysteries*. Accessed November 2023, https://www.bps.org.uk/psychologist/allure-mysteries.
York, R.A. *Power and Illusion* (Crime Files) (New York: Palgrave Macmillan, 2007).

1

The Innocence Project

The Murder of Roger Ackroyd

The Murder of Roger Ackroyd is famous for its narrator and the technical bravado with which guilt is hidden, but the mystery's power also derives from its concern with complex moral and psychological questions involving innocence. The issue of innocence mainly concerns the character of young Ralph Paton. The nephew of the victim, Roger Ackroyd, Ralph Paton is rapidly established as the most likely suspect. Ralph owns the shoes whose footprints track the garden. And it is Ralph whose mysterious disappearance is tantamount to a confession of guilt. Despite this incriminating evidence, for Hercule Poirot, Ralph's innocence must be established—who *did not* kill Roger Ackroyd is as important as who did.

This emphasis on Paton is on one level a clever misdirection. Christie has turned Poirot's attention to the rescue of Paton rather than to the detection of who killed Roger Ackroyd. Indeed, many of the novel's dramatis personae—such as Ackroyd's housekeeper, Miss Russell, and her illegitimate son, Charles Kent—are there to preoccupy us so we do not notice anything suspicious about the narrator. These characters are also there to serve minor supplementary roles in the murderer's plan: Geoffrey Raymond in making the presence of the all-important Dictaphone unexceptional; Charles Kent in making the phone call that seemingly exonerates Dr. James Sheppard from any scintilla of suspicion; Ralph's voluntary disappearance as a way to create a most likely suspect. While the novel's most likely suspect is Ralph, its least likely suspect is Sheppard, not just because he is Ralph's seeming protector but because he is telling us the story and, since Sherlock Holmes and his Dr. Watson, we are used to trusting the self-effacing first-person point of view, the Horatio to the Hamlet of the Great Detective.

As Christie concentrates on issues of innocence and guilt, we begin to lose touch with the victim, even though it is Hercule Poirot's task to pair the victim with his murderer. Roger Ackroyd had appeared to be a generic country squire, praised by Sheppard as "the life and soul of our peaceful village of King's Abbot." There is nevertheless a theatricality about him—he reminds Sheppard "of the red-faced sportsmen who always appeared early in the first act of an old-fashioned musical comedy, the setting being the village green" (7).

Ackroyd is not a longstanding member of the community and is instead the impersonation of a type that once did exist in King's Abbot. His identity is, in other words, a performance, a role just waiting to be filled for the benefit of the community of King's Abbot, whose very name, especially as compared to the quirkily humble names of other small localities in Christie's novels, invokes two very suitable traditional institutions—church and state. And on the surface, King's Abbot appears a very traditional place, perfect for the old-fashioned country squire Ackroyd very much pretends to be. One might even say that, for Christie, the pretentious aspirations of Ackroyd mean that one need go no further to establish his undesirability, indeed, his disposability. His murderer, Dr Sheppard is a different kind of cultural stereotype, but this is also a performance—his performance as the good doctor is one of the ways he conceals his identity as the murderer of Roger Ackroyd.

Christie's construction of narrative suggests that everyone in the social circle of Roger Ackroyd could cheerfully murder Ackroyd, but we exclude our trusted storyteller; our assumption is that he is exempt from murderous impulses. Additionally, Sheppard's crime of murdering Roger Ackroyd is compounded by a second crime: his plan to engineer the arrest and execution of Ralph Paton. It is this situation that both Christie and her detective make a top priority. Poirot's determination to restore Ralph's innocence and keep Dr. Sheppard in a zone of safety is such that one can conclude that the case Poirot is really making is that, if only Ralph is rescued, and any other local suspect exonerated, no one will really care who killed Roger Ackroyd.

In Edmund Wilson's essay "Who Cares Who Killed Roger Ackroyd?" Wilson failed to feel any particular interest in Christie's process of revealing who did and did not commit the crime. That Christie's narrative strategies consisted of a series of brilliant tactics to prepare us for her twist ending did not impress. It seems strange now to see Wilson exclude *The Murder of Roger Ackroyd* from the modernist canon. Wilson assumed—without particularly excoriating detective stories—that writers such as Christie were playing a different game than modernists such as James Joyce and Marcel Proust, whom he also, as evidenced in *Axel's Castle*, did not particularly like. Wilson's language in describing these modernist writers is notable: in trying to demolish the idea that detective fiction is appealing because there is no modernist innovation in his essay "Why Do People Read Detective Stories?" he said that Proust and Joyce also "have their various modern ways of boring and playing tricks on the reader." These narrative strategies place these two writers in a highbrow tradition, in the company of Sir Walter Scott, Victor Hugo, and William Makepeace Thackeray.

But Christie in *The Murder of Roger Ackroyd*, even as she never departs into the legendary tangents of Proust and Joyce, does consummately play tricks on the reader as well. Thus, even as her novel is a place in which Wilson suggests "pure storytelling survived," it is dominated by its plot twists. After Wayne C. Booth in *The Rhetoric of Fiction* in 1961 coined the term "unreliable narrator," the idea that the reader should not necessarily trust the narrator of any given text became a primary component of suspicious reading. The concept of the unreliable narrator soon became associated with the modernist novel; a sophisticated plot twist that modern readers understood and enjoyed. Ford Madox Ford's *The Good Soldier* is one example of what was considered an innovative, even experimental turn of plot.

Despite its title, Wilson does not actually mention *The Murder of Roger Ackroyd* in his short essay, but he did manage to call attention to a primal truth about Christie's novel: that its narratological plot twist makes it modernist. This becomes clearer if we see, chronologically, that the rise of the unreliable narrator occurs in the same period as the rise of stream-of-consciousness, interior monologue, *style indirect libre*, and other more officially approved modernist innovations.

The unreliability of Dr. James Sheppard—narrator, physician, and criminal—is at once the most determinate and indeterminate aspect of the book. He killed Roger Ackroyd, no doubt about it, and he confesses to it, but he is also the most indeterminate and the most modernist, because detecting Dr. Sheppard defies the rules of the genre. Not only is the story supposed to play fair with the reader, but the Watson figure from Conan Doyle onward has been there to report the story as a reliable intermediary between detective and reader, but who in himself presented no problems or any dramatic interest.

That the Watson figure has little life of his own is illustrated in the ostensible reason given for James Sheppard's narrating *The Murder of Roger Ackroyd*. In *The Murder on the Links*, Christie's previous novel involving Poirot and Hastings, she had married off Hastings to a young woman named Dulcie Duveen, and the couple had moved to Argentina. The reader of *The Murder on the Links* understood that while Christie deployed Hastings as the trope of the Watson figure, she was in effect burying Hastings through the English novel's two time-honored devices for burying a character one no longer needed: marrying them off and escorting them to a colonial or New World situation. The reader of *The Murder of Roger Ackroyd* who has read *The Murder on the Links* earlier is thus the purest audience for what Christie was staging tactically by using the unreliable narrator.

Given the fame of *Roger Ackroyd*, most readers today read this novel before they will even consider reading *The Murder on the Links*, which means practically that *The Murder of Roger Ackroyd's* readership will assume that Christie, having rid herself of Hastings, realized she needed another Watson figure. They will assume that Christie found it ridiculous to have Hastings suddenly come back from his estancia and have Poirot murmur, "Returned so soon, *mon cher*," and so improvises another narrator. But the unexpected and slightly absurd return of Hastings—who is not an established part of the world of King's Abbot—would arouse suspicion, as he has now become, in a way, a stranger from Argentina.

On the other hand, Poirot's ostensibly retiring to grow vegetable marrows is a narrative strategy that might reassure the reader that Christie elected to follow the example of Hastings, and, settling Poirot in King's Abbot, will have him gracefully leave the stage after one last adventure. Readers could assume that this would solve the issue of the way Christie has defied realism and let Poirot, a Belgian refugee who was already elderly when he arrived in England during World War I, continue solving crimes into a preposterously extreme old age.

These are factors endemic to Christie's framing of Poirot in this and the previous novel, which lead the reader to assume Sheppard is there simply as a replacement for Hastings, differing from Hastings only by remaining unmarried and living with an elderly spinster sister; he is kept well outside the marriage plot. He could even have been considered a figure who would continue to chronicle other cases in which Poirot might take an interest. Sheppard also has the advantage of being a physician like the original Watson—otherwise Sheppard has no more a life of his own than did Watson, originally. For all that *The Man in the Brown Suit* is described as a precursor to Christie's use of the culprit as a narrator in *The Murder of Roger Ackroyd*, it is *The Murder on the Links* that in narrative terms helps arrange for the surprise twist.

To illustrate what Christie is doing with seriality, we can look at an instance that does not involve reliability of narration but does involve establishing readerly expectations and then exploiting that establishment to surprise the reader with the identity of the criminal. In Christie's short story collection *Partners in Crime*, published in 1929 but containing stories published earlier in the 1920s, Tommy and Tuppence, the young detecting couple, are often assisted by a helpful Scotland Yard man, Inspector

Marriot. Even the most diligent of inspectors, though, must take vacations or travel to investigate a case, and when, in the story "The Adventure of the Sinister Stranger," Inspector Dymchurch shows up, saying he is a friend of Marriot's, there is no reason for him to be distrusted. Dymchurch, though, turns out to be a criminal and impostor; and we realize that we only trusted him because the unobtrusive Marriot had, and as with the sturdy Watsonesque Hastings, we are so accustomed to routine reliability that we do not find a similar substitute suspicious.

Sheppard fools us not because he deftly disguises his unreliability but because we have made assumptions about reliability, we have invested perhaps too much credence in the viability of the reliable narrator, and thus we are fooled (as Poirot is not). The detectives Tommy and Tuppence, as it turned out, were also never really taken in by the bogus Dymchurch. That "The Adventure of the Sinister Stranger" was, like *The Man in the Brown Suit*, first published in 1924, shows that the narrative strategies of *Ackroyd* have substantial continuity with Christie's work in the 1920s and is not a singular, calisthenic performance.

One can also conclude that Christie had the idea of an Evil Watson in the back of her mind during or even before the writing of *The Murder on the Links*. It was clear that she could not use Hastings himself as this figure—the betrayal would be too great, and the revelation of a dissociated dark side in our Captain Hastings would strain credulity. She could, however, use a replacement to whom her readers are not attached. Having accomplished assigning guilt to her detective's Watson-like sidekick in *The Murder of Roger Ackroyd*, however, Christie did feel it was safe to restore Hastings in six other novels. But she abandoned him after *Dumb Witness* in 1937, retrieving him only for Poirot's last case, *Curtain*, in 1975, a novel originally written during World War II. This means that Hastings was never a part of Christie's postwar work.

Hastings has some similarities to Mr. Satterthwaite in Christie's *Mysterious Mr. Quin* stories (published 1930), who also is a prewar figure, also is a narrator-interpreter of the mysterious detective, also is a tedious man whose life is made far more interesting by the charismatic sleuth with whom he is paired, and also leads us to assume his reliability. Dispatching Hastings can also suggest that Christie was considering narrative strategies for Poirot novels that did not require a Sherlockian Dr. Watson, or that could instead use a less conventional sidekick—Ariadne Oliver can be said to be one. Hastings was a version of Conan Doyle's Watson, and one can conclude that Christie was beginning to feel this character was no longer on the *dernier cri* side, especially as she developed her sense of the narrative possibilities of the mystery form, including a fruitful relationship with her parallel Mary Westmacott novels.

In *The Murder of Roger Ackroyd*, Christie did, however, bring Poirot's helpful companion closer to that of Conan Doyle's by also making him a doctor. Christie often includes a physician in her list of suspects, for very likely many reasons, including their generic identity as one that is considered most trustworthy. But that Dr. Sheppard is a doctor not only makes him a generic Good Doctor, but his identity as a doctor will also reassure the reader through its mirroring of Conan Doyle's more famous doctor-colleague. It is in *The Murder of Roger Ackroyd* that brings us the appalling, certain truth that Poirot's Dr. Watson murdered Roger Ackroyd, providing the novel's subversion of an entire genre. Indeed. it is striking, though not in literary-historical terms unusual, that the novel that most subverts the traditional paradigm becomes most famous as an instance of it.

Sheppard's real success, though, lies not just in committing the crime and temporarily deceiving Poirot, but in deceiving the reader. He has played fair to the reader, never lying, never delivering false information—only omitting certain details, a tactic routinely practiced in the real world by people who do not thereby perceive themselves as dishonest. Vera Tobin points out that Sheppard's "scrupulous phrasing" (211), even if it is only omitting the truth and not concealing it, betrays a certain self-satisfaction, a quality which bleeds into the egotistical mentality of a hardened criminal.

He does indeed congratulate himself on his masterful deception, only revealing at the end his selfish and ruthless murder of Ackroyd who was about to find out he has been blackmailing Mrs. Ferrars, extorting money from her to compensate for his stock market losses in return for his silence about her murder of her unpleasant husband. He conceals from the reader not only his killing of Ackroyd but his financial failures and the murder of Mrs. Ferrars—presumably, much on his mind. The novel thus explains the narrative strategy as a product of Sheppard's need to suppress awareness of any culpability—much of the novel's enunciation is to keep the reader from knowing anything about Sheppard's true interior life. The journal he is writing, then, is part of his performance.

At the end of his journal, however, Sheppard himself calls attention to the way he has carefully constructed his narrative. Soon after this admission, we learn that Sheppard himself is the criminal he had been purporting to help detect. He has simply been controlling the transmission of information to us in such a way that we failed to see the whole truth. This means that quite early in the novel, Dr. Sheppard was describing his murder of Roger Ackroyd to us without our knowing it. He tells us what happened in this famous passage: "The letter had been brought in at twenty minutes to nine. It was just ten minutes to nine when I left him, the letter still unread. I hesitated with my hands on the door handle, looking back and wondering if there was anything I had left undone. I could think of nothing. With a shake of the head, I passed out and closed the door behind me" (47).

This is, in a way, the written confession Poirot has been seeking; this is when Dr. Sheppard tells us he has murdered Roger Ackroyd. His tactical withholding of information, however, means that it is not until the last pages will we be required to recalibrate and reconsider not only what Dr. Sheppard has told us, but also the way he has done the telling.

Christie has, however, planted clues to Sheppard's identity as the murderous mastermind throughout the narrative. The exotic Tunisian dagger, the moved chair, the Dictaphone, and most importantly the journal itself are all part of a logical design. Sheppard's clever crime, however, does perhaps strain credulity—we must believe that Sheppard would be able to carry a receptacle containing a dagger, a pair of shoes, and a Dictaphone transformed into an alarm clock; later, he must also be able to tramp around the garden in said shoes unnoticed to implicate the very man he appears to be protecting. As Richard York notes, Christie's murders are strange, fantastic, and extraordinary—and a demonstration of great ingenuity and imagination.

Two phrases are of interest in the novel regarding "the good Sheppard." One pertains to the crime itself and the other to the fate of the perpetrator. The first is the phrase overheard by Geoffrey Raymond, Ackroyd's secretary, namely "the calls on my purse have been so frequent as of late." This is interpreted to mean that Ackroyd had been turning down requests for money and then been killed in reprisal. The importance of the phrase, however, is not what is said, but that it is said from Ackroyd's dictating machine, which Sheppard had turned on after stabbing him with a Tunisian dagger, so as to mislead people into thinking Ackroyd was still alive. The phrase "the calls on my purse have been so frequent as of late" was surely uttered by Ackroyd as he was composing a form letter turning down a request for charitable donation by someone personally known to him and therefore deserving of a formal reply.

The "calls on my purse" phrase is the most stock of stock phrases. But as something uttered posthumously, dictated into a machine as a kind of ghost-speech, it is redolent, in these 21st-century days, of artificial intelligence, of how speech can be non-human or post-human. The phrase and the issue of the dictation machine in the murder also speak to the mechanization or automation of language, which is another aspect of Modernism, visible in different ways from futurism to surrealism (as well as in Henry James using dictation machines to write his most complex novels) and which also links the novel unexpectedly to a general modernity. The phrase is also notable because it does foreshadow the real motive for Sheppard's having murdered both Roger Ackroyd and Mrs. Ferrars—his financial precariousness. It is his humiliating improvidence that has driven him to murder. The words that suggest a lack of cash in hand, which are not intended to be uttered by Ackroyd to accuse his murderer, ends up doing so, not in terms of intent, but eloquently in terms of utterance.

The second phrase relevant to Sheppard is the one Poirot utters, and which induces the doctor's face-saving suicide: "the truth goes to Inspector Raglan in the morning. But for the sake of your good sister, I am willing to give you another way out. But Ralph Paton must be cleared, understand?" (301). Poirot is giving Sheppard a decent interval to do what Poirot believes is the right thing. The visual imagery, though, of morning as the time of truth, of Poirot waiting into day to make revelation clear, is striking. When combined with the light and greenery of the summerhouse and the happiness achieved by Flora Ackroyd with her flowery name, it contributes to a sense of dawn after dark and tragedy.

Though *The Murder of Roger Ackroyd* in many ways establishes the genre of what George Grella has called "the formal detective novel." It also goes beyond this genre's inferred bounds by providing a sense of generosity and compassion to the wrongly accused. This is pure novelistic storytelling, surpassing the murder-as-narrator twist as fictional trope, as well as the very real havoc the crime wreaks upon the small world of King's Abbot. The dark unreliable narrator and the light-filled summerhouse represent polarities that are both paradoxically reliant on each other to be fully realized.

Ackroyd's trampled garden is evidence of Sheppard's quick incrimination of Ralph. Poirot's garden, next to the Sheppard home, is, however, a still intact version of pastoral as if a metaphor for the growing friendship between the doctor and the detective. The most important friendship in the novel is between Poirot and Sheppard, two confirmed bachelors who appear to have constructed a happy and quirky partnership. But this friendship is, on one level, a false one. This clever narrative strategy, in which Poirot is deceiving Sheppard as much as Sheppard is deceiving him, is a good example, to use Wilson's term again of "pure storytelling." Indeed, for all the narrative ingenuity of the unreliable narrator-as-murderer plot, unless there were not also traditional novelistic concerns in the book, the shock and surprise of the narrative gambit would not succeed.

These novelistic aspects are largely evoked in the romantic relationship between Ursula Bourne and Ralph Paton, strengthening this plot as the needed counterpoint to Dr. Sheppard's guilt. Without the presence of this resonant summerhouse—where Ursula and Ralph have their surreptitious meeting, which in the end gives Ralph his alibi—the novel would be drained of much of its power. The love story between Ursula and Ralph is a strong one, one of the strongest in Christie's entire oeuvre, because it involves what traditionally has been the largest barrier to romantic love in English society: social class. Ursula is described as the daughter of "impoverished Irish gentlefolk," which means that, on the death of her father, she has had little choice but to earn her living as a parlormaid.

Ursula and Ralph have fallen in love and have secretly married, but to stay in the good graces of his irascible and controlling uncle Roger, Ralph has had to conceal this and remain betrothed *en titre* to Flora, whose interest in Ralph is primarily financial and primarily spurred by her ambitious mother Mrs. Ackroyd. Ursula's meeting with Ralph in the summerhouse is an unquestionable allusion to Samuel Richardson's *Pamela*, in which a summerhouse also plays a large role, and which also concerns the romance between a nobleman and his female servant. But not only is Ralph far more a gentleman than is Mr. B in *Pamela*, Ursula is not actually working-class but a member of the distressed Irish Protestant Ascendancy. The family would deem the penniless Ursula as an unsuitable mate for Ralph—and in any event Roger Ackroyd would prefer Ralph marry Flora, just to consolidate the family. Ursula is nevertheless born a lady.

So, although Christie does not upend class barriers even to the modest extent that did Richardson, the romance between Ursula and Ralph is nevertheless affecting both because it celebrates love defying money, class, and social custom and provides a sense of hope and futurity. Moreover, the fairly obvious reference to Richardson gives the lie to, for example, I.I. Revzin's contention that Christie's book lacks "any artistic pretensions" (Revzin 385). This literary genealogy additionally, is one of compassion and advocacy. Ursula is exonerated and permitted to chart her own autonomous course much as did Pamela in Richardson's novel. Poirot abets the seemingly subversive relationship of Ralph and Ursula even before the solving of the crime releases them from any further subterfuge. Note, for instance, the avuncular way he elicits information from Ursula: "Poirot leant forward, looking at her. 'See now, mademoiselle'" he said very gently, "it is Papa Poirot who asks you this. The old Papa Poirot who has such knowledge and much experience. I would not seek to entrap you, mademoiselle. Will you not trust me—and tell me where Ralph Paton is hiding?" (151).

Once again, this is not about who killed Roger Ackroyd—Poirot's concentration on finding Paton is about who did *not* kill Roger Ackroyd, and about who must *not* be accused of such a crime, and who must *not* suffer the consequences. His gentle manner with Ursula should suggest to the reader that she is a key figure in a love story that must also not be damaged.

Ursula Bourne is not just a suspect who keeps us from investigating the identity of the criminal. She, and her marriage to Ralph, are the alternative to the criminal; they are conventional counterpoint to Sheppard's bachelorhood. Though it is true that this seeming privilege of social normativity is potentially (on the part of the author) a scapegoating of Sheppard—in that the alternative to his schemes are two young people seeking romantic happiness—is vital to the grammar of the plot. Heidi Armbruster's compelling dramatization of *The Murder of Roger Ackroyd* for the Hudson Valley Shakespeare Festival in 2024, which radically stripped down the cast of characters and doubled many of the roles, demonstrates this by dramatically placing Ursula in stark opposition to Sheppard.

Christie also uses Ursula Bourne to critique the British class system, and underscore the repulsive nature of Ackroyd's parsimony, conformity, and snobbery. She is given her reference as a parlormaid by Mrs. Folliott, her sister, who has married well and is using her new social cachet to place Ursula at Fernly. There is an intriguing mirroring between Mrs. Folliott and the novel's first murder victim, Mrs. Ferrars—both middle-aged married women with unusual names beginning with F—which ties together the love plot and the murder plot, as both Mrs. F's are absent but crucially necessary people in the story's mechanism. As the first Mrs. F is Sheppard's victim and is blackmailed by the doctor precisely because she fears the highly respectable Ackroyd will despise her for murdering her impossible husband, the two Mrs. Fs are allied as people in a minimal relation to the formative, conventional order represented by Ackroyd.

Ursula Bourne, though, is also a married woman. Indeed, the big reveal in the book is not that she and Ralph are a couple or that she is a woman of good class background masquerading as a servant, but that she is, as Poirot dramatically announces, "Mrs. Ralph Paton" (259). In an age where women were addressed routinely not just by the man's surname but by his entire name, as "Mrs. Ralph Paton," Ursula is revealed as a woman of unimpeachable morality; her relationship with Ralph as not just true love but, to use Shakespeare's phrase, "married chastity." Ralph is revealed as a model husband, chivalrous and altruistic, a more superior model not just to Ackroyd and Sheppard but to the absent figure whose malice in a sense set off all the tragic events of the novel: the drunken Mr. Ferrars, whose intolerable abuse had led his wife to poison him in what is the most understandable and forgivable of the three murders in the novel. While the Ferrars marriage had been the worst possible both in experience and outcome, the Paton marriage promises a change for the better. This is a marriage that will be filled with mutual regard and a sense of a love that can withstand and overcome adversity.

Something similar happens with Flora and Major Blunt. Flora reluctantly accepts the mandate to marry Ralph, not knowing her stepcousin is already married. But she finds she much prefers the deep and empathic understanding of Major Blunt. That Major Blunt is not a member of the Ackroyd family is an added advantage. Although Ralph and Flora are not blood relatives, avoiding any family connection also evades any incest taboo, something figuratively important as cousin marriage was much less prevalent in England of the 20th century than it had been in the 19th. Even though old enough to be her father, and, like Sheppard and Poirot, somewhat taciturn, Major Blunt is identified by Poirot as someone who can up his game and become a romantic possibility for Flora.

It is here that Poirot once again reminds us of his role as a mender of destinies: he takes Hector Blunt aside and tells him: "You love Mademoiselle Flora. You seek to conceal that fact from the world … do not conceal it from Mademoiselle herself." Poirot here has understood that Blunt is more sensitive than his stereotype (or his name) would permit. Indeed, Major Blunt is the consummate example of a character Christie relies on being read as a stereotype to subvert our expectations by having him emerge as far more agile, more romantic, and more modern than we might suppose.

Similarly subverting expectations is Dr. Sheppard's sister Caroline. She is never considered a suspect, and yet is both part of the story and, in a subtler way, part of the puzzle. Caroline is folded into the cognitive layer of the narrative in more than one way. She is enlisted as someone who helps detect the crime, following the pattern Poirot has created with Sheppard—he has deliberately adopted Sheppard as his "Watson," his helpful partner, and similarly is very open to whatever Caroline has discovered. And it may be likely that, like Poirot, the perspicacious Caroline finds her brother suspect. She hints at his weakness, complains about his withholding of information, and wonders about how he has spent his time. This has led the French literary critic and psychoanalyst Pierre Bayard to suggest in his book that Caroline herself killed Roger Ackroyd to protect her weaker sibling. Bayard's reading of Ackroyd, unquestionably more useful to the practical reader than Lacan's analysis of Poe's Purloined Letter, is far less compelling as an exercise in literary theory.

Indeed, Bayard was writing at the time when the transgressive French literary theorist had become as much commodity as the cozy, puzzle-oriented English detective story; and when you shake each to its core, Christie's narrative emerges as less commodified than Bayard's reading of it.

Bayard's theory is in a very modernist way somewhat like Freud's insistence that Dora in his famous case study was in love with her rival Frau K. There is in both Freud's and Bayard's analysis a sense that femininity itself is the culprit and that the true cause of the problems must be a woman. In Ackroyd, the ostensible scenario of the man-as-villain is somehow, at least in Sheppard's case, unacceptable—he rescues Sheppard and shifts accountability to the other gender. But what Bayard, for all the vertiginous quality of his analysis, resorts to is—for a French theorist—a curiously determinate solution to the crime. As Alastair Rolls and Jesper Gulddal argue, Bayard's mode of reading tends to privilege indeterminacy in one direction just so it can be determinate in another.

Christie's actual practice is at once looser and more fine-grained than this. Caroline is an enigma and remains enigmatic. Like Poirot, however, we do know that Caroline can detect what is underneath her brother's Good Doctor persona; she can face her brother's dark side more than he himself can. Unlike the rest of King's Abbot, she, like the future Miss Marple on whom she is based, can sense the dark powers simmering under the surface of everyone's psyche, including her own.

One motive for Dr. Sheppard's suicide was his wish to protect Caroline from the truth—but it may be that she had already concluded that her brother had killed Roger Ackroyd. The death of Dr. Sheppard may mean that the secret stays locked in the heart of the detective, but the secret very likely also stay locked in the heart of the murderer's sister—it is these two, of all in King's Abbot, who possess the darkest knowledge.

The murder itself remains officially unsolved. Everyone, anticipating Edmund Wilson, has lost interest in the murderer of Roger Ackroyd; even though we know he has confessed to Poirot before his suicide, Sheppard officially remains undetected, unpunished, and unrepentant. But at least the reader knows there has also been no miscarriage of justice—there has been no conviction and punishment of a person for a crime he did not commit.

And although W.H. Auden's response to Wilson in his essay "The Guilty Vicarage," defending Christie's mystery, may at first suggest that most readers did, indeed, care who killed Roger Ackroyd, Auden agrees with Wilson. This Christie mystery, Auden noted, was not about the detection of guilt, but the protection of innocence. Poirot here can be said to be in advance of the current legal practice of "innocence projects" in which defense lawyers will take on the cases of those falsely accused (see Norris). Christie's mystery itself is also an "innocence project," akin to the current organization of that name created to right wrongful conviction.

As Auden correctly understood, Christie has raised reader anxieties about justice, speaking to a "wrong man" fear, the fear that a man will be accused and punished for a crime he did not commit. The need to secure the innocence of a wrongly accused character is often deployed in Christie's mysteries and is often as important as finding and exposing the true culprit. Here, especially, Hercule Poirot investigates this case as much to save Ralph Paton as he is to expose Dr. Sheppard. Christie needs Poirot to do this to misdirect the reader, keep the reader following the wrong man, which means we are told that finding and exonerating Ralph Paton is a crucial task of the utmost urgency; but she is also doing this because this is a mystery whose mission is to both expose guilt and at the same time secure the innocence of all the characters in the novel, including in this case the innocence of the murderer himself.

One of the reasons to hold Bayard's "solution" to the mystery at some critical distance is that interpretive strategies that cast someone other than Sheppard as the murderer are mirroring, on an interpretive level, what was precisely Sheppard's strategy—to make it look as if someone other than he had committed the crime. What might seem to be a liberating, disruptive reading may end up cementing ingrained prejudices. In having Caroline Sheppard be the murderer, Bayard is potentially punishing an inquisitive, curious woman, keeping Dr. Sheppard in a zone of safety. Although it may be that, if Poirot had not detected Dr. Sheppard's crimes, it might have come down to Dr. Sheppard choosing to kill his beloved sister who he at last understands may know too much.

That Sheppard is a man whose intra-textual narrative authority is mirrored by the social prestige he enjoys because of his professional status and gender renders the existing solution of *Ackroyd* socially disruptive, even if—as with all unreliable narrators—indicating unreliability in the narrator in many ways simply serves to reinforce the reliability of the overall narrative strategy. This is something Bayard realizes, and which made him understandably eager for an alternative nexus of solutions. Even though the world of *Ackroyd* is not multiracial, in protecting both Caroline Sheppard and Ursula Bourne from mistaken allegations of culpability, Christie's plot, like the innocence projects in our society, helps ensure that people are not falsely accused simply for inhabiting the wrong bodies or the wrong identities.

Dr. Sheppard's deliberate shifting of suspicion to Ralph compounds the evil he has done. Or for some, the framing of Ralph is worse than murder, and that sending an innocent man to his death is a special kind of cold-hearted evil. It is a form of "false witness" in which an innocent man would receive the punishment that should be directed at the guilty man. This premise is reflected in Christie's narrative strategies, which prevent us from jumping quickly to a conclusion about guilt or innocence but asks instead that we wait—and allow Poirot to discover the truth. To do this, Poirot must first raise the prospect of punishing the "wrong man," and then rescue the community from that moral injury.

Edgar Allan Poe, who invented the detective story, not only created the first super-sleuth, but his genius is also proven by his inclusion of a "wrong man" thread through the suspicions cast on a man aptly named Le Bon. Poe's detective then not only uncovers the truth and identifies the guilty, but he also secures the innocence of a falsely accused man. Here one might note that, although Poirot was a detective created to rival Sherlock Holmes, Christie has cleverly modeled her detective on the detective that inspired Conan Doyle to create his English Sherlock, namely the European C. Auguste Dupin.

Hercule Poirot in this mystery is very much in the business not only of detection but exoneration, and not only of Ralph Paton. He exonerates the other suspects by consulting Inspector Raglan and coming up with a story that will suggest the killer of Roger Ackroyd was never a member of the community at all—that the murderer was very likely the mysterious anonymous itinerant stranger mentioned earlier, or someone very like. We learn a stranger was lurking about on the evening of Ackroyd's death—Charles Kent, the son of Miss Russell, who has come to a bad end as a drug addict and is seeking funds from his unhappy mother. Although his mother is an important member of the Fernly staff, the lurking Kent remains an "outsider" figure, not a part of the community, and will easily make credible the "stranger theory" or even morph into that stranger whom Poirot will assure all and sundry will be arrested by Raglan. That means that there is no story to tell, there is nothing more the community needs to know, all can disperse and go home.

Auden in his essay suggested that Christie's mystery wanted to evoke the "thrill of innocence" (Auden 24) when guilt is lifted off the suspects and by inference the reader, a thrill so intense it produces a striking incuriosity concerning the true killer. In other words, once Poirot clears them all of suspicion, no one in King's Abbot cares who killed Roger Ackroyd any more than Edmund Wilson did. Given that this is the case, Poirot can allow Sheppard to evade the entire system of justice, with its procedures and punishment, and substitute a looser and untidier conclusion.

Poirot has mirrored Sheppard's reticence with his own. That Sheppard complains in his journal that Poirot is holding back information hints to the reader that Poirot has been in the process of constructing a counternarrative almost from the start. As Sheppard writes, Poirot rewrites. One of the revelations at the end of the novel is that Poirot has been deliberately befriending the man he found most suspect. It is the nature of this friendship that is one of the novel's great subjects. Detective and criminal are here working in tandem, even as they work against one another. In *The Murder of Roger Ackroyd*, the friendship with the murderer is one that is forged mutually. Sheppard is determined to keep on top of what Poirot sees and learns; Poirot, in turn, makes Sheppard into the new Hastings—noting that Sheppard never leaves his side, he suggests that Sheppard must have been heaven-sent to replace his former colleague, and immediately proposes that together they begin their partnership with an investigation of the summerhouse.

This episode calls our attention to the idyllic summerhouse, symbolically adjacent to the home of the malevolent Sheppard—its importance is such that we return to it in the novel's final chapter. In the last chapter, Poirot reveals that he very early had identified Sheppard as the murderer through the little discrepancy in time he had mentioned the very evening the two visited the summerhouse: the very evening that Poirot invites Sheppard to become his Watson, Sheppard moments earlier had told Poirot it takes five minutes to walk the lodge to Ackroyd's house, but then soon after informed Poirot that it took him ten minutes to do the same walk on the evening of the Ackroyd murder.

This then, is the moment Poirot knew that Sheppard had given himself away—and soon after Poirot invites Sheppard to become his colleague. In the last chapter, we understand that beginning with the conversation about the five or ten-minute walk from Sheppard's house to Fernly, Poirot has been shaping Sheppard's narrative in a way that is a significant alternative to Sheppard's. Having reshaped Sheppard's narrative from this moment on, in the last two chapters it is Poirot's narrative that prevails. One might even say he wrestles the story away from Sheppard. But the last two chapters, which contain the novel's surprises and shocks, contrast in curious ways. The chapter in which Poirot gathers all the suspects to his home in The Larches features a Poirot full of bombast and drama. Sheppard himself comments on Poirot's sudden histrionics, and indeed Poirot is consciously delivering a performance.

It is here that the deliberately stagy and theatrical Poirot produces Ralph Paton and informs the gathered suspects that the real killer of Roger Ackroyd is in the room with them—is one of them. But when Poirot offers the murderer a chance to exonerate Ralph Paton and confess, no one does so; after the accusation and the consequent conspicuous silence, all but Sheppard to go home—it's the last we see of them. We are left with only Poirot and Sheppard—as Poirot's right-hand man, Sheppard has naturally stayed behind.

It is here that Poirot, still in his dramatic mode, identifies him as the killer of Roger Ackroyd. In this construction as if of a deliberately staged one-act play, these chapters come as close as this mystery will come to publicly exposing Dr. Sheppard. Poirot's histrionic identification of Sheppard as the murderer of Roger Ackroyd concludes the chapter, as if the final gesture in the performance he has been delivering. But unlike his public exposure of Ralph as the wrongly accused, this identification of the real killer is hidden from the others.

While this chapter discloses the truth, the dramatic identification of Sheppard as the murderer is essentially make-believe, since Poirot has no intention of publicly exposing or humiliating Dr. Sheppard. And although he very loudly accuses Sheppard, no one is there, no one can witness. Poirot knew from that start of the meeting at the Larches that, excepting Dr. Sheppard, none of the suspects were guilty—the only reason for them to be gathered was for the benefit of Dr. Sheppard, to demonstrate one frightening way his story could end—that is, with a devastating public disclosure.

This bombastic chapter contrasts with the final chapter, which features Poirot and Sheppard in quiet conversation, as if now backstage. Poirot suggests that the guilty Sheppard quietly commit suicide to protect the innocent from any residual upset his crime may have created. He suggests that he will want to protect his sister Caroline from being shadowed by his crime—any guilt or guilt-by-association must be lifted off her. He also suggests that suicide will allow Sheppard to practice some self-care; an empathic Poirot counsels his friend to do what, in the long run, is best for him as well as for his sister—best for all concerned. In this way, Sheppard, too, will remain an innocent man.

Poirot quietly works out a plan to protect Sheppard from public exposure without obvious theatricality. Sheppard will accept his defeat; he will transcribe his confession, repurpose his final entry in his journal as a suicide note, and in so doing achieve some level of inner peace. This is an unexpectedly thoughtful ending; no handcuffs, no arrest, no jail, but simply a final glimpse into the inner life of the murderer as he accepts his fate. In the final chapter, when Poirot quietly proves him to be the murderer, he is calm and quiet. One can conclude that the overplayed, temperamental performance Poirot delivers in the earlier chapter will also help convince King's Abbot that Poirot was engaged in a process of elimination; when there is no confession, he can conclude that the guilt belongs to someone outside the community—very likely that itinerant stranger introduced as an alternative to our gathered suspects. All the insiders in the community have gone back to their lives with the assurance that they are "safe," as will be, in a way, Sheppard himself. It is an empathic, reflective, somewhat melancholy Poirot who is disclosed in the final chapter—the man behind the showy, flamboyant mask of the stage Frenchman.

Poirot engineers a sense not of retribution but restoration within the community of King's Abbot, and to do so Sheppard must also be found innocent. Cleared of any involvement in the murder, the people of King's Abbot can dissociate from the shame of the crime and the criminal, even as they do not simply go back to the way things were. Instead, there is a clearing or space for a better future.

This pleasant outcome, however, is not how the mystery ends—it ends with the voice of the murderer, who expresses regret not that he murdered Roger Ackroyd (about this he seems utterly unrepentant) but only that Hercule Poirot chose to retire and grow vegetable marrows in the cottage next door. Christie sustains the mood of her last chapter with a rueful tribute on the part of the murderer to the superior powers of the detective but also invites us to consider the meeting of their two minds and how cat and mouse became, in a way, priest and penitent.

The community itself apparently will not only be incurious about the murderer of Roger Ackroyd, but also the suspiciously coincidental death by suicide of Dr. Sheppard will cause no great reckoning. Or it may be that, as Winnie Verloc said in Joseph Conrad's *The Secret Agent*, that it will be the intuitive consensus of the community that "things don't bear much looking into very much" (Conrad 194).

It may be that Poirot counts on the community's maintaining a very British reticence about the entire messy business, now that everyone is once again safe and happy, and that, instead of the public exposure of Sheppard or all the grueling procedures of the justice system, the newspapers, etc., the good people of King's Abbot will rather just let it go.

Or it may be that Sheppard's diary was eventually published when it was deemed safe to do so and is the book we are in fact reading. It is possible that in the last analysis everybody unquestionably knows everything. This kind of speculation is engendered by Poirot's cagey management of the outcome, activating a deeper speculation on the part of the readers. Here we are in a liminal space in which Christie's legendary somewhat untidy endings can be said to cross over into an enriching intricacy consisting of tantalizing fragments of possible stories.

Chapter References

Auden, W.H. "The Guilty Vicarage," in Robin W. Winks, ed., *Detective Fiction: A Collection of Critical Essays* (Englewood Cliffs, NJ: Prentice-Hall, 1980), p. 24.
Bayard, Pierre. *Who Killed Roger Ackroyd? The Mystery Behind the Agatha Christie Mystery* (New York: The New Press, 2005).
Christie, Agatha. *The Murder of Roger Ackroyd* (New York: Triangle, 1943).
Christie, Agatha. *The Mysterious Mr. Quin* (London: Collins, 1930).
Christie, Agatha. *Partners in Crime* (London: Collins, 1929).
Conrad, Joseph. *The Secret Agent.* Macmillan Collector's Library (New York: Macmillan, 2005).
Freud, Sigmund. *A Case of Hysteria (Dora).* Trans. Anthea Bell and Ritchie Robertson (London: Oxford University Press, 2013).
Grella, George. "Murder and Manners: The Formal Detective Novel." *NOVEL: A Forum on Fiction*, vol. 4, no. 1, 1970, pp. 30–48.
Norris, Robert J. *Exonerated: A History of the Innocence Movements* (New York: New York University Press, 2017).

Rolls, Alistair, and Jesper Gulddal. "Pierre Bayard and the Ironies of Detective Criticism: From Text Back to Work." *Comparative Literature Studies*, vol. 53, no. 1, 2016, pp. 150–69.
Shakespeare, William. "The Phoenix and the Turtle." Accessed August 13, 2024, https://www.poetryfoundation.org/poems/45085/the-phoenix-and-the-turtle-56d2246f86c06.
Spiro, Daniel. "On Absurdity: Allen Ginsberg and the Oneness: Everybody Knows Everything." Spiritual Fringe, American Religion in the Margins, September 30, 2015. https://www.spiritualfringe.com/spiritual-fringe/on-absurdity.
Tobin, Vera. *Elements of Surprise: Our Mental Limits and the Satisfactions of Plot* (Cambridge: Harvard University Press, 2018).
Wilson, Edmund. "Why Do People Read Detective Stories?" January 20, 1945. http://www.crazyoik.co.uk/workshop/edmund_wilson_on_crime_fiction.htm/.

2

The Guilty Vicarage

The Murder at the Vicarage

The Murder at the Vicarage is the first book appearance of Miss Marple, who had earlier been portrayed in a series of short stories beginning with 1927's "The Tuesday Night Club." Mark Aldridge notes, though, that it is "a common misconception" (15) to see the Vicarage novel as Miss Marple's first appearance, since the Tuesday club stories already established her as "a remarkable analyst of human nature" (Aldridge 19), and introducing essential characters in the Marple world such as Raymond West and Sir Henry Clithering. *The Murder at the Vicarage*, however, is a novel that begins to actively develop Marple's character and context. Set in her home in the old-fashioned English village of St. Mary Mead, the town's vicarage can call to mind Rupert Brooke's poem "The Old Vicarage, Grantchester," in which, despite the incursions of the 20th century, the Church clock "yet stands at ten to three," seemingly for all eternity.

Miss Marple's nephew Raymond himself dismissively compares St. Mary Mead to a "stagnant pool" (149)—a line K.D.M. Snell took as a title for an entire study of British detective fiction of the period—and his aunt Jane Marple as "a survivor" (149). But although Raymond, whose poems are described as "the essence of modernity" (149), views St. Mary Mead as hopelessly behind the times, modernity has found its way within its gates. Despite the evocation of an old-fashioned Vicarage in the novel's title, modernity will encroach in ways that can be said to presage a cultural shift.

At the start, it is in St. Mary Mead that we find the specter of staunch conservativism imperiled, what with churchwarden and local magistrate Colonel Protheroe found murdered in the cozy Vicarage study; the victim the village's most redoubtable Old School champion, whose moralistic pomposity is already proudly out of date. The Colonel is a comfortably off, hard-of-heart pillar of the community who believes it is his mission to heroically maintain no-nonsense Victorian values. So that when a pound note is missing from the collection plate, his reaction is a harsh and uncharitable one. He believes in merciless retributive justice, and he is eager to visit the parishioner responsible for the missing money. While modern and more sophisticated ideas of justice will later be taken up in greater depth by the Vicar and the village Doctor, at the start of this novel it is the Colonel's moral philosophy that prevails, even as, at the same time, this philosophy is far from popular.

It is Protheroe who can be said to be developing into the poster boy for the entire Church of England; and that this is so suggests a crisis not simply for St. Mary Mead, but for the country as a whole. That Protheroe's prohibitive, censorious approach is taken for what the Church has become in the eyes of the younger generation is the issue this mystery will address and attempt to rectify.

Although Protheroe appears to be the voice and face of the Church for the new generation, it is true that St. Mary Mead's chief constable, Colonel Melchett, and the Rev. Leonard Clement both prefer what is suggested in the Vicar's surname—a greater sense of clemency.

Nevertheless, the Vicar may be a little too much like his churchwarden Protheroe, as if Protheroe, who dies in the Vicarage in the Vicar's study, is a kind of evil twin. For instance, even though each enjoys a status as the very soul of respectability, both Protheroe and Clement have married much younger, more modern women. As has happened in Protheroe's marriage, there is a danger that the Vicar himself may also be prone to a Protheroe-like censoriousness that could alienate his young wife and drive her into the arms of another. This potential dark side is particularly important because Leonard Clement is not simply a suspect but the novel's narrator, the village's Vicar, and, as a champion of Miss Marple, also its Watson.

It is Anne Protheroe, the Colonel's wife, who, in tandem with her lover Lawrence Redding, is responsible for the ingenious murder of her husband. Their tactic is a classic Christie strategy—namely the "double bluff," in which we are directed away from the most obvious suspect. Although Protheroe's wife and her lover Lawrence each independently admit to the crime, each is ruled out. Their false confessions conceal the fact that the couple did conspire to murder the Colonel.

Protheroe is found murdered with a bullet in the head in the vicarage study, the time of death made confusing by a clock deliberately set back in time. But a diagram of the Vicarage tells us that the mystery is as much about space as time—it is Anne Protheroe's location, rather than the time of her location, that turns out to be crucial. Indeed, an ambiguous visual field is at the heart of the puzzle—suitable in a story that features an artist-criminal; Miss Marple's task is to disengage from seeing Anne as she would like to be seen—as an observer, a witness—and instead see her as she is—as a player, a performer, a murderer.

Miss Marple herself does not understand Anne's true nature at the beginning; she is ambivalent about Anne, saying, "So Anne Protheroe says she killed her husband. Well, well. I don't think it's true. No, I'm almost sure it isn't true. Not with a woman like Anne Protheroe" (61). Christie has Miss Marple rule Anne out, but at the same time has provided her with a vision of human nature dark enough to suspect any one of the denizens of St. Mary Mead of murder. Having ruled Anne out, and then right back in, the uncertainty of Anne's status is sustained from the start.

An experienced Christie reader will resist an early, easy answer to a murder mystery suggested by the confessions of Anne and Lawrence—that Anne and Lawrence could not have committed the crime because it is too easy and too soon. Chapter One is hardly the place for a whodunit to reach its conclusion. Instead, clues such as the deceptive clock, direct us to the possibility that an evil mastermind is trying to make the innocent Anne assume guilt for a crime she did not commit

Another source of obstruction is the obtuse Inspector Slack, who, despite his name, possesses energy such that he refuses to allow the Vicar or Miss Marple to complete a sentence. He is an over-confident and patronizing foil for Miss Marple, but in terms of narrative strategy is a welcome, intrusive distraction. These impediments are one way Christie is giving us a time to think; a solution is kept out of our reach to keep us bewildered, encouraging greater cognitive activity on the part of the reader as a result.

Yet another temporizing tactic is the use of the Vicar as the narrator, which deliberately blocks us from allowing Miss Marple to take center stage. Like Watson, he narrates the story of the greater detective and is there to recommend this unexpected super sleuth, but as was true of Sherlock Holmes, the intruding voice of this novel's Watson keeps the detective a little in the shadows. Miss Marple is very much in the background, and characteristically reticent. And she produces an atmosphere of uncertainty that mirrors our own. For instance, although Miss Marple briefly considers Lawrence and then Anne in a back-and-forth way that could lead a vigilant reader to consider complicity, on the surface Miss Marple appears to dither, forestalling a solution.

Christie further blocks us from considering the two lovers as complicit by directing us to suspects who could very well live up to Miss Marple's dark view of human nature. Some suspects are incomers, such as the archaeologist Stone and his secretary Miss Cram, or Mrs. Lestrange, who it is revealed is the estranged ex-wife of Colonel Protheroe. Their daughter,

Lettice, has an old-fashioned name in keeping with her father's conservatism. A more familiar version is Letitia, but in either case, it is quite an old name, dating back to medieval times. The name contrasts with the actual modernity of Lettice, who dislikes her traditionalist father, and in defiance has accepted the risqué invitation to pose in her bathing suit for one of Lawrence's paintings. Lettice's stepmother Anne's name is also a contrast to her character since it is also an old name—in this case, the name of a saint, the mother of Mary.

The vengeful poacher with the appropriate name of Archer is yet another suspect—he has been sent to jail by Protheroe. His retributive motives are fairly transparent, but other possibilities include the Vicar's young frisky wife Griselda, who is no stranger to Laurence Redding and who has made a possibly incriminating phone call to the Vicar's impish nephew Dennis, her partner in crime as it were, a faint echo of the partnership of Anne and Lawrence. And it is Miss Marple's irreverent nephew Raymond who suggests the Vicar himself committed the crime.

The presence of Raymond as a modern literary man emphasizes Miss Marple's identity as a Victorian relic, an impression set up only to be dislodged by Miss Marple's phenomenal skills as a detective. Miss Marple's old fashioned spinsterhood can be said to summon onto the stage its opposite, the figure of the modern literary man, and with him a certain self-awareness and self-positioning. For instance, John Curran has found, in Christie's notebooks for the early 1960s novel *The Pale Horse*, an indication that Mark Easterbrook, the smug young literary man who is the detective figure in that non-series novel, was originally intended to be Raymond West's son (Curran 40) and thus Miss Marple's grandnephew. There is thus a curious interdependence between St. Mary Mead and literary modernity. It is as if literary modernity needs the village to fall back on as a substrate and the village needs literary modernity to be up to date. More literary than Miss Marple, and less literary than Raymond West, Christie positions herself as able to approach the former using the latter, but also able to puncture the pretensions of the latter using the former.

It is in the Marple books that Christie's oeuvre becomes closest to a *roman fleuve*, with familiar characters appearing and reappearing; a technique that has to be limited because too much familiarity will eventually preclude the possibility of their being plausible suspects, the major reason in general why, despite the phenomenon of series detectives, detective series are not *romans fleuves*; every book generally contains a fresh set of suspects.

More literary than one would imagine, the Marple books, as signaled by Leonard Clement as the narrator of *The Murder at the Vicarage*, are also more religious in tone and theme than Christie's other novels. Part of this can be attributed to the village setting and the importance, as with the Reverend Harmon in *A Murder Is Announced*, of the local church in the village. But, as we shall see in our discussion of *At Bertram's Hotel*, the pronounced religious tone of that London-set novel, with its meditations on sin, forgiveness, and retribution, also tells us about that religion in the Marple books does not just mean an unthinking conformity to an established, conservative institution. Indeed, through *The Murder at the Vicarage*, Christie raises the specter of such a conservatism only to banish it.

Thus both the modish literary man and the local vicar are enmeshed in a much larger discursive context in Christie's oeuvre, a context which illuminates their interaction in *The Murder at the Vicarage*. As a member of the younger generation, Raymond teases Clement with the modern psychoanalytic theory that his motive for murder is his inferiority complex. Raymond's suggestion about Clement's culpability, while inaccurate, is not untrue in textual terms. *The Murder at the Vicarage* is unusual among the Miss Marple mysteries because it is the only one that is narrated in the first person—in this case, the Vicar.

This narrative strategy is surely because Christie did not necessarily intend to make Miss Marple a series detective. Miss Marple appears to us at first as she appears to Leonard Clement, but in subsequent novels is presented in a more omniscient way; that the reader already knows she is the detective means her insights are to be trusted and her perspective is nearly infallible. In the first book in which she appears, these aspects of her identity are far more contingent. Yet she is intended throughout by the author as the major character of the book—in this way is very unlike the notorious appearance of Albert Campion in Margery Allingham's first novel, *The Crime at Black Dudley*, in which Allingham not only does not have Campion solve the crime but also did not intend him as a central character.

That Christie, on the other hand, intends Clement as the narrator means that our first experience of Miss Marple is filtered through his perspective, and somewhat distorted. In addition, there are two issues concerning Clement as a first-person narrator. First, Christie has already shown a penchant for unreliable, criminal first-person narrators. One who is a cleric is not necessarily exempt from that category; indeed, it would be the religious complement to the secular malefactor of Dr. Sheppard in *The Murder of Roger Ackroyd*. Second, even if he is not a criminal, an autobiographical account by a priest is ipso facto a confessional. That Clement has nothing to confess except his feelings of inadequacy as Griselda's husband and an almost expected sense of self-deprecation as a spiritual guide does not mitigate the inherent vestige of the confession in his narration. The fiery sermon Clement gives at the climax of the book can also be said to be a confession, at least in the sense that it is using language to speak from the heart. This is a canny aspect of Christie's narrative strategies here, since there is a motif of confession throughout the novel, beginning with Anne and Lawrence, through Griselda and Lettice, and reaching a culmination in Hawes, the curate who has been primed to be found guilty of the murder of Protheroe.

Though Clement is not a criminal and has nothing to hide, indeed is the uncomplicated if imperfect country parson he says he is, his first-person narration does nevertheless sustain the reader's interest in him and his fortunes. The novel begins with the narrator saying he does know exactly where to begin; a device which both conveys to the reader the subjectivity of the narrator's viewpoint and encourages the reader to trust the narrator as guileless, as if he will not himself quite know the truth until he finished his story.

If Miss Marple is famously like Caroline Sheppard in *The Murder of Roger Ackroyd*—-a spinster whose gossipy curiosity leads to deep critical (and criminal) revelations—then it should also be recognized that Colonel Protheroe is like Roger Ackroyd. Just as James Sheppard—on the face of it, at least—finds Ackroyd a somewhat uncomfortable colleague, so does Clement find Colonel Protheroe difficult to handle, although in the latter case the nearly inevitable problem, for a priest, of a rebarbative but indispensable parishioner is something that Clement by his very vocation would have had to anticipate, even if never easy to suffer.

The name of Clement's wife Griselda is Trollopian—Griselda Clement has far more the aspect of Griselda Grantly in the Barchester books than Chaucer or Boccaccio's "patient Griselda"—and the position in the Clements' marriage and the Vicar's philosophy as one of advanced liberal-conservatism, is also consummately Trollopian. But Trollope wrote long books, whereas Christie wrote short ones. While Trollope found it necessary to move on from his characters, even those his readers loved, Christie found in Miss Marple a sustainable figure who, despite her advanced age when we first see her, appears in many future novels.

Though Miss Marple is not a particularly religious figure—indeed, far less than more actual provincial Englishwomen of her generation and background would have been—and although her wisdom about life is both determinedly practical and secular, her adventures start with a clerical situation in which the patience, integrity, and percipience of a clergyman is tried and tested. If the Miss Marple stories are neither religious nor prescriptively moralistic, they are nonetheless, in a soft-focus way, ethical. Her mysteries concern how people live together, the true or false faces people present to others, and the secrets that people keep, some socially necessary (such as Lettice Protheroe hiding the fact that Mrs. Lestrange is her mother) and some simply abominable (such as Anne Protheroe's affair with Lawrence Redding, which leads to the murder of her husband).

Lettice seems a callow, narcissistic teenager but her care for her dying mother shows her capable of altruism, a promising sign for the future. Megan Hoffman has spoken of the novel's representation of motherhood as more "expansive" (Hoffman 56) than the time's cultural expectations, and motherhood is another area where *The Murder at the Vicarage* is less nostalgic and recuperative than stereotypes would have it. There is an aspect to the ending of Lettice's story that is encouraging moral advance, as is the baby expected by Leonard and Griselda. Christie's solution to these ethical issues is not a religious one, but the moral texture is nevertheless enriched by the "churchiness" of this first Marple mystery.

The archaeological aspect of the book is also quite salient. *The Murder at the Vicarage* is the first Christie novel in which archaeology plays a role. It is not easy to determine the precise chronology of the novel's composition and whether Christie had met her future husband, the archaeologist Max Mallowan, before she began work on the novel; but certainly, her meeting Mallowan, in February 1930, preceded the publication of *The Murder at the Vicarage*, which features the character of Dr. Stone, an archaeologist excavating a barrow on Protheroe's land.

But whether she had met Mallowan or not, Christie had already become interested in archaeology, visiting the Woolley expedition excavating the ancient Sumerian city of Ur in "Winter 1928" (Thompson 272). She did not become interested in archaeology because she married Mallowan, but rather met Mallowan after she was already pursuing her interest in archaeology. Moreover, the archaeologist is a kind of detective: a detective of the past, a detective of the earth, someone who similarly seeks to patch together meaning out of a series of disparate clues.

This archaeological interest is reflected in Stone's presence in the novel. The criminal Redding, as Desirée Prideaux (110) points out, and the detective (Miss Marple) together both sense Stone's fraudulence; therefore, Stone brings out a moment when detective and criminal are of one mind, and points to the archetypal intimacy between detective and criminal that is always a feature of the mystery form. Mark Aldridge comments that Cram and Stone are "generally removed from adaptations" (*Agatha Christie's Marple* 34). But they are a crucial part of the novel's articulation of its own provincial English setting.

This tactic of a man merely impersonating an archeologist will later be found in *Murder in Mesopotamia*. If one compares the archaeological plots of *Murder in Mesopotamia* and *They Came to Baghdad* with that of *The Murder at the Vicarage*, there are two interesting commonalities, one obvious, the other subtle. The first is that the two Mesopotamian novels both feature younger female protagonists, Amy Leatherman and Victoria Jones, and that, in a case that is "determinedly prosaic" (Thompson 286) they detect the criminality of the imposters partially through their skeptical reception of male expertise. Though Miss Marple is not of an age that would make any travel to Iraq feasible, nonetheless her detecting of Stone (even though Stone is not the murderer) involves not just an awareness of human character but a certain detachment, an impartiality, a distancing— so that as present as she is in St. Mary Mead, like Poirot, she also comes from Someplace Else, namely the pre-war past.

The other, more subtle commonality between *The Murder at the Vicarage* and Christie's archaeological mysteries set in Iraq is, given that Dr. Stone is said to be interested in excavating a "barrow" on Protheroe's land, he is excavating a neolithic site of an age comparable to the Mesopotamian sites excavated by Mallowan. There is a sense that Jerusalem (or, in this case, Babylon), could also be found in a sleepy village in England's green and pleasant land. The same techniques British archaeologists applied in sites of empire, colonization, and exoticism such as Iraq could also, in what James Buzard has termed an "autoethnographic" way, be applied in England itself.

Although at home in St. Mary Mead as a community, Miss Marple must also look at it as an archaeologist might, which she can do in that she is in a way only visiting the present—she is still on one level living in her Victorian past. In this regard, Miss Marple is not quite so different from Hercule Poirot. The "generic village" (Thompson 278) of St. Mary Mead where Miss Marple finds herself able to investigate and overcome first false impressions must rely on the aptitude or the distance of an outsider. But the archeological thread in *The Murder at the Vicarage* shows us that, as is true in much British literature of the Victorian and modern periods, there is a reflexivity, an interchange, between abroad and home that enriches the text and makes the domestic not merely domestic.

Moreover, the detective and the archaeologist, in sounding the depths of peoples' souls, have aspects in common with a priest, such as Leonard Clement, and with a psychiatrist or psychoanalyst. Freudian psychoanalysis, even though not overtly appearing in *The Murder at the Vicarage*, is something all but the most blinkered resident of St. Mary Mead would know about. And, most likely known also by the more-aware-than-he-seems Colonel Protheroe, who knows enough to ratify the parallel between (fake) archaeologist and (amateur) detective. Additionally, we know Miss Marple's nephew Raymond demonstrates his knowledge of the latest psychology, and Christie herself was by this time in therapy.

But Miss Marple deploys Sherlockian observation as much as she does modern psychology. It is the discovery of the gun in the potted palm that

2. The Guilty Vicarage

leads Miss Marple to realize she had been wrong about her "lone killer" theory, concluding that Anne and Lawrence were working together. Interestingly, Miss Marple allows herself to be wrong, perhaps more easily than her counterpart, Hercule Poirot. But Poirot will also admit to having, at first, been wrong, each reminding us that being wrong prepares alternative viewpoints, and other possibilities, and preserves the agility of intellect necessary to dismantle one idea to be open to another.

Ultimately, we learn that Anne and Protheroe have staged a performance to deceive witnesses. Redding is the mastermind, arranging to have Anne hide the pistol in the potted palm, staging Anne's lack of a purse to prove she was carrying no weapon into the Vicarage, arranging the false gunshot in the woods, pinching a letter the colonel had written to Clement that incriminated the curate Hawes, and changing the pills Hawes was taking for his health problems and staging his suicide as an admission of guilt.

Hawes, then, is also a victim of Lawrence and Anne; they have plotted to blame the crime on him because he suffers from *Encephalitis lethargica*, whose symptoms include confusions that would allow Hawes to be a convenient scapegoat for the crime the couple had committed. Also, Hawes "doubles" with Dennis Clement: both are younger men under Leonard Clement's protection and are in some way trained or nurtured by him. Dennis, however, is actively interested in Lettice; Hawes's High Church predilections may preclude romance. But in trying to blame Hawes and sentence him to the electric chair, Lawrence and Anne, who see themselves as young lovers blocked by the elderly Protheroe, are preventing the next generation of youth from emerging, often an issue in a Christie mystery.

Even as Clement is trying to mentor Hawes so that he can eventually be a good priest, Redding is trying to prevent Hawes's career from ever happening. It is also interesting that Redding's studio is next to Clement's study, which in retrospect suggests the proximity of Redding to the crime scene, as well as the proximity of an artist to the crime scene, suggesting this is a crime that indeed required artistry. The proximity might also suggest that the Vicar Clement may need to acquire some of the disinhibition and passion of the young artist Redding if he is to avoid becoming another Protheroe, who is not only a censorious moralist, but very much represents that "stagnant pool" that St. Mary Mead threatens to become. There is a deadness to Protheroe even when alive—and rather than revitalize him, his deadening control has the effect of suppressing his wife Anne's own youthful vitality. Only falling in love with the bold and inventive modern artist Redding brings her back to life.

Although Redding is the clever and daring mastermind, Miss Marple identifies Anne almost from the start as the partner who pulled the trigger. Although Miss Marple reconsiders Anne's character as quiet and ladylike it is when she welcomes the associations of her memory that she can reconsider who Anne is and what she is capable of doing. For Miss Marple, memory is key: it is when she recalls a man who "gets the wrong idea into his head," as Marple herself does, that she begins to detect the motive she was missing for Anne Protheroe. Marple remembers Joe Bucknell, the keeper of a pub, and the "to-do about his daughter carrying on with young Bailey. And all the time it was that minx of a wife of his" (17). It is this memory that leads Miss Marple to reconceive Anna Protheroe as more minx than lady, a sexual being who would stop at nothing once her passions were aroused. Anne on her own is one sort of person; Anne in love is another. This theme of the strange, dark emotions of a woman in love will return in other of Christie's novels. It can also be said to be a theme that makes its first appearance in her novels only after her own well-known breakdown and disappearance in 1925.

Related to the identification of Anne as the killer is Christie's introduction of the once notorious Constance Kent case (1860–65) in which Constance Kent confessed to the murder of her little half-brother. As others have noted, an echo of this crime is reflected in the way Inspector Slack may be named for another Mr. Slack, the man in charge of the Constance Kent case. And Miss Marple's recalling from Edwardian times of a sweet young girl who tries to murder her little brother also calls to mind the Constance Kent crime. The purpose of these references is to encourage us to consider the possibility that a woman can be a murderer, rather than rule Anne out with the suggestion that a woman like Anne is not capable of violence, which in a Victorian way preserves the "angel in the house" image of women that, while appearing to give them an upgrade, at the same time impoverishes them or invalids them out in terms of the full reality of human nature. Similarly, Miss Marple herself is not the fluffy old party she appears to be, and her friend Griselda is not all sugar and spice either. This selection of women breaking out of a limiting gender box may be the reason Christie dedicated this novel to her daughter, Rosalind.

The other important love story in this mystery is that of the Vicar and his wife, Griselda, who make their first appearance in this novel, but continue to turn up in Miss Marple mysteries, notably, in *The Body in the Library* and *The 4.50 from Paddington*. Here, however, they are newlyweds. Tensions in the marriage, plus the presence of the attractive Redding, draw both the Vicar and his wife into the circle of suspects. Miss Marple particularly suspects Griselda, noting how clever she was at concealing her previous romance with the younger Redding. Griselda was an unlikely partner for Len, although, for each of them, their marriage is an unconventional disruptive choice. Marrying the pretty twenty-years-younger Griselda in haste at the end of 24 hours of courtship, the Vicar at leisure struggles with his apprehensions about marriage to a fancy-free wife, which Griselda reinforces through her refusal to take responsibility for the management of the Vicar's household. The domestic disorder, combined with the inaccurate clock in the Vicar's study suggests that in some way "the time is out of joint," at least as far as the Vicar's life is concerned. But since the Vicar is so central to this village, there is a suggestion that the entire community may be affected.

In the end, Griselda herself finds she can contribute to the Vicarage—she realizes that the vicarage is not meant to be a stick-in-the-mud place, but a place that will welcome her youthful perspective. Clement has been rejuvenated by his marriage to the bright young modern Griselda, but we learn he saw it at first as his mission to "form her mind," something he failed to do since Griselda already had a mind of her own. His mistake was in setting himself up as an authoritative father figure, a status he does not relinquish until the final pages of the novel. He does not undergo the necessary transformation until he demonstrates some genuine passion, overcoming his reserve and risking vulnerability by admitting to Griselda how deeply he loves her. When Griselda asks, "Could you say, just for once, that you love me madly?" Clement responds: "Griselda," I said, "I adore you! I worship you! I am wildly, hopelessly, and quite unclerically crazy about you." He adds, "My wife gave a deep and contented sigh" (230).

Griselda has early in the novel longed for Len to admit that he adores her madly, but it takes the murder and its solution before Clement will do so. That pattern here is the classic comedic yielding of Senex to Joven, but Christie also transforms Griselda into a mature wife and mother, whose sense of responsibility has developed such that she has bought a book on Household Management and one on Mother Love. Having previously dismissed all forms of domestic accomplishment as of little interest to her and the other "bright young things" of her generation, Griselda has developed a new respect for the idea of a well-run vicarage, a vicarage that deserves special care and special status, a vicarage that can take its place in the modern world.

Len himself has been transformed from a seasoned vicar to a romantic lover, and overcoming the Victorian inhibitions of the traditional Church, almost automatically becomes a liberalizing figure. Interestingly there is an echo of this pattern in a later Marple, *Nemesis*, when the solution of the mystery leads Archdeacon Brabazon, a particularly high-ranking clergyman, to help doomed young lovers Michael Rafiel and Verity Hunt. In so doing he also demonstrates his status as a change agent and signals a changing church. The future now belongs to both Griselda and Len—modern innovation and the traditions work together, so that as Len avoids the rigidity of Colonel Protheroe and Griselda develops gravitas, traditions are updated, refreshed, and made new by such an unlikely figure as the previously frivolous too-young Vicar's wife.

While Leonard Clement is keeping us up to speed on unfolding events, Miss Marple has retired to deliberate, ponder, muse, and meditate, so it comes as something of a surprise when she is suddenly quite present, just as it comes as a surprise to find that Len and Griselda have found a new and happier way to be married. Is there some relationship between the detecting of an evildoer and the strengthening of the novel's love story? Very often in Christie, a mystery and its solution seem to unblock a love problem, and allow it the liberty to both express itself and represent the way the arc of universe ultimately works the good. But Marple's investigation into this mystery also introduces Griselda to the existence of the dark side of human nature. Miss Marple has noted that Griselda is too young to appreciate the reality of the evil heart, but Marple's detection of such has led to a new maturity in Griselda, a maturity that appears as if by magic only after the evil-hearted couple have been exposed. Somehow, the identification of the dark side leads to love; once Griselda is enmeshed in a murder mystery, it is as if the forces of love which have been working their power in secret off-stage or underneath the mystery plot can be considered as the transcendent solution to all that the crime metaphysically represents.

That Dr. Haydock is so close to the Vicar suggests they are a Flaubertian duo of the man of science and the man of religion. That Haydock and Miss Marple live so near each other, as shown on the map in the book, and that their phone numbers are inversion of each other (35 and 53 as the last digits) suggest Miss Marple's informal but thorough moral knowledge can complement the expertise of both men of formal authority. But in this novel, Haydock and the Vicar are resisting complementarity and have become oppositional.

At first the modern doctor and the traditional vicar are at odds with one another in what is an ongoing debate that Christie threads throughout this novel, in tandem with the murder investigation. Colonel Protheroe first raises the issue when he asks: "Why should a man escape the consequences of his acts just because he whines about the wife and children? It's all the same to me—no matter what a man is—doctor, lawyer, clergyman, poacher, drunken wastrel—if you catch him on the wrong side of the law, let the law punish him" (28). For Colonel Protheroe, there are no extenuating circumstances, mitigating explanations, or special cases—there are not even individual cases. Even at the start, however, the Vicar cannot agree with the way Protheroe sees the world in black and white. In considering his eventual Day of Judgement, for instance, he admits "I should be sorry if the only plea I had to offer was that of justice. Because it might mean that only justice would be meted out to me" (29). His last name is, after all, Clement. But it will take the murder mystery to make the Vicar sufficiently distant from Colonel Protheroe.

Part of this ongoing project to make sure that Clement is not the new Protheroe of St. Mary Mead requires the Vicar to debate the issue of crime and punishment with the more modern Dr. Haydock, who strongly disagrees with him about the nature of sin and personal responsibility. The Doctor takes a scientific view, suggesting that the evil of criminality is a form of chemical imbalance for which the culprit cannot be responsible, and for which he should not be punished. The Vicar insists on the concept of sin, a moral and not a biological category. It is when—and only when—the Vicar and the Doctor consider the curate who was manipulated into becoming the prime suspect, that they come to an amicable conclusion.

Although Redding has successfully pointed the figure of guilt at the curate Hawes by placing an accusatory letter of Protheroe's among Hawes' effects, it is Len who is responsible for activating suggestible Hawes' guilty conscience, goading him into a confession provoked by Len's fiery sermon calling sinners to repentance. Hawes is upset to such an extent that he later makes a truly heartfelt confession—that is, a confession he believes to be true. For Len, he is confessing to the murder of Protheroe, although Hawes is in reality confessing to having taken the missing church money that so vexed Protheroe—something Miss Marple discerns when she mentions that Hawes reminded her of an organist who had taken the money meant for the church Choir Boys' Outing.

In another twist, when it is discovered that Hawes has suffered from an illness that has affected him psychologically to such an extent that he is not in his right mind, the Vicar immediately adopts the doctor's perspective. He concludes that the Curate's recent conduct is a biological circumstance for which he cannot be responsible. The Doctor, on the other hand, unexpectedly takes the moral high ground when he learns Anne and Redding are the murderers. Here Christie sets the heartlessness of Anne and Lawrence as a contrast to the helplessness of Mr. Hawes. Anne and Lawrence's confessions are cynical, insincere, and intend to deceive; Mr. Hawes' confession, although the outcome of his clouded mind, is sincere.

The doctor at this point cannot possibly interpret the conduct of Anne and Redding as indicative of a medical problem. As the Vicar notes, "Haydock's views appeared to have undergone a complete transformation. He would, I think, have liked Lawrence Redding's head on a charger" (225). The doctor's outrage, however, is not a reaction to Lawrence's role in the murder of Colonel Protheroe; instead, the doctor is sensitive to the injustice of Redding's arranging to punish an innocent man. Once again, Christie introduces as a source of anxiety the transgressive identification of the "wrong man." Hawes is only one example of the numerous false murderers in Christie's work who have persuaded themselves or have been persuaded that it is they who are the evildoers.

Our opinion of Hawes will vary depending on whether we suspect him of murder. For instance, when Hawes is near death, the Vicar does not want to revive him once he assumes he is guilty—that Hawes will take his own life was somehow just. But had Hawes been perceived as innocent, his death would have been considered an appalling tragedy—and he would have been described as yet another victim of the real criminal. Anne and Lawrence, on the other hand, are far more in their right minds than is Hawes and are hiding behind a façade of innocence—unlike Hawes who presents a visage of guilt, their guilt is true guilt.

From the start, when C. Auguste Dupin must rescue the aptly named Adolphe LeBon from the false accusation of murder, the figure of the wrongly accused suspect is hard-wired into the mystery form's moral/emotional lexicon and is often formidably deployed in Christie's work. As W.H. Auden suggested in his essay "The Guilty Vicarage," it may even be that the specter of a guilty person remaining undetected is less disturbing than the possibility that the innocent person will be assigned false guilt. Auden conjectured that readers of mysteries will also somehow begin to feel guilt and anxiety that is only dispelled when the true murderer is found out. It is as if the reader is likely to be as suggestible as Hawes himself and requires a similar exoneration.

Dr. Haydock's sudden understanding of the evil of assigning guilt to an innocent man also brings with it a surge of sympathy for Hawes—Haydock's feelings are engaged; his previously detached, one-size-fits-all medical perspective is found inadequate. Here Christie may be suggesting that if morality is divorced from human sympathy, it is less likely to be truly moral.

As a result of the situation with Hawes, the Vicar, and Dr. Haydock switch sides. The Doctor's sympathetic feeling leads him to roundly condemn the man who was going to exploit and sacrifice the innocent Hawes—he will accept no defense involving mitigating psychological circumstances. As Haydock reinstates the idea of sin, the Vicar realizes that his threatening sermon does not apply to the curate, whose problem he concludes is not sin, but sickness. How Dr. Haydock and the Vicar can take the other's point of view is, yet another example of the way tradition and innovation can work as it also does in the Griselda-Len marriage; both are about the dialogue between modernity and tradition, and in each case there is a way for these two seemingly opposite perspectives to work together, pretty much on a case-by-case basis.

That justice requires nuance and calibration is suggested by the

Vicar's challenging question to Haydock: "Haydock," I said, "if you suspected—if you know—that a certain person was a murderer, would you give that person up to the law, or would you be tempted to shield him?" (99). Here the Vicar is finding a weakness in Haydock's theory of criminality, suggesting that Haydock would establish a morally dubious complicity with a murderer, protecting this criminal from exposure or punishment if he felt there were palliative circumstances. This question is dropped in this novel, but it will surface in other of Christie's mysteries in ways that are unexpected and provocative.

Hawes' confession is a voluntary false confession, the result of his impaired mental faculties. But the confession was also a coercive one since it was precipitated by the Vicar in the character of an accusatory authority speaking directly from the pulpit. The Vicar's sermon was predicated on the reality of sin and guilt, the certainty that these evils lived in the hearts of us all. And in the curate's mind, these evils especially lived in his heart, even though Hawes never thought he murdered Colonel Protheroe; he thought he was confessing to the theft of a pound note from the offertory plate. Even the reality of that pound-note confession, however, is in doubt; there is a suggestion that Hawes suffered from a false memory or a false belief. His lack of self-confidence, his high levels of anxiety, his meek character, and his suggestibility had made him, of all in the congregation, especially open to persuasion that he was guilty of almost everything. Christie is here considering the hazards of sustaining a dark view of human nature—as if a certainty that evil lurks in the hearts of man could end in hundreds of people convicted, imprisoned, and sometimes sentenced to death after confessing to crimes they did not commit. In this case, however, Hawes has been happily exonerated and Redding correctly apprehended. It is interesting to note, however, that Christie herself has dismissed the initial mystery of Mrs. Price Ridley's missing pound note, suggesting that Mrs. Price Ridley herself should have simply let it go.

Miss Marple's secret is that she is an incredibly skilled detective, not just a dithery old lady—it's almost as if her disguise as an old lady conceals her modern superhero identity, in which she can be said to be not Miss Marple, but Ms. Marvel. Even as she approaches the moment of disclosure, however, there is still a pattern of obstruction that has pervaded this mystery—Miss Marple suspects Hawes of being guilty, but at the same time is kept from moving forward with this idea because of an intuition that it was not right. As she says, "Oh yes, it all fits in—the letter, and the overdose, and poor Mr. Hawes' state of mind and his confession. It all fits in—but it's wrong" (205).

That sense of it all being wrong that pervades this novel is also suggested by the way all is not as it should be with the church—poor Hawes is not quite in his right mind, Protheroe is a harsh and pompous moralist, and the Vicar is having marriage troubles. Perhaps the most haunting image of wrongness, however, is that of the almost gothic Mrs. Lestrange, who at times operates as if a ghost from the past, or a kind of summoner whose presence presages the death of her former husband Protheroe. That she is revealed as a dying woman only adds to her mystique as a retributive spirit.

Gladys Cram is another woman who at once keeps secrets yet is not a criminal. Gladys Cram, Stone's assistant, does not detect Mr. Stone—not all women possess Miss Marple's intuition. On the other hand, Cram acts in good faith, and even though she is serving an imposter, her service to him is pure. Much like Lettice, and Mrs. Lestrange, Gladys Cram ends up proving better than the most suspicious interpretation of her behavior would postulate. But Cram in the woods with a suitcase is an abiding image—showing that a woman at once can have something to hide while still innocent illuminates the feminine secrets of Lettice; Mrs. Lestrange; and even Griselda Clement, who has concealed her earlier relationship with Lawrence Redding.

As there are interesting similarities and differences among the suspects, so there are also among the detectives. The presence of a doubled regular police force, in the person of the police inspector and the county chief constable, is found in several of the Marple novels—e.g. Sir George Rydesdale and Dermot Craddock in *A Murder Is Announced*. But it finds its first expression in the presence of both Inspector Slack and Colonel Melchett in *The Murder at the Vicarage*. Slack and Melchett disagree at times (for instance, Slack at first correctly suspects Lawrence Redding, before incorrectly recanting) and both their collegial relationships and their occasional differences allow Miss Marple to insinuate herself into the investigating cadre as part of a consortium. Yet the same acuity that makes Miss Marple part of an investigation team also gives her some proximity to criminality. Clement, indeed, suggests that if she did commit a murder, her powers are such that she would never be found out.

This indicates a dark aspect of Miss Marple that must command respect, and which tells us that she is a creature of waters deeper than her nephew Raymond has understood. Along with introducing the possibility of a homicidal Miss Marple at story's end, Christie returns to the earlier view of Miss Marple as an incorrigible gossip. She has promised that Griselda's secret that she is pregnant is safe with her, but if she is still as she was at the start, that is, "the worst cat in the village," it is difficult to imagine that she can keep this juicy morsel to herself.

Gossip itself can be said to be a form of false witness. Refraining from false witness, or spreading a false report is one of the Ten Commandments, and Dr. Haydock certainly perceived Redding's lies or false report as coming from a sinful human heart, from lack of empathy so profound as to become evil. But false witness can also include slander, rumor, and malicious gossip, and here we are straying into Miss Marple's territory. Her valuable memories are often those of crimes or other unpleasant personal information that, while correct, can be said to be examples of dishing the dirt. Despite her promise to Len, then, is it possible that Griselda's pregnancy will be old news for the village in a matter of hours?

Very early in the narrative, Miss Marple is compared to one of her fellow spinsters, Miss Wetherby, who is described by Clement as a mixture of "vinegar and gush," while it is the gentle white-haired Jane Marple who is "much the more dangerous" (14). But the last words uttered by Len in the novel demonstrate a new trust and affection for Miss Marple. There is here a narrative arc that takes Miss Marple up quite a few notches and suggests a certain transformation of character. This narrative arc can be said to be one Christie herself did not anticipate—she has said in her autobiography that not only did she not remember when or how she wrote *The Murder at the Vicarage*; she did not remember how or why she created the crafty old party from an unremarkable English village who would unexpectedly become a rival to Hercule Poirot (420). Because Christie was feeling her way through this first journey of Marple's, by the end of the story she is a different Marple. She is no longer the worst gossip in St. Mary Mead but someone the village Vicar can trust as a dear friend, someone who is now almost one of the family.

Marple has, then, moved from village gossip to crackerjack detective—this is her narrative arc. Miss Marple is not only far from cozy and old-fashioned, but also timeless and needful; her powers of memory and observation mean that she will ultimately always know and see all and, eventually, tell all. But this will not be gossip. The narrative arc has mellowed her in some way; retaining the intelligence but adding complementary kindness. Many readers of this first Marple novel do not think that the way Marple is depicted at the start is really "true Marple." Some readers find the Marple in this first mystery virtually unrecognizable. They miss the warmer and more empathic Marple of the later mysteries. And in imagining Miss Marple for future mysteries, it may be that Christie did understand the need to make her less one-dimensional, and, like Griselda, more responsible. Or it may be that the character itself, as characters often will, had insisted on an arc that brought her inside the Vicarage, rather than outside looking in, as she was in the first chapters of the novel. Inside the Vicarage she will be softer of heart, less of an indiscriminate teller of tales. She is now a trusted resource for not only the Vicar and his wife, but also for the many policemen who will look to her for guidance in future investigations. She will keep Griselda's secret.

Chapter References

Aldridge, Mark. *Agatha Christie's Marple: Expert on Mysteries* (London: HarperCollins, 2024).
Auden, W.H. "The Guilty Vicarage," in Robin W. Winks, ed., *Detective Fiction: A Collection of Critical Essays* (Englewood Cliffs, NJ: Prentice-Hall, 1980).
Brooke, Rupert. "The Old Vicarage, Grantchester." https://poetrysociety.org.uk/poems/the-old-vicarage-grantchester/.
Buzard, James. *Disorienting Fictions: The Autoethnographic Work of Nineteenth-Century British Novels* (Princeton: Princeton University Press, 1995).
Christie, Agatha. *The Murder at the Vicarage* (New York: Berkley, 1984).
Curran, John. *Agatha Christie's Secret Notebooks: Fifty Years of Mystery in the Making* (London: HarperCollins, 2010).
Hoffman, Megan. *Gender and Representation in British "Golden Age" Crime Fiction* (London: Palgrave, 2016).
Leo, Richard A. "False Confessions: Causes, Consequences, and Implications." *Journal of the American Academy of Psychiatry and the Law Online*, September 2009, pp. 332–343.
Prideaux, Desirée. *Sleuthing Miss Marple: Gender, Genre, and Agency in Agatha Christie's Crime Fiction* (Liverpool: Liverpool University Press, 2022).
Shaw, Marion, and Sabine Vanacker. *Reflecting on Miss Marple* (London: Routledge, 1991).
Snell, K.D.M. "A Drop of Water from a Stagnant Pool? Inter-War Detective Fiction and the Rural Community." *Social History*, vol. 35, no. 1, 2010, pp. 21–50.
Worsley, Lucy. *Agatha Christie: An Elusive Woman* (London: Pegasus, 2022).

3

Rough Justice

Murder on the Orient Express

The Orient Express begins where Shakespeare's Othello's account of himself ends—in Aleppo. As with Othello's account of himself once killing a circumcised dog, this great Syrian city is also a place of memory for Hercule Poirot, who has just solved a case of a murdered French soldier and has been successfully congratulated by a French general. This is at the height of French colonial control of Syria, under the Sykes–Picot agreement and the consequent League of Nations mandate. Notably, there is a sub-theme in certain of Christie's works of not just colonialism in the Middle East but French colonialism, as also found in the role of Father Lavigny in *Murder in Mesopotamia*, which has some links with *Murder on the Orient Express*. There is an unusual deployment of French throughout the novel (see Rolls)—Christie did always pepper her early novels with catch French phrases to reflect Poirot's Belgian origins, but here the language is more saturated with French, indicating in the winter of the early 1930s the last days of the French empire.

That his colleague M. Bouc, like Poirot, is not French or from France but a Francophone Belgian seems almost a deliberate attempt to deflect the reader from the fact of French colonialism in Syria, although certainly Belgium had its own tale of colonialism elsewhere. Yet despite the novel beginning in a highly colonial context in one of the world's most historic cities, it is not really a guide to the exotic East, nor does it involve geography, culture, or interwar politics. Indeed, the Orient Express, the train itself, is in the category of what Marc Augé called the "non-place." For most of the book, the train is trapped due to a snowstorm, made stationary in Croatia (then a part of Yugoslavia). But to maintain its status as a locked room mystery, the local people and culture never figure in the plot.

The train is stopped—and the mystery is detected—in a no-man's-land, an empty liminal zone, with no local color, no history: not

"Stamboul," not Aleppo, not even the Belgrade where Poirot steps out on the platform for a few minutes. Christie had gone in full Ruritanian mode concerning Eastern Europe in *The Secret of Chimneys*, but here Yugoslavia, "one of those Balkan things" (40) in Mrs. Hubbard's words, is just a train stop, or a series of them. It is a place where a murder can be committed that is very nearly the perfect crime, as the subjects are all transient individuals and there seems no basis to pin the crime on any one of them. The suspects are an international group, but their cosmopolitanism does not make the train itself a particularly interesting or unusual site. It is a vehicle, a mode of conveyance, a place people are passing through.

This is one of the reasons the murder plot very nearly succeeds. As Poirot points out, the people on the train are, or at least in theory should be, a random group, together for three days but never to see each other again. It is a motley congeries of people, seemingly redolent of a mass, global society of the 20th century. But the grouping on the train is a different sort of mass: a mass murderer, not in the sense of one person killing many people but in the reverse sense of many people killing one. This is a 20th-century world and to describe it we need not, as Mr. Bouc would say, possess "the pen of a Balzac" but the pen of a Christie. That the murder plot revolves around an American family shows us that it is inflected with cosmopolitanism as a new world and makes the transnational space more modern.

This new modern world is one of immigrants and refugees. Princess Dragomiroff is described as "a cosmopolitan" (25) but she is so as an exile, an émigré, someone who lost her station in her home country after the Russian Revolution. Foscarelli's is a new sort of cosmopolitanism, as he is part of an American society inherently polyglot and multiethnic so that he is identified, within a few sentences (142) as both an Italian and an American. Poirot discerns the traces of an "Anglo-Saxon" (146) rather than "Latin" (146) mentality in the crime; but the crime involves both—as a collective act it evades ethnic stereotyping of a single murderer, and, so, tacitly, does the incipient melting pot of America, a country "where many nationalities drift" (216), including those with "a strain of Jewish" (216); a country, as Dr. Constantine says in his interior monologue, "so progressive" (209) it can include an Armstrong and a Van der Halt (the family of Colonel Armstrong's mother) but also a Foscarelli. Furthermore, the French and English may have the empires and the prestige, but the Americans have the money. Christie, whose father was American, portrays an America that, despite the manifest isolationism of its postwar retreat from the world in its refusal to sign the Treaty of Versailles, is nonetheless ineluctably global and indelibly influencing old Europe.

We are in a Europe that is in some way still imperial, where the British and French are the upper crust of the continent, not to mention the Middle East, but that in other ways is changing. Colonel Arbuthnot does not come back from India to England on the British P&O train, which shows that Britain no longer has a hold on a possible means of transport between East and West. The mixing and mingling of nationalities is also suggested by the way Colonel Arbuthnot and Mary Debenham are identifiable as members of the same English social class but only because they both know what a *pukka sahib* means.

Colonel Arbuthnot, however, more seriously represents a sense of Britishness on the train. His name is Celtic, and, while slightly comical, points to the various onomastic and cultural elements of Britain. Even as the train is a transnational space, featuring a Belgian detective and a cosmopolitan cast of characters, the mystery is nonetheless written by a British-born person and published in the first instance in British print culture. But it also shows a Britain very much connected to Europe, and Christie was deliberately leaving her typical English country setting for a more global milieu. Indeed, in this novel Hercule Poirot, perhaps bolstered by the presence of his countryman Bouc, seems at his most Belgian, interviewing Hildegarde Schmidt in German and even going so far as to start to interview Colonel Arbuthnot in French, before switching to English after the Colonel demonstrably cannot speak that language. That Poirot, a man who would have been resident in England for twenty years, interviews Colonel Arbuthnot at first in French tells us he is demonstrating more than a touch of the Continental—being outside England reignites the European in him. The extraordinary amount of French in the book resituates Poirot not as a comical Francophone person in an Anglophone world but as an assured man at the center of things, in his "métier" (210), that is, "the elucidation of crime" (201) on the Continent.

The elegance of the Orient Express is tinged with nostalgia but is also a modern elegance that comes with the quintessentially modern mode of rail travel and the mobility and transposability it implies. But even though affirming the same basic conceptional model of the "Berlin to Baghdad" railway so feared by the Allies before the first World War, it is decentered, denationalized, not run in the service of any group that is sovereign. This unraveling of the Austro-Hungarian Empire is tacitly acknowledged. The city associated with the Orient Express is Istanbul, or as Christie chooses to call it, the Graham Greenish "Stamboul," is a city in literature often connected with intrigue and mystery, but it is also now a modern city.

While "Stamboul" was once the capital for the people living in what later became Yugoslavia during the Ottoman Empire and other larger, hegemonic empires, Yugoslavia is in the time of Christie's novel a unified nation of Slavic-speaking peoples. Hungary is also an independent nation that can send Count Andrenyi to Washington and provide him with a Hungarian diplomatic passport. Nevertheless, although "Stamboul" is as it was then a major city in Turkey, in *Murder on the Orient Express* it is still a transnational space, poised between the imperial and the decentered, the archaic and the modern. Given that Christie so associated the Orient Express with her travel to Mesopotamia and there meeting her future husband archeologist Max Mallowan, the Orient Express is also potentially transtemporal, a train into the past.

This transnational space, furthermore, includes a Jewish component; Count Andrenyi may come from a storied aristocratic family, but his wife is a Jew, Helena Goldenberg; and, since her sister was the mother of the murdered Daisy Armstrong, the victim of Ratchett/Cassetti, one can conclude that Daisy was a Jewish baby. Given that the Armstrong baby's death was modeled on the death of the Lindbergh baby, and given the anti–Semitism associated with both the Lindbergh parents, Christie—in contrast to her own parlor anti–Semitism in work earlier and even later than this novel—creates a reasonably Philo-Semitic cosmopolitan space.

The Orient Express itself is associated with comfort, luxury, and haute cuisine—on one level, the ambiance is positively cozy. Although on one level the Orient Express is the height of exotica, one that has led both novel and author to become associated with the glamour of the Orient Express legend. In terms of its actual place in this novel, it is a non-space—that is, it is in-between. It is like the venue in Christie's Mary Westmacott novel *Absent in the Spring*, in which Joan Scudamore is on a platform somewhere in Europe, between trains, a vantage point for which she assesses her life. The Orient Express is a different, if comparable, non-place in which informal justice can be meted out in a way which brackets the usual processes of sovereign states. In each case, that liminal space will appear to stop time, but once the mystery is solved, the train will leave the past behind, and move not both space and time, starting the clock that will once again lead into the future.

Christie has also made this a space that is composed of an entire Long Island great house, complete with family and staff; the railway car is also a crime scene and is then consequently converted into a kind of courtroom in which a verdict must be delivered. The railway car is also a classic "locked room," since the snowstorm has prevented any exits or entrances, and in its hermetic separation from the outside world, and in the improbability of the crime itself, the railway car can also be said to be transformed into a kind of Shakespearean magic forest, free of ordinary rules, outside the accepted social system. Christie herself mentions Shakespeare's magical Forest of Arden. But she also more emphatically mentions Macbeth's three murderers, invoked even before we discover that the murder is collective, or know they are like Macbeth's murderers in their anonymity. In this mysterious space, we discover each murderer has assumed a false identity and a false name, as does their victim; their disguises make them doubly strange and doubly "disorienting."

In addition to the Orient Express and its providential snowstorm, the other inspiration for this novel was the kidnapping and murder of the son of the famous and beloved American aviator Charles Lindbergh in 1932, just before the book was written. Christie creates in Daisy Armstrong an image of the victimized child, but concentrates on her kidnapper, who is this mystery's murder victim and whose hardened, corrupt character is an exquisite contrast to his own victim, the innocent Daisy. Unlike the guileless Daisy, the murdered murderer has masked his identity in such a way that, for Poirot to solve this crime, he must know the identity of the victim—once he ascertains a profile of the victim, he is then able to deduce the probable murderer or murderers.

Samuel Edward Ratchett has fashioned a new identity for himself, which is true of all the suspects as well. It is only in the last section that the true professions and associations with the Armstrong family are revealed. The question of identity—or indeed the mystery of identity—is crucial to solving this mystery. It is not only necessary to know who the victim is, but the true identities of the murderers also supply a motive for the crime. Ratchett's identity as a respectably wealthy man conceals the reality of a heartless criminal, identified only as Cassetti. Moreover, he is attached to the American world of organized crime, a criminal underworld, in which he appears to specialize in profitable kidnappings. His surface identity as a harmless businessman and collector of antique pottery conceals a dark and evil heart.

The suspects have also changed their names and are in disguise; some of them have insinuated themselves into Ratchett's employ, as part of a patient, well-planned conspiracy to murder him on the Orient Express. The murderers of Ratchett, then, comprise what is left of the Armstrong family and the employees, servants, and associates who felt equally invested in avenging the death of Daisy. This group is made up of different nationalities, social classes, and ages so that it is not simply a family but an entire society. It is only in the last section that everyone's true professions and associations with the Armstrong family are revealed. along with the reality that all of those suspected of the crime were indeed guilty of the crime. No one is innocent. The inability to secure innocence in this novel may suggest that, for this little train car community, innocence died with the death of Daisy Armstrong.

That 12 murderers are working together to execute a well-planned attack on Ratchett is significant. We learn that the murderers are motivated by their grief and anger at the loss of Daisy and are united in their mission not only to avenge themselves against Ratchett but also to serve the interests of their society and justice itself. The identity of the group as representing a social consensus is important—their sense of good mission and sense of empowerment comes out of consensus. It is unlikely that any of these murderers would have acted on an individual basis. It is as if together they create a second self, a team consciousness that can permit and enable their collective action.

As particular individuals, none of the murderers possess the sociopathy or depravity Ratchett's persona conceals. It is important to Christie that she does not dissolve her murderer's individual identities completely into an anonymous consensus. She spends considerable time establishing their particularity, beginning with the way Poirot not only interviews all 12 individually, but interviews them in a manner commensurate with who they are, as people. Jesper Gulddal's contention that the they-all-did-it solution is commensurate with Poirot's authority as the detective illustrates a fundamental tension in the book: that as revelatory and almost even sublime as the collective dénouement is, in another sense, it is unsatisfying precisely because the possible individual culprits are so specifically delineated. As Gulddal contends, the murderers exist on one level in a near-perfect tension between the collective and the individual, between collective innocence and individual guilt, but are on another level riven by that essential contradiction.

Because the murders are both individual and collective, the most specific clues, therefore, can be what one can call illuminating misdirections. One particularly specific clue is a linen handkerchief embroidered with the Cyrillic initial "H." Princess Dragomiroff's first name is Natalia, which calls attention not only to her Russian origins, but also to the fact that the train itself is stalled on the border between the Latin and Cyrillic alphabet in eastern Croatia. Poirot and Bouc are staggered by the symbol H representing the sound N in the Cyrillic alphabet, which is another instance of the way the Francophone characters, despite their ostensible cosmopolitanism, orientalize Eastern Europe, as Bouc certainly does in his brief interior monologue. The exotic handkerchief, specific to Natalia Dragomiroff, singles her out also as an especially important murderer, whose identity is explored in greater detail. Significantly, she is a character who has no disguise—or another way of putting it is that her aristocratic pedigree is almost a kind of armor that requires no added defense.

Other clues can be said to be an indication of variety. Especially interesting in this regard are the stab wounds on Ratchett's body—which run from the savage to the tentative, suggesting a difference in temperament, even as it is mandatory that all must use the same knife, and all must stab the body; all must share the guilt. Individual difference, however, is also established—we note who in the group end in tears: Hildegarde Schmidt, Greta Ohlsson, Antonio Foscarelli, and Mary Debenham all break into tears at one time or another. Others, like Princess Dragomiroff, are as if made of steel. Although individual differences of temperament and social class may divide them, however, they all unite on this one thing—to rid the world of Ratchett. Part of this sense of commonality is reached through the way each is part of a larger plan—is each has a part to play in a performance staged to hide any connection with the Armstrong case.

Especially true in this regard is Caroline Hubbard. Investigating the identity of Mrs. Hubbard is a crucial task since her identity is at the heart of the crime. Mrs. Hubbard is one of the novel's most outstanding misdirections: a kind of false fool, endlessly talking about her daughter and behaving like a classic noisy American. It is eventually revealed that she is Linda Arden, the acclaimed Hollywood actress, and grandmother of the murdered Armstrong baby, demonstrating that the stock figure she has portrayed aboard the train is her ultimate dramatic achievement.

It is Mrs. Hubbard/Linda Arden who is the 12th murderer, the last to stab Ratchett, the one who will make sure the deed is done, summoning up some of the cold resolve she must have used when she also notably performed Lady Macbeth. Interestingly, although the name Linda Arden is meant to mirror Rosalind in *As You Like It*, Mrs. Hubbard plays a character on the train who most discloses her true self—her identity as Daisy Armstrong's grandmother, and the mother of Sonia Armstrong, who did not survive the tragic loss of her little girl. Constantly talking of a daughter whom she has just been visiting, she shares her maternal identity with that of her true self, Linda Arden, as if Mrs. Hubbard cannot help but be who she truly is. Even her false name points to a maternal identity, calling to mind the Old Mother Hubbard nursery rhyme:

> Old Mother Hubbard
> Went to the cupboard,
> To give the poor dog a bone:
> When she came there,
> The cupboard was bare,
> And so the poor dog had none.

It is interesting also to note also that Sonia and her sister Helena were originally Goldenbergs, the daughters of Arden's marriage to a man named Goldenberg, whose name may have been chosen to echo that of Lindbergh and the Lindbergh tragedy.

As both the mastermind and the major maternal presence, Linda Arden eloquently confesses all to Poirot and bravely offers to take full responsibility for the crime. It is her maternal identity that can be said to establish her as the beating heart of the conspiracy; that a mother is the mastermind of this crime needs no further explanation.

Poirot initially identified the murder of Ratchett as a "woman's crime" and indeed women are central to the success of the murder. Second in command is Mary Debenham, who Poirot calls "the strongest character among us." It is she who possesses a head cool enough to organize and coordinate this complicated plan and see to it that it goes like clockwork. If Mrs. Hubbard/Linda is the heart of the group, Mary Debenham can be said to be its brain. Christie particularizes the women in the group not only through their interviews with Poirot, but also through one could call the Mystery of the Scarlet Kimono. Someone has planted a woman's scarlet kimono in Poirot's suitcase, leading him to investigate by means of the strangely intimate process of examining each woman's dressing gown.

Looking for the owner of the red kimono once again points to the general importance of women in masterminding the plot and allows Christie to once again consider the issue of identity through the medium of the dressing gowns. We learn that the Princess Dragomiroff's gown is of black satin, that the Countess Andrenyi owns a gown of "corn-colored chiffon," but that Greta Ohlsson's is a "good comfortable dressing gown" of Jaeger wool and that the similar working-class gown of Hildegarde Schmidt is of blue flannel. Mary Debenham's, on the other hand, possesses the more ambiguous "pale mauve abba," abba being Arabic for a robe-like dressing-gown, and mauve giving us the only hint of red in any of the gowns examined.

One purpose of this investigation into dressing gowns is to make the point that underneath each woman's false identity are dressing gowns that suggest that on one level they are not far from their actual social identities—the common flannel gown of Hildegarde Schmidt, for instance, tells us something about who she really is and suggests what role she might play in the life of the Armstrong family. We do not find in these suspects the double or even dissociated identity of one of Christie's classic murderers; there is no radical discrepancy between surface and depth, reminding us that none of the murderers on this train fit the profile of a cold-blooded murderer. These murderers are not truly two-faced.

The scarlet kimono itself, however, does not tell us much about social class—it's neither an aristocratic satin gown nor a sensible working-class robe. It is the color, not the fashion or the fabric that is the message. Red is a color that raises the heart rate and blood pressure. It's a passionate color and can also be associated with anger and aggression. It is the universal color of danger. It can also be interpreted as a way to warn Poirot, a way to point him toward a motive for the crime as one of high emotion. That it was given to Poirot deliberately can be said to be an invitation to become as one with the women in what he so often calls a "woman's crime." That Poirot is in possession of the scarlet gown points to the way the identity of the criminal is at first theoretically posited as that of a "womanish man," which can be said to point strangely to Poirot himself.

Bernthal points out (101, 102) that Christie frequently uses "womanish" to describe men who are atypical in their behavior or presentation. Poirot, who in his presentation of self is fussy, and dainty, and who is described in Dr. Constantine's interior monologue as a "queer" (209) little man, can be said to become a member of the Dressing Gown Club through the placement of the kimono in his suitcase. Thus, the clue of the kimono, a bright, shiny distraction for the investigating authorities, can be said to be an indication of not simply sexual fluidity, but his complicity.

The scarlet gown, however, signifies more than Poirot's own solidarity with the women in the group. The use of the word "scarlet" has led some readers to recall Arthur Conan Doyle's first Sherlock Holmes mystery, "A Study in Scarlet," which finds Holmes encountering a corpse and a wall of which the French word "Rache" has been written in blood. It is in this novel that Holmes says, famously, "There is the scarlet thread of murder, running through the colorless skein of life." The scarlet threads of the kimono, then, can point to vengeful murder, since *rache* itself, when translated. means "revenge"—it is as if the scarlet kimono is a deliberate repetition of the lurid scrawl of "rache" in the first of the Sherlock Holmes novels.

The sexuality of red can also suggest the body—but although we have a dressing gown, there is no body for it. That sense of a missing body and the intense passions associated with the color red can lead to the conclusion that the red kimono represents the avenging spirit of Sonia, Daisy's mother, a figure whose memory is animating the entire project, but whose death precludes her participation. Interestingly, the red color is also associated with fertility and ovulation—an indication of maternity in its most bodily form. The scarlet kimono and the empty berth, then, can be said on one level to be a symbol of the mother of Daisy—the missing body of Sonia Armstrong.

Even had she been alive, however, it is doubtful that this grief-stricken woman would have been able to take part in the murder. Christie has indeed deliberately made it impossible for her to be a part of the vengeful plan. Her sister Helena is also recused from participation—her husband, the Count Andrenyi, will replace her. Her recusal is likely because she is too close in body and spirit to her sister Sonia—in fact one might conclude that the countess would have been the most likely suspect, had there been evidence of her participation. The depiction of Helena as in need of protection and care can be said to mirror what would also have been the situation of the actual mother, who must not be subjected to either the trauma or the transgression of the crime—she has been through enough.

The black satin gown of the Princess Dragomiroff suggests power, authority, and a certain sense of the absolute. Unlike some of the others, the Princess has no reservations about the crime—to quote the Victorian prime minister Benjamin Disraeli, she will never complain, never explain. She and Poirot develop a special rapport; she also is elderly, and elderly in such a way that it is almost as if she is a visitor from the Other Side. Certainly, her identity as a Russian aristocrat and her great age suggests she has her roots in the "other country of the past" a country that brings with it a sense of moral authority, as if it is her roots in the deep past that permit her to judge what is right and what is correct, and what is not. She is not only a princess, Dragomiroff is the godmother of Daisy Armstrong—the word "god" and "mother" put together suggests the nature of her high status. Her function as the wise Old One is to give the group her blessing.

As Mrs. Hubbard is the group's heart, and Mary its mind, one can call Princess Dragomiroff its soul. And as is true of Poirot as well, she is there to "make right" the murder of Ratchett. Princess Dragomiroff immediately understands this when, after Poirot introduces herself, there is a moment of silence before she repeats his name and says, "Yes. I remember now. This is Destiny" (66). Characteristically, Christie does not amplify—it is up to the reader to interpret what the Princess might be saying. By this time, however, the reader might understand that providence has already been at work—the paralyzing snowstorm is providential; Poirot's overhearing the conversation between Mary Debenham and Colonel Arbuthnot before he boards the train is providential.

There is also a hint of what is in the cards or in the stars in Poirot's refusal to use his powers to help detect any potential murder plot against Ratchett—this anticipates Poirot's final position, which is in solidarity with Ratchett's murderers. If, as Jesper Gulddal puts it, Poirot does not, in his investigation of the murder of Ratchett, operate according to rational investigative premises, instead wielding an "freewheeling imagination communicated apodictically" (14), this may be because, as textually conceived and dramatically claimed, he does not want to convict parties for the murder but instead absolve the complicit parties of legal liability. When putting together the picture of the crime, Poirot is not a rational detective, and his solution to the crime is not a consummate ratiocinative triumph. He, and the reader are required to do much fancy stepping between the category of guilt and that of innocence.

It also can be said to be providential that there is an empty berth available for Poirot. The berth is for a Mr. Harris, whom Poirot immediately recognizes as an imaginary character in Dickens' *Martin Chuzzlewit*. He understands the providential nature of this available berth when he pronounces the name Mr. Harris as one of good omen. Knowing Mr. Harris will never come, he accepts M. Bouc's invitation to use that berth, the only one left in the car. The next night, however, M Bouc gives up his berth to Poirot—this berth is, providentially, right next to the berth of Mr. Ratchett. This Mr. Harris berth may have been taken out of commission so that only the 12 murderers and their victim were able to be in the car; but it is as if it was made to be empty so that Hercule Poirot would take his place in the same railway car as his suspects, establishing an unusual intimacy between the murderers and their detective.

As we subtract the victim Ratchett as the 13th character in the car, we add the detective Poirot. But all this still does not address Princess Dragomiroff's comment about the way Poirot was destined to be on the Orient Express. It is as if Poirot, as an agent of justice, manifests whenever there is a disturbance in the good order of things. His more specific role is not to prosecute the murderers, or punish them, or expose them—he is fortuitously there to help them. In introducing a sense of legal procedure—the staging of a judge and jury—he will restore the wheels of justice, but even more this is Poirot's way of doing what Dragomiroff also did—give his blessing.

For Poirot to completely make things right, however, he must secure a consensus with M. Bouc and Dr. Constantine—a collaboration that mirrors the collaboration of the murderers. Bouc is the great enigma of *Murder on the Orient Express*. The least captivating aspect of the novel, he is yet essential to its plot and situation. Kenneth Branagh's 2017 film adaptation drastically changes the character by making him a younger, more English, and more interesting figure. As he is presented in the novel, Bouc is just a procedural figure, so colorless as to make Christie's English policemen Inspector Japp and Superintendent Battle look like Walter Pater and Oscar Wilde. He is not an official presence, although as a Belgian helpmeet he can be said to be a kind of trusted brother to Poirot. It is Bouc who agrees to the first untrue solution of the murder—and who must be perceived to agree as a representative of the Orient Express.

Even in a transnational space, in an emergency Poirot feels the need to be correct by perpetually consulting with M. Bouc over every suspicion and investigation. This keeps us up to speed, but at the same time establishes a narrative that can deceive us. That Bouc, as a director of the company, is a private official, not a member of the police force, is appropriate for the crime itself—which is carried out for private reasons and in which justice is done privately. It is "private vengeance" (131) of a "self-appointed jury" (258) and is privileged over "law and order" (131).

It is notable also that the 2017 film had to "borrow" the character of Pilar Estravados from the (wrongly) far less esteemed *Hercule Poirot's Christmas*. This spoke to a larger aspect of the *Orient Express* cast of characters: that they are actually not as colorful and as varied as Christie's usual cast, that the interrelationships and lines of affiliation and conflict are not as rich. As noted earlier, they are, indeed, revealed as by and large simply ordinary, decent people, without the dark secrets one may find in her *Mystery of the Blue Train*, or her country house mysteries.

Christie's four most famed plots—*And Then There Were None*, *The ABC Murders*, *Murder on the Orient Express*, and *The Murder of Roger Ackroyd*—rely upon a juxtaposition of the one and the many. In *Roger Ackroyd*—the one, the narrator, the person who above all is indubitable—is exposed as fallible, and all the many are innocent. All of King's Abbot is innocent! In *And Then There Were None* ten guilty people die, and only one of them is the guilty killer of all. In *The ABC Murders*, what seems a series of random murders is only one murder, with the others there as misdirection. In *Murder on the Orient Express*, on the other hand, there is not one criminal, but many.

Indeed, in *Orient Express* Christie gently mocks herself, as the usual assemblages of suspects with the opportunity and means to commit murder are revealed as all criminals—they are an intentional assemblage, working together and competing (although not against each other) in a kind of innocence contest. They are all, however, not guilty, unlike the guilty guests of the hanging judge in *And Then There Were None*. In arranging the execution of Ratchett, the murderers establish themselves as agents of justice—much as did Judge Wargrave in *And Then There Were None*, but in a far more morally attractive way.

It is interesting here to consider Richard Alewyn's opinion that the detective novel, far from being systemic and public in its orientation, is private and relies on "the liberalistic spirit of 'self-help,'" using the agency of its characters (65). This is true of the ultimate resolution of the plot of *Murder in the Orient Express*. And their revenge is undertaken privately—outside the legal system, outside any public framework of accountability and culpability—something which coincides with the private ownership of the Orient Express. As M. Bouc is there to remind us, the Orient Express belongs to no nation, no public transportation agency but is owned by a private consortium—operating outside of avowedly public space.

A fascinating and little-noticed aspect of *Murder on the Orient Express* is the short interior monologues of M. Bouc and Dr. Constantine. Brief and straightforward in content as they are, they are as much interior monologues as those of Molly Bloom and Septimus Warren Smith, and Christie here once again shows she is no stranger to the modernist techniques developed *entre deux guerres*. Bouc's monologue is somewhat of a technical triumph, as he is revealed as very judgmental of both the English and the local Yugoslav police and at the same time so banal as to have his inner life match the banality of his outer exterior.

The surface and depth here are perfectly mirrored. Dr. Constantine's monologue is even more interesting, as it gives the readers of an inner life that refers to people and places otherwise unmentioned in the text. Although the name of Dr. Constantine reminds us that the emperor Constantine was born in Nis, not far from the trajectory followed by the Orient Express, the doctor's relationships are farther flung. Constantine says that when he gets home "I must get hold of Demetrius Zagone—he has been to America he has all the modern ideas." Then he thinks: "I wonder what Zia is thinking at this moment. If my wife ever finds out—" (209). Then the monologue breaks off, and the narrator informs us that Constantine's "thoughts went on to entirely private matters" (209), presumably sexual thoughts of Zia, who is presumably the doctor's mistress.

These two interior monologues are a bravura instance of technique that, if we allowed ourselves to look to Christie for models of writerly excellence, we would see them as worthy of her contemporaries, laureled for their innovative styles. But even as Christie is teasing the reader through interior monologues that take us out of the plot momentarily, at the same time she clouds our minds with information that is not germane to the crime, even as the criminals do the same with their clues. This can be said to be the significance of the interior monologues of M. Bouc and Dr. Constantine.

Poirot's two companions can decide that one of Ratchett's enemies boarded the train at the last stop in an earlier time zone, murdered Ratchett, and then escaped. Or they can accept the confession of Mrs. Hubbard, who speaks for the group when she reveals all to Poirot in a kind of showdown, and which establishes a surprising intimacy between the mastermind of the murder and the investigating detective that erodes their binary opposition. The confession of Mrs. Hubbard means Bouc and Constantine can conclude that all 12 people in the railway car conspired to murder the 13th passenger and must be handed over to the authorities. But after Bouc and Constantine agree with some alacrity that one of Ratchett's enemies must have secretly boarded the train, Poirot falls silent.

Throughout this novel, Poirot mirrors some of the chattiness of Mrs. Hubbard, just as in *The Murder of Roger Ackroyd* he mirrored Dr. Sheppard's reticence—but after announcing he has retired from the case, he falls silent.

That silence opens a space for the reader to react. What can it mean that Poirot has decided to simply leave well enough alone? The reader, like a jury, is asked to consider the evidence and listen to the closing arguments, just as the 12 murderers have also mysteriously morphed into a jury, which has not only found Ratchett guilty, but it has also carried out his execution.

But it is those who are reading the novel who are now invited to be a part of this consensus—the sense of suspension and silence at the end is to make room for the reader's response to the way Poirot has recontextualized the crime. He tells the Countess Andrenyi that the reason for the devastating tragedy that had darkened her life lay in the past, namely the terrible kidnapping and murder of innocent Little Daisy. It is only when Poirot introduces this original tragedy that we understand that heartbreaks created in the surviving 12 people in consequence of the crime produced a condition of such anger and despair such that there could be no peace of mind until the murderer was removed from society in a drastic way.

Daisy's inexplicable and unjustifiable murder inspired a great outpouring of both grief and anger—emotions run high in our 12 murderers, and color our judgments as well. In the end, Ratchett is more a murderer than a victim; the Armstrong household members are more victims than a murderer; and Poirot himself begins to abandon his status as a detective and become something of an accomplice—as perhaps does the reader as well.

A final problem concerns the psychological cost of the crime for those who have committed it. Will their inner lives always be shadowed by what they have done? It is in the individual case that the question of innocence remains unresolved. The sobriety of the ending suggests that the lives of all 12 murderers will carry the weight of the crime into the future, each in their own way. A BBC production of the mystery is noted for especially layering this possibility into its ending even as the combined imprimaturs of Princess Dragomiroff and Hercule Poirot are an insistent counterpoint. This leftover question, however, means that Christie brings us not to a festive but to a reflective conclusion. Our detective has retreated, leaving the reader to consider crime, punishment, and the unstrained quality of mercy without further assistance from Poirot. We are now on our own.

Chapter References

Alewyn, Richard. "The Origin of the Detective Novel," in *The Poetics of Murder: Detective Fiction and Literary Theory*, eds. Glenn W. Most and William W. Stowe (New York: Harcourt Brace, 1983), pp. 62–78.

Augé, Marc. *Non-Places: An Introduction to Supermodernity*, trans. John Howe (London: Verso, 2009).

Christie, Agatha. *Murder on the Orient Express* (New York: Putnam Berkley, 1991).

Gulddal, Jesper. "'Beautiful Shining Order': Detective Authority in Agatha Christie's

Murder on the Orient Express." *Clues: A Journal of Detection*, vol. 34, no. 1, 2016, pp. 11–21.

Most, Glenn W., and William W. Stowe, eds. *The Poetics of Murder: Detective Fiction and Literary Theory* (New York: Harcourt Brace, 1983).

Rolls, Alistair. "*Ex Uno Plures*: Global French in, on and of the Rue Morgue and the Orient Express." *Arcadia*, vol. 53, no. 1, June 2018, pp. 39–60.

4

The Wheel of Fortune

The ABC Murders

Unlike the closed circle of suspects in a single village in *The Murder at the Vicarage*, *The ABC Murders* multiplies its venues for the crime and widens the list of suspects considerably. This is unusual because, as Poirot himself notes, the crimes he has solved in the past have always been what he calls the *"crime intime"* within a manageable setting and list of suspects. Additionally the series of murders in this novel moves outside Christie's usual upper middle- to upper-class settings into what Hastings finds are rather dull workaday venues that have nothing of the appeal of a gracious English country house, or the appeal of romantic venues such as the Blue Train, or exotic settings such as the Orient Express. And previous crimes have clearly not been of the cold, impersonal kind we associate with the random, impersonal choices of a serial killer.

The mystery in this novel concerns what appears to be a killer who is murdering people in an arbitrary way involving alphabetical serial order: first Alice Ascher of Andover in Hampshire, secondly Betty Barnard of Bexhill-on-Sea in Sussex, then Sir Carmichael Clarke of Churston Ferrers in Devon. The victims are selected in the basis of their names, as is the locale, which can be anywhere in England. The field is so large, the victims so various, and the motive so irrational as to confound the possibility of detection. Though the locales are all real places, and, except for the final and atypical locale of Doncaster in South Yorkshire, are all in the south of England, there is an arbitrariness to them which is suggestive of both textual play and of the mechanization and a mass economy that are in turn the products of an atomized modernity. Indeed, what seems to be a serial killer is very fitting: a mass murderer for a mass economy and what Chris Ewers calls "a world of mobility" (Ewers 98). A series of seemingly random, alphabetized crimes speak to the anonymity of 20th-century society.

There is a very loose genre into which *The ABC Murders* falls and of which it was the first example—novels about serial killings by detective writers who usually do not write about such things. In both Margery Allingham's *The Tiger in the Smoke* and Ellery Queen's *Cat of Many Tails*, the killers' relationship to their crimes seem arbitrary, even if eventually exposed as more personal than originally understood. In the case of all three of these novels, the writers genuinely wish to evoke the senselessness, randomness, and terror, of modern serial killing.

The killer himself does, however, narrow the field for us in a variety of ways, and slowly Christie negotiates her narrative back into a *crime intime*. By the end of the novel, we know that the seriality and randomness was itself a cover, a distraction. Only one letter in the ABC sequence mattered; the rest were there as kind of null sets to distract the police and make the authorities look for a culprit who was not committing the crimes out of any personal motives.

Instead of a "general" killer, the solution to the mystery lies in the motives of a "specific" killer, whose strategy requires that he impersonate a serial killer. But the reader cannot forget the terror and the sociological and psychological windows opened by the specter of the "general." That the killer leaves an ABC Rail Guide suggests that he can strike in any town that begins with the right letter, once again leaving the field very open. The killer does, however, narrow the field in important ways that allows Poirot to begin to create a psychological profile. He sets up a "dueling minds" challenge to Poirot sending a series of taunting letters before each crime telling him where and when each murder will take place, but too late for intervention.

Just as the first two victims are revealed as pawns in the killer's game, so the killer has decided to manipulate Poirot as well into what he considered his airtight master plan. That the killer has the individual sensibility to engage Poirot suggests the exceptional nature of his crime, but also, *sub rosa*, a desire to engage in an individual contest, to register as an individual, as "somebody," and not exclusively subject to the more procedural and routine investigation of the police.

The first two victims are what one could call useful idiots for the killer—he has no personal grudge against them, they are simply useful alphabetically. But it is significant that the first two victims are from a socioeconomic class that one does not associate with Christie territory. The master plan requires disposable victims, all chosen from a far lower rung on the social ladder. The serial killer himself, however, is a member of the upper classes. The first victim chosen by the aristocratic Franklin Clarke is Alice Ascher, an old woman who owns a tobacco shop and, as Captain Hastings notes, "This sordid murder of an old woman in a back street shop was so like the usual type of crime reported in the newspapers that it failed to strike a significant note" (21).

This humble little crime (reminiscent slightly of Raskolnikov's in Dostoyevsky's *Crime and Punishment*) is important as a part of the puzzle. But it is also here to give a more sympathetic look at representative of England's "nation of shopkeepers." Additionally, Mrs. Ascher's abusive German husband, Franz, is briefly a suspect, but Christie may also be indicating in a minor way the trauma of the First World War, something that will eventually develop into one of the narrative's major themes. Franz Ascher is also a stranger in England whose foreign name automatically makes him a bit more of a suspect than he otherwise would be. Highly aware of British xenophobia, Christie will use it as a red herring to misdirect her readers, as she does here.

Clarke's murder of the flirty working-class waitress Betty Barnard is even more emotionally resonant, since the crime engages the reader sympathetically with a more suitable romance between Betty's earnest fiancé Donald Fraser and her true-blue older sister Megan. Christie makes the Barnard strand central, providing us with the major marriage-plot ending of the book. On the team that is helping Poirot investigate the murder of Betty, Donald Fraser is also this story's romantic lead as well as one of its suspects. Donald was genuinely jealous of Betty's flirtations. That he dreams of strangling Betty with a rope only to find that in the dream she has turned into Megan, intensifies his sense of guilt as well as revealing a doubleness that speaks to an unconscious attraction to Betty's sister. Both Alice Ascher and Betty Barnard are, as Hastings notes, everyday people, and although not very special, that they have been used as part of Clarke's master plan reminds us that they have been treated as disposable and unworthy of respect. Christie, on the other hand, takes care to humanize the lower classes and make us feel some affection for the milieu, a sentiment which eventually comes into play as well in our view of the world of Alexander Bonaparte Cust.

The Donald Fraser–Megan Barnard plot, even as it provides the novel's happy ending, also demonstrates some class anxieties. The competent, steely, imperturbable Megan is a more admirable woman than the flirty, frivolous, and inconstant Betty. This makes the sisters seem like people of almost two different backgrounds, particularly since the name "Megan" especially at that time possessed an upper-class inflection in contrast to the rather "common" Betty. That Betty's is a meaningless killing by a heartless murderer who is using her death to hide his own stake in another murder does render her tragedy poignant, and underscores her unjust superfluity. But Megan is so far preferable to Betty that Donald might feel guilty for not just falling in love with one sister while mourning the other—he might also feel guilty that he had somehow lucked into somebody of far greater quality. Luck will prove to be a deep subject in this novel, but the first indication of luck are the unfortunate and arbitrary deaths of Mrs. Ascher and Betty. The substitution of the more ladylike Megan for the fickle Betty, conversely, can be considered a stroke of good luck for Donald.

Megan pleases as a modern woman in her sense of agency and her confident bearing, but also as more old-fashioned than her sister in both her propriety and discretion. Ultimately Fraser's story is a love story, but he is a suspect at first, and then possibly a victim. There is the intriguing detail that Donald Fraser's name begins with "F" and that the reader perhaps suspects the sequence will continue long enough for him to be one of the serial killer's targets.

The title of the novel and the premise for the murders does at first suggest that what Dan W. Clanton calls the "seemingly maniacal killer" (Clanton 123) will relentlessly plow through the entire alphabet. But Christie has limited the premise exclusively to the letters in the title, namely ABC. The "D" crime is a more casual one—the crime seems sloppy, Clarke no longer really interested, having successfully committed the crime that mattered to him. The victim of the "D" crime, Earlsfield, is robbed even of the dignity of being supposed Clarke's intended, who was a man named Downes. Clarke had just assumed someone named D would be nearby and did not even know or research Downes in particular. It is the "C" murder that counted, and that murder is accomplished not in remote Doncaster, but in Churston Ferrers, where Agatha Christie and Max Mallowan were themselves eventually to live.

And it is the final "C" murder that is different in many ways from the earlier two. As the ABC killer, Franklin Clarke has deliberately misdirected a letter to Poirot about this crime, so that Poirot is offered no possibility of intervening. And the crime receives more attention than the other two because it is Sir Carmichael Clarke who is murdered, and because once he is murdered the ABC sequence stops in substantive terms at "C" with the "D" as a cover. Christie cleverly begins to re-establish the classic Christie pattern of a closed circle of suspects, moving back from atomized modernity into the more intimate and traditional set of candidates. We have moved from the murder of a woman who runs a shop, and a woman who was a waitress in a café, to the murder of a titled aristocrat with a sizeable fortune. This shift to aristocracy disrupts the pattern—we have been in working-class England and are suddenly back at a stately manor house. Not only is the victim of a different order, but so are the suspects. This twist not only works as a narrative strategy, but it also allows Christie to explore both the humble and high aspects of British society, pointing to social and economic inequities while also noting that murder suspects are classless.

We eventually learn the entire ABC conceit is a way to conceal the murderer of Sir Carmichael Clarke. Sir Carmichael's younger brother Franklin has ingeniously hidden his crime in the misleading pattern, providing information that acted as a form of clever misdirection. The murderer is not a mad serial killer, but someone from the inside—in fact the murderer represents the very *crime intime* discounted by Poirot at the outset, featuring a rivalry between Sir Carmichael and his younger brother Franklin, as well as a large inheritance and a beautiful, young personal assistant, Thora Grey. We learn that Franklin has created a bizarre design that sacrifices innocent victims to hide the only crime that mattered to him. The mastermind made random choices of his first two victims because they simply had the bad luck to have their names begin with the wrong letter. The victims cannot be said to have crossed the murderer in any way, but are instead arbitrarily pulled into the cold, impersonal design, and serve only as pawns in his game.

This means that Franklin Clarke is not actually a classic serial killer—but only an emulation or impersonation of one. At the same time, Franklin, in his making the murder of his brother his only priority, can be said to in a way conform to the theory that a serial killer is killing the same person over and over again. The concentrated effort, concentrated deliberation evidenced in the first three crimes suggest that Alice and Megan can be said to be proxies for Sir Carmichael, or rehearsals. The messiness of the "D" crime after the murder of Sir Carmichael at first suggests to the reader a simple loss of interest once Franklin's actual target has been murdered. But Franklin Clarke is not being simply careless—he deliberately disrupts the airtight ABC pattern. The fourth victim, George Earlsfield of Doncaster, has a first name that begins with a G and a last name with an E: the more logical victim, a man names Downes, was sitting two seats away. This at first suggests that the serial killer slipped up. But Downes' first name is Roger, which is also not a part of the pattern, leading us to conclude that the sustaining of the design was virtually pointless for a man who was, in fact, no serial killer. Here, Christie engages in what Shosuke Kinugawa calls her "secret fair play" (Kinugawa 163), as the breakdown of the pattern provides a clue to the reader that the plot is not as abecedarian as the criminal ostensibly contends and as the investigating authorities assumed.

Franklin's goal was the elimination of his brother; once that is accomplished, it is as if he has no incentive, no motive to continue the killings. His need to murder Sir Carmichael had to do with the way the imminent death of Lady Clarke will change the status of Sir Carmichael to widower and will change his secretary Thora Grey into a potential new mate. Time, then, is of the essence. But once Sir Carmichael has died, Franklin can relax into the baronetcy and into his inheritance; he has only to arrange the fourth crime as one that will expose and arrest the man he has designated as the ABC killer. Which, indeed, is what happens. The strange skipping from "D" to "E" in the name of this fourth victim is a clue to alert us to the way the murderer is giving pride of place to "C" which fulfills the message of the Railway Guide, which also stops at "C." But the stopping of the pattern through the confession of Cust allows Christie to direct us away from the design of the crime to its designer, who at first appears to be the man who has confessed to the murders, Alexander Bonaparte Cust.

Christie would not write a pure puzzle mystery without narrative surprise. For all her skill as a deviser of puzzles Christie always puts her mystery in the context of a story that will activate the reader's emotional intelligence. This means that the solution to the puzzle also discloses the mind of the puzzle-maker. We learn that Franklin has developed his ABC design to not only hide the only victim that matters, but to also ruthlessly deflect guilt onto an innocent bystander. The way he has arranged for Alexander Cust, a fragile veteran of the Great War, to take the blame, in fact, is more central to this novel than are the actual murders. Franklin has made the incoherence of the "D" crime mirror the incoherence of Cust himself. The ABC rail guide Franklin leaves beside each victim is also way to draw attention to the way the crime involves travelling, part of a pattern of false clues that lead to the travelling salesman Alexander Bonaparte Cust, a man Franklin met in a chance encounter in a pub.

Christie's narrative strategy has led readers to believe that the murderer is someone other than Franklin, who is virtuously a member of the investigative team helping Poirot. No one can imagine that Franklin's plan is to deflect guilt onto Cust, an ideal scapegoat. Not only are his initials ABC, but he is cognitively impaired, something expressed in the confusions of the "D" crime. As a name, Alexander Bonaparte Cust combines three different military conquerors (General Custer the last). The name also points to those who have distinguished themselves for good or for ill through what Anthony Powell called "the soldier's art," suggesting that Cust too deserves respect. But Clarke sees the name as an ironic one, because, far from a war hero, Cust has merged from the Great War as a damaged, vulnerable veteran. As an epileptic traveling salesman selling women's stockings, Cust is an itinerant, vagrant figure, perhaps one and a half steps above a hobo or a homeless man. As Richard York points out, Cust impresses with "a forceful sense of the fragility of personality, of a person subject to emotions beyond his rational control" (York 29).

Franklin has insinuated himself into the life of this Cust, has hired him to become a travelling salesman working door-to-door, has typed his letters to Poirot on a typewriter residing in Cust's home, and has arranged to have Cust visit all three of the future victims in their various locales in order to sell them stockings. In other words, Franklin has staged something of a performance that will point the finger of guilt at Cust. He knows Cust is a confused and wounded war veteran; in an almost Nietzschean way, Clarke values himself as one of the higher men who exploit the lower man Cust as expendable cannon fodder for his own profit.

Franklin Clarke has exploited Cust's vulnerabilities to the point that Cust himself is convinced he is the murderer; Franklin has not only been building his serial-killer pattern, the murder also increasingly weakens and confuses Cust, clouding his mind and culminating in his confessing to the "D" murder, which was indeed intended to convince Cust that he is, somehow, the criminal mastermind behind the ABC murders. Cust's epilepsy means there are moments when he blacks out, leading him to believe he may have done things he does not remember doing during that time—things that are wrong, transgressive. He suffers such a blackout at the Doncaster movie house at which he has been placed by Franklin Clarke so that later, discovering the murder weapon that Franklin has put in his pocket, he goes to the police, and confesses. in this regard Cust anticipates such future victims of false witness in Christie's mysteries—such as Norma Restarick in *Third Girl*.

The reader is privy to the troubled nature of Cust's interior consciousness, which is interspersed with the main line of the ABC investigations. Because we are drawn close to Cust's point of view, we suspect him of the crimes—that his dazed and bewildered character is one that we can profile as that of a serial killer. There is mystery and suspense in the Cust narrative—we feel it is leading us to some kind of crisis. This was unconventional for Christie, whose art as a storyteller and mystery writer is so premised on withholding information—here, in an unusual way, we are invited to live within the troubled mind of the man who will be identified as the murderer. Certainly, later in her career, however, as in the psychopath in *Endless Night*, she will construct stories based on first-person confessions of those of unsound mind. But here, just as the reader is fooled, so is Cust himself—he has been tricked into thinking that he is, indeed, a murderer. The letter "C" is indeed not only the most important letter in the murder of Clarke; Franklin arranges that this will be the letter of the ostensible murderer, not to mention the letter of the true one.

Even more interesting is the way that Christie, who deceives the reader, and Clarke, who deceives Cust, both have names beginning with "C" and ending with "E." And as Carmichael resides in Churston Ferrers, Devon, so eventually will Christie. The letter "C" then provides a linkage that doubles the mastermind within the narrative with the mastermind who is its author, as well as doubling the compositional structure that is its backbone.

4. The Wheel of Fortune 77

That she and Cust share a "C" name points to a recurring theme in Christie's work, and which has its source in her own well known amnesiac disappearance in 1925—her own blackout. Part of our interest in the design is the way in which it weaves poor Cust into it—he is prey to something larger than himself. Cust believes that some hidden part of himself took control of his actions, although in fact it is the fragility of his personality that has led to his being the subject of another powerful controlling mind who has trapped him in his intricate plan. This is yet another reason this mystery interests us—the design appeals to our intellect, but innocent victims appeal to our moral feeling. Not only are Ascher, Barnard, and Sir Carmichael Clarke victims, Cust himself is meant to be the final sacrificial victim, taking the blame for Franklin's crimes. In turn, the ABC plot advertised by the novel's title and its seeming premise is a false bottom, as the ABC is a feint designed to conceal one specific crime. Readers—who think they have been allowed privileged access to the alleged murderer Cust's point-of-view—have been nearly tricked as the police almost were.

Even though Cust is set up as a likely suspect, there is much about his character that makes it difficult for us to suspect him—or, indeed, to want to suspect him. He may remind us of the curate Hawes in *The Murder at the Vicarage*, suffering from nervous exhaustion or illness, and equally as suggestible. Like Cust, Hawes too was almost victimized by a more personable, presentable, and masterful figure—the Lawrence Redding figure for Hawes becomes Franklin Clarke for Cust. Even before we discover how Clarke took advantage of Cust, it is striking that even as Britain enters the 1930s, Cust, somewhat like Septimus Warren Smith in Virginia Woolf's *Mrs. Dalloway*, still suffers consequences of the Great War—and as such enlists the reader's sympathies.

Poirot himself also guides the reader away from Cust as the culprit when he identifies in the profile of the criminal two separate people who contradict each other—as if a gentle, confused nature has somehow become mixed into a criminal mind. Hastings' narrative tone also shifts from a more detached perspective to an empathic one, which replicates that sense of paradoxical doubleness. The resourceful and daring is paired with the vacillating and suggestible, as if there are two modes of consciousness in one body, as if what is going on inside Cust is a split personality.

Cust, with his ABC name and his perpetually bewildered personality, is another unlucky victim of our serial killer. As we see in other Christie mysteries, what seemed to be a murder game becomes something more tragic. While Christie's puzzle brings to the novel a playfulness that will activate our intellects and make them more agile, our moral compass and our empathy are also gradually activated when we understand that not only are there three murder victims, Cust himself is meant to be the final one. That apprehension about the wrong man identified as the criminal is one that Christie will layer into many of her novels—her novels are not only about Poirot's identification of the murderer, but they are also about Poirot's protection of the innocent from false accusation, false witness. Along with our wish to see the guilty identified, there is a more subtle need to make sure we have not only sorted out the good from the evil, but that we have not got it wrong.

As it turns out, however, it is Franklin who has unwittingly elevated the fortunes of his victim Cust by bringing his story to the attention of his society. Franklin's own clever plan had not considered the skill of his opponent Poirot, nor his tenacity and the percipience. Franklin had originally constructed a game of wits only as a subterfuge, but in doing so he had unwittingly engaged a great and powerful rival. Poirot's exposure of Franklin's plan will bring good luck at last to Cust—the unrecognized soldier will receive medical help and, as the fortuneteller predicted, he will be celebrated for his service in all the papers. His rescue is interestingly, also within a military context—Poirot enlists a selection of helpers related in one way or another to one of the victims, and together they become his "Legion," calling to mind the ancient Roman legions.

This collaboration of the loved ones of the victims is one of the most memorable aspects of the novel, and extends the network of investigation beyond the police, as represented by Inspector Japp, and even beyond the genius private investigator, as represented by Poirot, into a network of concerned people. Franklin Clarke, Alice Ascher's niece Mary Drower, Donald Fraser, Megan Barnard, and Sir Carmichael's secretary Thora Grey all become detectives—but, as Poirot well knows, he has also gathered together his suspects. That the culprit himself turns out to be Franklin Clarke, himself a member of the Legion, is the ultimate betrayal; but it renders the work of Mary Drower (an understated though important character in the novel), Donald Fraser and Megan Barnard as something that is one of the most constructive and affirmative aspects of the book, and supplies a needed moral and attitudinal balance to the sheer evil and manipulativeness of the murderer.

Franklin's bad luck, in turn, generates Cust's rising fortune—rather than facing imprisonment, Cust is promised medical attention that will cure the headaches that led him to feel so often confused. He also acquires enough money so that he can buy a wedding present for Lily Marbury, the landlady's daughter who remained loyal to him in the teeth of the evidence. Here, however, Christie is not only establishing a just outcome to Poirot's investigation, but she also asking us to consider the strangeness in the sudden reversal of fortune in this novel, in which Franklin's fortunes fall, and Cust's rise.

4. The Wheel of Fortune

In keeping with the entire theme of the random crime, towards the end of the novel Poirot makes references to a game of chance—the roulette wheel—as a symbol of the mysterious way luck can turn. It is Poirot who officially introduces the concept of luck into the novel through this reference. When consoling a distraught Thora Grey, he suggests that there will be a change of fortunes, simply, because "the red succeeds the black" (119). Explaining to Hastings that he "speaks the language of the tables" (119), he points out that although there may be a long run on the black, sooner or later the red will come up. The laws of chance promise that luck will turn. He characterizes any murderer as "a supreme kind of gambler" who in committing the crime has risked his life but has failed to understand that his success is unsustainable (224).

Poirot notes that although the murderer believes he has been clever enough to get away with his crime, Franklin did not anticipate the mysterious workings of the wheel of fortune. One day, his run of color will be over as the roulette wheel hits *rouge*, in this novel designated as Poirot's color against Franklin's *noir*. Although Poirot himself is a mastermind, the vagaries of luck are out of Poirot's hands—he is not the power that makes the red succeed the black. Here Christie suggests there are large mysterious forces that Poirot respects, and of which Franklin is ignorant.

The roulette wheel is associated with posh gambling establishments, but in this case, it has turned against the wealthy and insulated Clarke, and his aristocratic world is exposed as decadent and declining; there will be no more marriages, no future generations for the Carmichaels. This suggests not simply blind luck, but turns of luck, as in a cycle, which is represented in this novel by the roulette wheel. The introduction of this wheel of fortune suggests we step back and look at the big picture, in which luck is turning, and those on the bottom are rising, and those at the top are declining. At this point in British history, economic, social and political forces are leading to the greater power of the modern working and middle classes, and the lesser power of the previous and increasingly discredited ruling class—which indeed is what is happening as well in her novel, and which is indeed also tied to the Wheel of Fortune.

The introduction of the wheel moves beyond the image of luck as chaotically random—in a game of chance some balancing occurs when one person has bad luck and another good luck. As e.e. cummings said, "nobody loses all the time" (cummings n.p.). While the idea of the roulette wheel only surfaces in the end of the book, Poirot early establishes the motif of luck. He tells Hastings, "whereas one cannot command a crime to order? Very true." He sighed. "But I believe in luck—in destiny, if you will" (6). It is as if, in a situation in which a change of luck will right a wrong, Poirot will manifest to preside over this transition, as if he himself is an agent of destiny—which he suggests can present the appearance of luck but is part of a larger metaphysical system premised on inevitable changes in fortune. Christie is using the ideas of fortune and luck to help us see the common vulnerability shared by all social classes, all members of society—no one is immune to the randomness of death, violence or shifts in economic fortune.

The Clarke family represents the larger reality of patrician decay, and, conversely, a time in which the common man is elevated. Within this inexorable rise and fall of people from positions of power and privilege, Franklin is himself a fool of fortune, having unwittingly been the agent of his victim Cust's good turn of luck. As every gambler knows, the roulette wheel is then not an image of rigidity or inflexibility—it is an image of energy, and as it spins, a change can come out of the blue—a break in the order of things.

Christie is here taking the idea of the random winds of change and placing it at the same time into the context of a force behind the workings of the world—something known as fate or Fortuna in the Middle Ages, which became our contemporary image of fortune. That Poirot mentions the word luck and the word destiny in the same sentence as virtual equivalents suggests that Christie is entertaining the idea of a hidden order in the randomness of chance. In this regard, Christie has intuitively allied herself with the findings of modern mathematicians—according to Kevin Hartnett, it has been discovered that the moment when a random system seems most chaotic, a hidden geometric order will manifest. She is also addressing the same issues that preoccupied Tolstoy in *War and Peace*—namely, the great and mysterious historical forces bringing things about in the first half of the 19th century. Why do things change, how do they change, how does change come about? Do we change history, or does history change us? Are we the agents of historical processes we cannot understand?

Christie mentions the word "luck" more than twenty times in this novel, and also references the roulette wheel several times. Poirot talks about luck as an integral part of life in such a way that not one of us can ever be in total control of the outcome of our actions. But it is Franklin Clarke, the criminal himself, who evokes luck, the chancy competition between the red and the black—when, caught by Poirot, he says: "Rouge, impair, manque!—You win, M. Poirot! But it was worth trying!" (177). Franklin Clarke's crimes were committed with a pattern he engineered within the seemingly arbitrary atomized ABC Murders—but he did not admit that he also relied on luck. Poirot warns, however, one day the run of luck will end, the croupier calling out "rouge" and indeed Franklin does imitate the voice of a croupier doing just that. Here he acknowledges at last a force greater than himself—something which reintroduces an element of chance and unpredictability as well as giving rise to a mystical sense of wheels within wheels that suggest not accident, but inevitability. Franklin attempts suicide with a small gun from which Poirot had removed the bullets, so there is no escape from this novel's victory of red over black.

Although the battle of wits at the start was part of Franklin's plan of misdirection, the face-to face showdown with Poirot has now become a reality. Here Christie reminds us that on one level, there will always be the game. Her novels are on one level about the game the author and the reader are playing with each other; author and reader are embedded in her stories in an invisible way, but both must be present, and must understand their connection to each other. And this is also a game played between Clarke and Poirot. Clarke's ingenuity and cool, composed demeanor—not to mention his conceit—make him evenly matched with Poirot, which means that Poirot does admit that the criminal mind he is tracking is giving him a game worth playing.

Furthermore, in seeking out England's most famous detective, Franklin perhaps unconsciously expects Poirot to find him. This psychological subtext once again can be said to conform to the psychology of some serial killers, who also seem motivated by a need for recognition, and perhaps a wish to be caught. There is in Clarke this kind of sociopathy that desires a star status, and wants to be perceived as a mastermind. So although the crime is a typically intimate one characteristic of those Poirot usually detects, it is clear that some of the twisted psychology of the serial killer still seems to be an aspect of Franklin's mind-set.

Christie has blocked us from confidently identifying Franklin as the culprit because, as Poirot has noted, we can only do so if we identified him as someone who would create a bizarre design that sacrifices innocent victims to hide the only crime that mattered to him. We must stretch our minds to accommodate Franklin's extremely self-interested, essentially sociopathic logic. The need to understand the mind of Franklin establishes this novel as one of Christie's most psychological. Clarke is a good example of the kind of criminal characteristic of a Christie novel—the murderer is not a poor, deluded man fumbling about without really understanding what's happening to him, but someone who instead has gone to quite a lot of trouble to make careful plans. We will find other villains in Christie who demonstrate a similar tenacity and ingenuity.

That said, there are also some similarities between Clarke and Cust, and some meaningful contrasts. For one thing, both are unmarried and nonreproductive males. This similarity is concealed because Clarke seems so much more presentable and polished. As Poirot points out, the down-at-heel, nearly homeless Cust was totally incapable of making "the click" (169) with the impressionable, boy-crazy Betty Barnard, whereas the suave, polished Franklin does so with ease (only to lure poor Betty to her death). But Franklin is no more capable of an actual relationship with an adult woman than is Cust, and part of his rage at his brother Sir Carmichael is not only his greater success and renown, but that Sir Carmichael has achieved a traditional marriage with Lady Clarke and is poised, even at an advanced age, to do so again with the congenial and willing Thora. Indeed, Clarke can even be seen to be inferior to Cust in this respect.

However incapable Cust might have been of making "the click" with the alluring, available Betty, he is more than capable of wishing his landlady's daughter Lily Marbury well in her marriage to Tom Hartigan (even though Hartigan at one point suspected him of the murder). Though Cust cannot fully function in the way Donald Fraser does in his courtship of Megan, the blessing of his loyal friend Lily's marriage shows his attitude towards the happiness of others is the opposite of the malevolence and exploitation of Franklin Clarke. His concern for others (also expressed in the way he thanks Poirot and even Captain Hastings at the end of the book) means that even though he will never (even after his exculpation and prospective medical treatment) be "whole" he can still care for others.

Franklin, on the other hand, is so personable, so seamlessly integrated into the social system, that exposure as the psychopathic master planner and serial killer is shocking. This is where Christie is hoping to block us from confidently identifying Franklin as the culprit; we can only do so if we understand his mind, and she is assuming that we will not identify him as someone who would create a bizarre design that sacrifices innocent victims to hide the only crime that mattered to him. We must stretch our minds to accommodate Franklin's extremely self-interested, essentially sociopathic logic.

As is so often in Christie, the solution to this crime runs as much to psychology as to clues—Poirot's task is to build a profile of the killer. He even traps Clarke using psychology, lying about finding fingerprints on the gun to rattle him and, as he says, to please Hastings, who also, like Clarke, requires material evidence. Poirot's approach, however, is psychological, assuring Hastings that although they have no material clues, the killer has already thrown light on himself though through the extraordinary plan he is executing. He notes that conceit and self-confidence are two qualities that belong to the inventor of this crime—the crimes reveal his arrogant belief that he is an invulnerable mastermind.

Poirot also suggests that the killer was once a resentful, humiliated child needing recompense for his neglect—and unfortunately remained that way even as an adult. In the case of both the false murderer (Cust) and the true murderer (Clarke), the invocation of the first three letters of

4. The Wheel of Fortune

the alphabet suggests some kind of arrested maturation. In Cust's case, it is as if he is now a neglected and abandoned child, has lost any sense of adult agency. Franklin, on the other hand is depicted as something of a Peter Pan, or someone who has an advanced mind but a stunted character. Poirot notes Franklin's immature "railway mindedness" (246) and points out that Franklin had recently been reading a classic of children's literature, E. Nesbit's *The Railway Children*. It is interesting to further note that the father of the children in the Nesbit story has been falsely imprisoned for the crime of espionage, as if the Nesbit's plot has inspired Franklin to take similar advantage of Cust.

Poirot continues to suggest arrested development in Franklin when he speculates that the criminal grew up "with an inward sense of inferiority—warring with a sense of injustice" and an "inner urge—to assert himself—to focus attention on himself ever becoming stronger, and events, circumstances—crushing it down—heaping, perhaps, more humiliations on him. And inwardly the match is set to the powder train…." (67).

On one level, this is a novel about a modern society in which Agatha Christie lived and in which her publishing career flourished. Without the mass readership of the 20th century, Christie's phenomenal commercial success would have been more difficult to achieve. And yet Christie was herself born in the 19th century, and knew a different world, a more intimate world, a world where individuals—and individual pain, individual resentment—mattered. It is thus important to note that the ABC pattern of this crime recalls childhood, a time when we are all learning our ABC's and can appear to indicate that the murderer is deliberately playing a childish alphabet game, but abstracted in a way that would require railway travel.

Although Franklin's is an adult scheming mastermind, it was the earlier injuries of his childhood that are echoed in the residual childishness of his ABC design. A collateral consequence of Franklin's childish compensatory construction of an identity as an invulnerable mastermind is that he underestimates Poirot when he establishes himself as an intellectual and social superior to the Belgian incomer. Equally damning is Poirot's remark that the murderer is unsporting, that our damaged war hero has been bullied by a stronger and more ruthless man who has every advantage and who has in an unsportsmanlike way preyed upon a troubled and needy veteran, using him as his dupe. That reference to cheating as if in a competition also lightens the mood and reminds once again that this has been a game played between Clarke and Poirot. Poirot adds insult to injury when he explains that Franklin is the type of man who preys on people with who are vulnerable, such as a patient, a child, an old person, someone under stress or psychologically impaired people. Their status as low hanging fruit means that our criminal mastermind is not only immoral, but he has also actually had to cheat to win. Perhaps he cheats at cards as well; here Poirot is exposing him as not only a callous criminal but a very poor example of an English gentleman.

In a related thread of the plot, the attractive Thora, who had been set to inherit the estate through her anticipated marriage to Sir Carmichael, has her luck turn bad as well. The good hearted and dependable girls like Lily, Cust's loyal friend, and Betty's sister Megan, on the other hand, end by hearing wedding bells, as if as much a reward as a twist of fate. But although Poirot suggests that murder is a great matchmaker, the reader may have been surprised that Thora Grey has lost three potential husbands by the end of this story—Sir Carmichael is dead; Franklin has been arrested for his murder; and Hastings, so smitten at first, is no longer interested. Thora, who moves among the upper echelons and who entertained great expectations therein, has now become collateral damage as the Wheel of Fortune turns for the Clarke clan. Her potential as the rejuvenator of the Clarke line through potential children has been demolished; there will be no more Clarkes. Thora's downfall is somehow part of her punishment for not only being a fortune hunter but also a social climber, since it is clear she was hoping to improve her social status through possible marriage to Sir Carmichael.

Social class is very much an issue in this novel—Christie has given us a broader-than-usual picture of a British society which includes both the upper and working classes. Significantly, Thora is the only one of the three women to be moving in patrician circles, and the only woman to fall from grace. Having attached herself to the Clarke world, she, too, will be attached to its declining status. Poirot's task at this juncture is to facilitate a good outcome especially for the younger generation; but within the cyclical wheel of time he can even be elevated to the general status of "mender of destinies" or, as found in its source in the Book of Isaiah, the hero who is "the repairer of the breach, the restorer of paths."

Poirot is the hero who does the right thing at the right time in tandem with the turning of the wheel of fortune; here Poirot serves a power greater than the workings of an arrogant mastermind, and indeed a power greater than himself. And indeed in solving this mystery Poirot does mend the paths of Alexander Cusk, Donald Fraser, and Megan Barnard so they can fulfill their intended destinies.

Christie keeps open the ambiguous relationship between fate and luck, so the mystery of chance itself can be said to remain. It is the random that corrects the ambitions of the human mastermind, and instead of a closed, hermetically sealed master plan, the surprises of the random becomes a breath of fresh air, an escape from the cold schemer always at the heart of crime in a Christie novel. But chance is ultimately the mysterious weapon of a Higher Power. Christie is as if of one mind with a thinker like the poet Gerard Manley Hopkins, who noted in his nature journals, that "chance left free to act falls into an order as well as purpose." The troubled situations of Ascher, Barnard, and Alexander Bonaparte Cust suggests bad luck had drawn more bad luck to them, as if a dark raven has settled in their households; but in the end there is a sense not simply of unpredictable twists of fate, but of enigmatic symmetries that will lead to the inevitable achievement of justice, social justice, and recuperated true love.

Chapter References

Christie, Agatha. *The ABC Murders* (New York: Pocket Books, 1944).
Clanton, Dan W., Jr. *God and the Little Grey Cells: Religion in Agatha Christie's Hercule Poirot Stories* (London; T.T Clark/Bloomsbury, 2024).
cummings, e.e. "Nobody Loses All the Time." https://hellopoetry.com/poem/1628/nobody-loses-all-the-time/.
Ewers, Chris. "Genre in Transit: Agatha Christie, Trains, and the Whodunit." *Journal of Narrative Theory*, vol. 46, no. 1, 2016, pp. 97–120.
Grafe, Adrian. "Hopkins's Saltationism." *Études anglaises*, vol. 64, 2011, pp. 236–248. https://www.cairn.info/revue-etudes-anglaises-2011-2-page-236.htm.
Hartnett, Kevin. "Random Surfaces Hide an Intricate Order." *Quantum Magazine*, July 2, 2019. https://www.quantamagazine.org/random-surfaces-hide-an-intricate-order-20190702/.
Isaiah 58:12. Bible Gateway. https://www.biblegateway.com.
Kinugawa, Shosuke. "Agatha Christie's Secret Fair Play." *Narrative*, vol. 26, no. 2, 2018, pp. 163–180. Project MUSE, https://doi.org/10.1353/nar.2018.0009.
Powell, Anthony. *The Soldier's Art* (London: Heinemann, 1966).
Rezvin, I.I., and Julian Graffy. "Semiotic Analysis of Detective Novels: With Examples from the Novels of Agatha Christie." *New Literary History*, vol. 9, no. 2, 1978, pp. 385–388.
Tolstoy, Leo. *War and Peace* (New York: Vintage, 2008), Part Four, p. 258.
York, R.A. *Agatha Christie: Power and Illusion* (Crime Files) (New York: Palgrave Macmillan 2007).

5

Patriots and Traitors

N or M?

This chapter will explore the role of the Tommy and Tuppence mysteries in Christie's oeuvre. In a tightly linked sequence, the mysteries refer to each other more than do the Poirot and Marple books. Indeed, the inconsistencies that readers often note in the Tommy and Tuppence books are salient precisely because the books are otherwise so tightly linked that no one expects them. That one can take these mysteries as a whole suggests that before going on to our analysis of *N or M?* it is important to comment on the entire sequence. The Tommy and Tuppence canon is also unusual in that short stories (all collected in *Partners in Crime*) play a major role in its construction.

Though Christie's short fiction is criminally (as it were) underrated, the stories involving Poirot and Marple do not substantially contribute to how these detectives are defined over their truly prodigious oeuvre. Within the smaller canon and the more temporally progressive pace of Tommy and Tuppence, though the short stories do matter. The reader of 1941 who had kept pace with all of Christie's work since the beginning saw Tommy and Tuppence not just as the one-time adventurers of *The Secret Adversary* but as veteran detectives who have, in the interwar period, learned enough about human nature to be able to face the challenge of two Nazi agents operating deep within middle England.

Tommy and Tuppence Beresford, as detectives, differ from Miss Marple and Hercule Poirot in being married (obviously to each other) and reproductive (their two children are the twins, Derek and Deborah), an early instance of the later-emerging habit of giving children alliterative names. Derek and Deborah also appropriately repeat the idea of a duo, as their parents are. These are two detectives married to each other; that they also work together is something that makes them distinctive. Another distinction is that Tommy and Tuppence change with time. Miss Marple and Poirot are old when we meet them—although they may be appreciably older in their final mystery (counting *Nemesis*, the last written, as the one in which Miss Marple is the most elderly), we do not see Poirot or Marple move from youth to age.

On the other hand, we watch Tommy and Tuppence travel from their exuberant 20s in *The Secret Adversary* to their brooding 70s in *Postern of Fate*. Of the five books devoted to them, two, *The Secret Adversary* and *Partners in Crime*, picture the couple in their twenties, and two, *By the Pricking of My Thumbs* and *Postern of Fate*, find them firmly in old age. Only *N or M?* presents them in what might be called their prime. As Megan Hoffman points out, between these spurts the couple seems to take a "hiatus from detection" (Hoffman 31). Their appearance and their aging have a punctuated, drastic aspect, more of a quantum leap than the gradual aging of a series protagonist, such as for instance, Rabbit Angstrom in the John Updike novels. Tommy and Tuppence's five books are more like a compressed version of Shakespeare's seven ages of man: youth, young adulthood, maturity, age, and the only end of age.

Although Tommy and Tuppence are unique in Christie's gallery of detectives in their husband-and-wife partnership, Poirot and Ariadne Oliver in *Third Girl* (1966) and *Hallowe'en Party* (1969) also feature a certain Tommy-and-Tuppence aspect, especially not unlike the Tommy and Tuppence we find in *By the Pricking of My Thumbs* (1968) and *Postern of Fate* (1973). Tuppence and Ariadne are similar in the way each undertake separate roles of detection and are redoubtable older women in the style perhaps of Christie herself as she was writing these books. In *Third Girl* and *By the Pricking of My Thumbs*, both Ariadne and Tuppence also receive concussions because of their detective efforts. But although Tuppence eventually advances into the dignity of old age, in the first two mysteries she and Tommy are young and in love. In *N or M?* they sustain an aura of the still-youthful, the still in love, despite middle age and parenthood. And although the never-youthful Hercule and Ariadne are just good friends, they work as a team, even if not a romantic one, making the Belgian bachelor a little more heteronormative, providing him a kind of female companionship.

One can even whisper that in those books Hercule Poirot has found a girlfriend, albeit in a very limited sense of the word. We can even see Ariadne Oliver's entrance into the section as a shock to the reader who had made certain assumptions about the detective and his Sherlockian distaste for or abstention from the female. And although in the earlier books, the young, adventurous and married Tommy and Tuppence were very different from the solitary, cerebral Poirot, in their final outings they have somewhat found their way into Poirot's more reflective territory.

This testifies to Christie's capacity to entertain unorthodox views of male-female relationships, views not necessarily bound by stereotypes of either the married or unmarried elderly person. For instance, as Philip Scowcroft has pointed out, we meet Tuppence first under her maiden name—Prudence Cowley (Scowcroft 12). This suggests that Tuppence will always be on one level independent of her marriage, her "own woman, well at ease, well off."

It is obvious that Miss Marple and Hercule Poirot are older than Christie and remain so even as Christie herself ages. Miss Marple is a portrait of a late-Victorian spinster, in the spirit of the generation of Christie's mother or even grandmother. Poirot is already an elderly refugee when he arrives in England during the First World War, and his survival into the 1960s is a magical-realist one. What has often been missed, though, is that Tommy and Tuppence are *younger* than Christie when we first meet them. As *The Secret Adversary* makes clear, they come to adulthood during the war and are still in their early twenties in this, their first mystery. Christie was a married woman by the time the war broke out and had her child at around the time *The Secret Adversary* was set. What Sarah Martin called Tuppence's "Flapper sleuth" identity (Martin 139) was hardly shared by Christie, a thirtyish wife and mother at the time she wrote the novel. In *Partners in Crime*. Tuppence is even said to be under 25, which would make her circa ten years younger than Christie herself.

Indeed, Christie is not only writing about people slightly younger than she is, but she is also writing about a different generation. One can see in her portrayal of Tommy and Tuppence as 1920's style Bright Young Things in *The Secret Adversary* and *Partners in Crime*, suggesting that Christie is probing into the workings of an essentially younger generation, a consequence of the "cultural upheaval" (Hoffman 33) of the First World War. Later, after the Second World War, she will do something similar in her portrayal of David Baker, "The Peacock," in *Third Girl*, a figure of the Swinging Sixties, albeit within a far longer spectrum of generational distance. In *N or M?* Tommy and Tuppence are in their forties while Christie is in her fifties, and in *Postern of Fate*, when Christie is 83, the couple is still only in their seventies.

In the penultimate Tommy and Tuppence, *By the Pricking of My Thumbs*, Tommy and Tuppence are in their late fifties or early sixties, noticeably younger than other characters in the novel, such as Mrs. Lancaster; Sir Philip Starke; Tommy's aunt, Ada Fanshawe (who dies in the novel, and probably not of natural causes); and Mrs. Moody (same). As commentators have noticed, the aging of Tommy and Tuppence (and of their children) is inconsistent, but there is one consistency: they are always younger than Christie when she wrote about them. Despite their relative youth, however, Christie decided to see the Beresfords through their entire lives, so that they, too, will one day become elderly detectives like Poirot and Miss Marple. The resources and continuing value of the older or the aged will then find a way into her Tommy and Tuppence series as well.

It is Tommy and Tuppence's youthful irreverence, however, that is foremost when we first meet them as barely post-teenagers in *The Secret Adversary*, giving that novel, as well as *Partners in Crime* a sense of lightness and zaniness redolent of the *joie de vivre* of youth, even and in a way especially, in the 1920s wake of the trauma of wartime slaughter and postwar disillusionment. Though these high spirits inevitably flag in the last three Tommy and Tuppence books, their mysteries are still celebrations of their life as a couple together, their clear mutual happiness and camaraderie. Yet Tommy and Tuppence are essentially fictional creations and not based on Christie or her relationships. After all, she wrote the first book while married to Archibald Christie, the book of short stories *Partners in Crime* while divorcing him, and the last three while married to Max Mallowan. Yet Tommy and Tuppence remain much the same, even as they age and their life circumstances change.

Tommy and Tuppence are relatively unobtrusive in their mysteries, although this is less true in *Partners in Crime* where they, and their bogus detective agency, are the common thread linking stories of heterogeneous situations that in turn parody previous detective writers. But, in general, their stories are not about their marriage. As compared to Nick and Nora Charles in Dashiell Hammett's *The Thin Man* novel, or Jerry and Pam North in Frances and Richard Lockridge's series about them, Tommy and Tuppence meld into the dark situations of their mysteries. This gives the Tommy and Tuppence novels a sober realism that lies behind, and buttresses, their "caper" quality, and their sense of irreverent humor. That such a high-spirited book as *N or M?* could be written not just during and about the Second World War but during and about Britain's finest and darkest hour in late 1940, when Britain stood alone and an imminent German invasion was feared, shows the effective interplay of a fun, frothy surface and a deeper, thoroughgoing realism, in which the couple investigate a crime but also acknowledge the dire social circumstances of the time.

Tommy and Tuppence stories have a playful aspect to them, most obviously in their youthful mysteries, but even their final adventure, *Postern of Fate*, is studded with allusions to old books which inevitably give it a self-referential quality but also a ludic aspect that is consonant with what we expect of Tommy and Tuppence, continuing the motif of the German spy that is at the center of the *N or M?* mystery. Throughout the oeuvre of Tommy and Tuppence, the two world wars loom large. *Postern of Fate* is about British xenophobia and the consequences of the way the British Mary Jordan is taken for a German spy. Given that the novel was published just after Great Britain entered the European Union, the novel thereby gained new relevance after Brexit in 2016. *Postern of Fate* is also one of the last works, in any genre, that refers to the First World War by someone of an age to have both witnessed the war as an adult and participated in it (as Christie did, albeit on the home front).

The narrative inevitably ponders the relation between Britain and Germany in peace and in war, and the role of suspicion and fear in local British communities that goes beyond, and to a darker place, beyond patriotism and national loyalty. *Postern of Fate* evinces a concern about right-wing tendencies in the village that might have seemed outdated in 1973, but prescient after 2016. The novel stretches through time in a meaningful way and although it is, as critics have noted, the work of an older writer not at the peak of her powers, it does touch upon several core aspects of Tommy and Tuppence and demonstrates why the couple are important to Christie's oeuvre. Foremost among these is the couple's link to military intelligence and foreign intrigue. Though all five of the books in which they appear occur entirely within England, there is always a link to the foreign and the transnational—in *Postern of Fate*, not just to Germany but to East Africa where the Beresfords' adopted daughter Betty works as an anthropologist. Nor is xenophobia and paranoia always dominant.

The reader of *The Secret Adversary* might think that Julius Hirsheimmer—businessman, American, and, quite possibly Jew—is the villain, but in fact, he is the book's secondary hero, who is rewarded with romance; the villain is the impeccably British and aristocratic Sir James Peel Edgerton. The book is an early venture in the transatlantic for Christie, literally so, in that the sinking of the *Lusitania* by German submarines in the mid–Atlantic is a major plot point, and more figuratively in its braiding of British and American characters, concerns, and culture in the wake of the unprecedented British-American military cooperation developed in the war.

In general, one would say that in their internationalism, the Beresfords are closer to Poirot, who even when he is not explicitly abroad is looking at England with a foreign eye that in critic Viktor Shklovsky's famous phrase "lays bare the device" by which Poirot investigates his cases, as opposed to Miss Marple, whose device is the memory of the Victorian/Edwardian past of England. One might say in general that Christie's non-series detective books (among which we might strategically class the Tommy and Tuppence books even though, in their modest way, they are also a series) are less rooted in the Englishness, or the English stereotypes of the foreigner than the Poirot and Marple books.

This is illustrated by the way that, in the 2023 BBC adaptation of Christie's *Murder Is Easy* (1939; also published as *Easy to Kill*) the detective figure, Luke Fitzwilliam, is represented as Nigerian. Luke Fitzwilliam appears only in that one book and is somewhat of a cipher, and is there only, the reader might feel, because Christie did not want to center this particular novel around Marple or Poirot. It makes as much sense to have Fitzwilliam be a Nigerian as any other alternative simply because Christie does not invest Fitzwilliam with any signifiers of national identity. Tommy and Tuppence, although certainly not represented as anything other than conventionally English, are not rooted in an archetypal English identity, as is Miss Marple, or in its inversion, as with Poirot. Both the Marple and Poirot series cannot help but be national in tincture, even though they represent very different versions of the national.

The Tommy and Tuppence stories, on the other hand, are grounded in a sense of the international, even those, unlike *N or M?* that are set during peacetime; their mysteries involve crimes that have to do with networks of interest that are continental (and this is true even of *By the Pricking of My Thumbs*). Beginning with *The Secret Adversary*, the international ground of the Beresford books is given new sobriety through the introduction of war. As Jessica Gildersleeve notes, "*The Secret Adversary* both conceals and reveals the traumatic impact of the First World War on British society. It is important that, unlike *early* Christie novels, the war is mentioned in *The Secret Adversary*, laying groundwork for the Second World War to become the background of *N or M?*"

Her novel *N or M?*, particularly, was set in a tremendous time of transition, so that, for instance, we speak today of post–World War II literature as a new era. The novel itself is very much a line of demarcation, ushering us into Christie's Middle Phase, beginning with the war. It is this novel that also shows Tommy and Tuppence in their Middle Years—perhaps at the top of their game. This may be especially true of Tuppence. As Mary Vipond says, "In *N or M?* Tuppence Beresford, by now a middle-aged woman with a grown family, fakes a telephone call, hides in a cupboard, and beats her husband Tommy to the scene of a spy investigation in which she then plays a major role" (119). The years have not made her matronly, or conventional, or sedentary.

Of all Christie's detectives, it is Tommy and Tuppence who enjoy adventure most. The novels in which they appear are more action-packed than her traditional mysteries. To some extent, Tommy is the brawn and Tuppence the brains, but one might say that each has a particular cognitive style that works for them as detectives. Tommy and Tuppence, while a twosome, are not mirror images; each has an individual approach to detection. Neither their partnership nor the marriage homogenizes the duo— each remains very much an individual with an individual style. Tuppence, for instance, is more impulsive—which is ironic, since her given name is

Prudence; Tommy, on the other hand, is slower and steadier. We see this dichotomy in another way in *N or M?*: while Tommy ponders the problem of having to deceive as necessary to spy work, Tuppence cheerfully insists she does not "mind lying in the least," and derives "artistic pleasure" from her deceptions (81).

Though not amateurs in the sense of Miss Marple, they are not professionals in the sense of the spymasters Mr. Carter or Mr. Grant, or official police detectives such as Superintendent Battle. As Lucy Hall and Gill Plain say, "Tommy and Tuppence are amateurs, dependent upon chance and inspiration. They defeat a ruthless, professionally trained enemy through common sense, creative thinking, and farce" (Hall and Plain 122). The word "farce" here points to certain silliness in the first two Tommy and Tuppence books, which had attenuated by *N or M?* although it is still there in the interstices, such as Tuppence's comical and only half-explicable choice of the surname Blenkensop as her alias, and Tommy's bemused reaction.

The alias of Blenkensop in *N or M?* raises the question of the names Tommy and Tuppence. Tuppence is the two-cent British coin. It is also considered a negligible amount, as in "not caring tuppence," but it is also both a coin and a word very much associated with England—America does not have an equivalent coin. The name Tommy originally meant "twin," which means that each name has an "it takes two" aspect, suitable for their partnership. Tommy's name also is redolent of Englishness; a popular given name among the British, it was also the nickname for the infantryman in the British army and had been so for centuries. "Tommy" was an especially popular name for the British soldier during World War I, which was Tommy Beresford's war. In their adventures, Tommy and Tuppence are usually defending England against one enemy or another, as one would in war.

To quote Philip Larkin, *N or M?* was set "in the depths of the Second World War" (Larkin 179). It was published in 1941. France has fallen, and so has the Netherlands; the Allied troops have been evacuated from Dunkirk; the Battle of Britain and the German bombing Blitzkrieg begins and continues into 1941, which also saw the fall of Yugoslavia and Greece. This novel was published, however, before the Japanese bombing of Pearl Harbor, and before America entered the war; it was also published before Germany suffered a setback at the hands of Russia. This means that when Christie wrote this novel, the UK was a country in crisis in which it was not at all clear that there would always be an England. Victory was far from assured; no one knew what the future held, certainly; neither Tommy nor Tuppence was certain of what would come next.

This mystery especially marks a transition into a world more serious for both Tommy and Tuppence, taking place as it does only a year or so after the beginning of the Second World War, when the outcome is far from certain. France had fallen, the British forces had narrowly managed to retreat at Dunkirk. Britain was experiencing the airborne assault of the Luftwaffe and fearing an imminent German invasion. Within this historical situation, Tommy and Tuppence's adventures are more sobering, given what Tuppence refers to as "the pity, the waste, and the horror" of the war. Generally, Christie does not refer to the war in her novels of that period; what makes "*N or M?*" unusual is the degree to which her depiction of the war was important to this narrative and has also proved of value to historians.

In keeping with Christie's "it takes two" motif, two spies for Germany will be uncovered by two detectives. A cryptic message from German intelligence mentions, "N or M. Song Susie," which is decoded as Sans Souci, a hotel in Leahampton, and "N and M" as spies for Germany, one male and one female. That the initial used for each are two letters next to each other in the alphabet suggests not only twinning, but a confusion of twins—we do not know if the mastermind is "N" or "M." That the German code includes the French name of the boarding house and a formulation known in England through its use in law courts and the Anglican Church, demonstrates the polyglot nature of this conspiracy. Indeed, the culprits turn out not to be Germans but English.

It is Tommy, posing as Mr. Meadowes, who tracks down the male spy, known as "M." "M" is Commander Haydock, who masks his actual status as a spy by bringing his spy paraphernalia out in the open, claiming that it is all left over from the time when German spies used the house in the First World War. But this spy equipment is not leftover technology, but new technology that can communicate with the Commander's staff officers at the Sans Souci hotel, who will carry out a plan for invasion.

Tommy cannot help but admire the ingenuity of the scheme he helps expose. Commander Haydock has been convincingly impersonating a hearty Englishman but is unmasked as a spy for Germany. As was true of Tuppence in her investigation, Tommy detects Commander Haydock by means of analogy, recalling an episode when a Prussian bully had berated a subordinate, reminding him of Commander Haydock to the letter. It should not go unremarked, however, that Tommy himself is impersonating yet another hearty Englishman, almost a mirror image of Haydock's equally staged version. The complexity of Haydock's character, however, is that he possesses a double articulation as that of both an Englishman and a German. At times he appears to be not only a German spy but is an example of the British Fifth Column, suggesting that the invasion by the Nazis he is planning may be not literal, but psychological and philosophical.

That is, for some Englishman, the Nazis have already arrived and installed themselves in their psyches. Commander Haydock's final speech to Tuppence, for instance, suggests that there are rather a lot of people in England who could be easily persuaded to serve the Nazi cause. With an arrogant and utopian ideology that shades very easily into the totalitarian, eugenically-minded Nazi philosophy, Haydock tells Tuppence: "Our leader does not intend to conquer this country in the sense that you all think. He aims at creating a new Britain—Britain strong in its power—ruled over, not by Germans, but by Englishmen. And the best type of Englishmen—Englishmen with brains and breeding and courage. A brave new world, as Shakespeare puts it" (213).

The last two sentences are especially telling—there is a certain eugenically-minded aspect to the reference to the "best type of Englishman." Huxley's dystopian novel, *Brave New World*, had been out for about a decade, so the phrase "brave new world" is associated less with the optimistic Miranda of Shakespeare's *Tempest*, and more with its ironic use as an image of a future in which humanity has lost its bearings. Haydock's belief in a future of British supermen, however, permits no doubts or questioning and instead encourages him to do whatever it takes to bring about that world. Here he identifies as a British man who would be the first to be rewarded with power should the German army succeed in invading England. Something similar had already happened in France, where the collaborationist government at Vichy, was composed of people who were often sympathetic to Nazi political views, but who also saw themselves as French patriots. From the perspective of most of the French however, and especially from the perspective of the French Resistance, these patriots were treasonous—the vice-president of the Vichy government was executed by a firing squad after the war. At the end of the Second World War, two prominent supporters of the British Union of Fascists, Oswald Mosley and William Joyce, who had fled to Nazi Germany, were arrested and tried for treason. Joyce ultimately was executed (Pugh 314).

The character of Haydock then takes on the aspect of a Fifth Columnist, a British man of some status whose sympathies are with the Nazis. Here Christie manages to deploy Haydock as a German spy and at the same time a redoubtable Englishman who is part of the Fifth Column of British nationals who support the enemy. The presence of a Fifth Column was an issue that was of concern throughout the country at the time, and concentration on local rather than invasive fascism is also something that works well within Christie's chosen world—her specialty is the menace coming from within intimate worlds, from inside the seemingly safe and protected world of the domestic and the everyday. Christie here is indeed suggesting that, to paraphrase Sinclair Lewis, "it can happen here," in England's own sceptered isle.

5. Patriots and Traitors

The most ingenious and least detectable disguise, however, is not Commander Haydock's "N," but "M," who, disguised as a Mrs. Sprot, appears to have fled London and the Blitz with her baby for the safety of the Sans Souci hotel. Tuppence, posing as a Mrs. Blenkensop, exposes this ruthless spy, who appears to be an ordinary young British mother, with bland gooseberry eyes that suggest she is a harmless Mum preoccupied with her baby daughter. Mrs. Sprot is the brains behind the powerful and complex espionage organization centered at Sans Souci. It is she who is the mastermind. The dissonance between her appearance and her reality makes this discovery preposterous, as Tuppence herself admits, and yet Christie makes it work. Very early, Tuppence thinks, "To believe in Sans Souci as a headquarters of the Fifth Column needed the mental equipment of the White Queen in Alice." To clarify this remark: the White Queen is the figure in *Alice in Wonderland* who was able to believe "six impossible things before breakfast." This means that Tuppence must imagine the unimaginable to detect Mrs. Sprot—and it will prove to be the case that imagining the unimaginable is a very good approach to the reality of Nazi Germany.

At first, Tuppence very early considers and discards Mrs. Sprot as the hidden traitor because of her status as a mother; but it is always important to take a second look at any suspect Christie appears to have discarded. Mrs. Sprot appears to be a generic mother—the issue here is stereotypes, which are meant to make us feel that everything is safe and in order, when in fact Christie suggests that a conventional appearance can easily be a disguise—it is the easy assurance of safety and security that their disguises encourage that allows our villains to be indistinguishable from anyone else's reassuring appearance. It is when Mrs. Sprot rather too resourcefully murders the woman we believe has kidnapped Betty that doubts begin to surface. At this point, readers might sense something "not right" about Mrs. Sprot and her baby Betty, even as the reader is still imprisoned in a narrative that prevents the recognition of the truth. When Mrs. Sprot shoots Vanda Polonska, we assume her motive is that of a mother lion protecting her young; it has not occurred to us that this is a cold-blooded murder of an innocent woman who is Betty's true mother. Mrs. Sprot is yet another example of the ingenious way in which Christie conceals her murderers; Mrs. Sprot not only keeps her true identity hidden, but her also seeming defense of baby Betty masks the crime as well. Like Commander Haydock's spy equipment, Mrs. Sprot's actions as a spy are hidden in plain sight. The one murder in the novel is at the time not identified as such by anyone, including the reader. The reality of this episode is that Mrs. Sprot is not shooting a woman to prevent her from kidnapping baby Betty—Mrs. Sprot is in a cold-blooded way murdering Betty's mother, Vanda Polonska, who is there to reclaim her own. We do not even think there is a murderer to hunt down, and we do not take Vanda Polonska for the victim she is.

Like Tommy, Tuppence is helped to penetrate Mrs. Sprot's disguise through analogy. When observing Mrs. Sprot as she murders the woman who is the true mother of the baby, Tuppence is reminded of the Biblical story of King Solomon and the two mothers each of whom claim possession of the same child: the mother most reluctant to endanger the baby is deemed the real mother. Similarly, Mrs. Sprot's need to silence Vanda was such that she readily endangered the life of baby Betty who was virtually in the line of fire. That Mrs. Sprot is a terrifying crack shot who can take Vanda Polonska out with cold detachment also shows us she does not fit into the persona of the ditzy but devoted Mum she has constructed for public consumption.

There is a mirroring shadow in the way in which Mrs. Sprot doubles for Tuppence, in that Mrs. Sprot is a kind of anti-mother to Tuppence's good mothering. The theme of motherhood is an important one in this novel, but Mrs. Sprot is the opposite of a real mother, only using this persona as a way to give aid to the enemy—her identity as a mother is simply a brilliant disguise. Christie provides a good outcome for baby Betty when she is adopted by Tommy and Tuppence—Betty will now once again have a truly devoted mother. And there is another Biblical reference concerning Tuppence that speaks more specifically to the idea of a good outcome—this is the reference to the slaying of the oppressive Canaanite ruler Sisera by the Israelite woman Jael, fulfilling the prophecy of Deborah that a woman would be victorious over the enemy of Israel, as Tuppence is victorious over Mrs. Sprot. This analogy also provides a bit of either prophecy or hope about the outcome of the war itself.

That we have mistaken the illusion for truth is also the case with baby Betty herself. As there is something not right about Mrs. Sprot, there is also something not right about Betty's baby talk. Her babbling can suggest that Betty has been listening to her Polish mother—that she had learned a different language earlier. One can even conclude that the babble is on the verge of revealing Mrs. Sprot's secrets—the "Nazer" word that surfaces among the nonsense syllabus especially suggests this, with its homophonic relationship to the word "Nazi." The nonsense talk of Betty is eventually something Tuppence herself employs when she mocks Commander Haydock with a defiant "goosey goosey gander" retort to his Nazi plans for world domination, suggesting that Tuppence is making the point that his precious Nazi ideology is in reality just nonsense, barely a cut above childish prattle (88).

In addition to the least-likely Mrs. Sprot, the Sans Souci boarding house is filled with more likely suspects, including two Irishwomen, the canny resident Mrs. O'Rourke, and the proprietress Mrs. Perenna. Mrs. Perenna, despite her seemingly Spanish or Portuguese name, is British-presenting and appears to have the usual British sympathies—but in fact, she is secretly a member of the I.R.A., some of whose leaders did at that time have links with Nazi Germany. She can also be said to shade into a Fifth Columnist. As Judy Suh demonstrates, though, Christie notably eschews the anti–Irish sentiment typical of British government propaganda at the time, "avoiding self-righteous judgment" (Suh 150), even as Mrs. Perenna's sympathies are not with England. Additionally, the dictatorial Mr. Cayley is an open admirer of the Nazi system. Then there is Tony Marsdon, the Beresford daughter Deborah's young man who presents himself as a helpmeet, but who is exposed as something of a colleague of Mrs. Sprot's. Aside from their status as suspects, Christie here is stocking her Bournemouth hotel with not-very-nice characters to such an extent that Tuppence struggles with having to admit the possibility that these people are truly typical of her fellow countrymen. One figure, Major Bletchley, in particular, echoes Commander Haydock in that he is an old-school military man who is so much a cliché that Tuppence suspects him of creating a false front. It was because of Major Bletchley that British intelligence MI5 investigated Christie (see Taylor) for fear that she knew something about what was going on in Bletchley Park, the legendary big mansion that housed all accomplished codebreakers.

Tuppence herself finds Bletchley irritating, as did Christie when interrogated about him—and in general, Tuppence finds all her fellow countrymen in the hotel so unpleasant that her favorite boarder is Carl von Deinim, supposedly a German refugee. Tuppence is gratified that here is a resident of the hotel who is not staging a virtue-signaling performance as a patriotic Englishman. But Carl was, as it happens, loyal to England, and had been working for British intelligence in Germany. To flee Germany, he has been impersonating his friend Carl, who had been murdered by the Nazis. He is then, once again in the liminal zone like Commander Haydock's, in which the German identity and the British identity mix and mingle in such a way that it is impossible to tell them apart. Here *N Or M?* deliberately unsettles the idea of a fixed British identity and deliberately and inventively blends it with its wartime enemy. If, as Judy Suh points out, "Christie has Major Bletchley also regularly conflating refugees and enemies" (Suh 143), Christie in turn unsettles any fixed sense that one can always distinguish between the enemies of the English and the English themselves.

Although British, Carl's time in Germany has ironically led him to feel so close to the German people as to become one of them, and he is concerned for the safety of his friends there. Tuppence shares his concern, explaining: "But when I think of individual Germans, mothers sitting anxiously waiting for news of their sons, and boys leaving home to fight ... and some of the nice kindly German people I know, I feel quite different. I know then they are just human beings and that we're all feeling alike. That's the real thing. The other is just the War mask that you put on. It's a part of War—probably a necessary part—but it's ephemeral" (96).

Christie is having Tuppence warn against the dehumanizing effects of war. Suh points out that another way Christie works to eliminate a sense of the demonized other is the way she suggests xenophobic prejudice "strongly deters refugees' considerable potential to contribute to the British war effort" (145). Turning the novel to recruiting those who can serve war effort, however, reinstates the very division between that this novel is determined to interrogate. Serving the war effort is less the topic of this novel than the development of a fresher and less familiar perspective, in which we are asked to develop a mentality that can imagine the cessation of mandatory national aggression.

Throughout this novel, Tommy and Tuppence have been considering the dangers of insular patriotism, from Mrs. Perenna to Carl, from Commander Haydock to Mrs. Sprot. Related to this theme is Tommy's introduction of Edith Cavell into the conversation. Edith Cavell was a nurse who famously cared for the ill no matter what their country of origin; as a result, she was shot as a spy by the Germans and is noted for the comment she made before her death, which is paraphrased by Tommy as "Patriotism is not enough.... I must have no hatred in my heart" (60). The prominent mention of Edith Cavell reminds us that, although this novel has been about treachery, it is also about mindful versus mindless patriotism. Christie's purpose here was to write against an impoverishing self-certainty and close-mindedness in England that might lead to the ruthlessness and insular nationalism associated with the other side. We can see that Christie feared her country would become a mirror-image of Germany's chauvinism—that is, would develop a similar aggressive irrational patriotism that could lead to persecution of particular religions, nationalities, and ethnicities.

N or M? also addresses how the force of German propaganda will appeal to the worst instincts of the English. British intelligence agent Grant suggests that Nazi propaganda appeals to "some desire or lust for power. These people were ready to betray their country not for money, but in a kind of megalomaniac pride in what they, *they*, were going to achieve for that country. In every land, it has been the same. It is the Cult of Lucifer—Lucifer, Son of the Morning. Pride and a desire for *personal glory!*" (225).

The mention of Lucifer in this paragraph is striking. Here Christie touches on that sense of the demonic found in other writings about the

Nazi movement—Klaus and Thomas Mann, or more recently Roberto Bolano's *2666*. But in general, this mystery is preparing for a return of peace, rather than an England always subject to a wartime mentality or the prominence of the military. Suh argues that the novel "utterly fails" (154) to provide a diagnosis of fascism. But one could argue conversely that Christie shows that English patriotism can elide into fascism if taken to an extreme, and that fascist sympathies can develop beneath the surface of familiar British insularity. Christie also suggests that the most compelling way to both ward off fascism and avoid having anti–Fascism become monstrous is to sustain empathy, cultivate critical intelligence—and keep calm, carry on with a normal life. There is a "fight the good fight" energy here, but on the other a certain moral clarity and reserve. Christie is certainly convinced of the threat of the Nazis and the need to win the war—she has the entire Beresford family involved in this effort. In her personal life, she gave her house over to the military for the duration of the war; additionally, her daughter Rosalind's first husband was killed in action. But choosing Tommy and Tuppence to preside over her war novel suggests that Christie is placing Britain within a sophisticated international context. Additionally, this novel is not a murder mystery; it is as if on one level Christie feels that her British readership has had enough of death and dying and that the anxiety of the war was all that was needed to create the necessary narrative tension. Our sole murder, for instance, does not allow for a whodunit motif, in which Christie would allow for quiet moments of reflection that in the crisis moment of this novel become too much of a luxury. In terms of negotiating the issues that faced the country in crisis, Christie knew that the task must be given to Tommy and Tuppence less in the context of a murder mystery, but more in the context of the contagion of a political philosophy that actually normalizes the crime of murder. For this she selected her still vigorous, dashing young iconic British moderns, who must find a way out of the fascist ideology itself that may be invading England, into their own humane peacetime futures, and the country's.

Chapter References

Christie, Agatha. *N or M?* (New York: Berkley Books, 1984).
Christie, Agatha. *Postern of Fate* (London: Collins, 1973).
Gartchev, Slav, and Howard Mancing. *Viktor Shklovsky's Heritage in Literature, Arts, and Philosophy* (Lanham: Lexington, 2019), p. 72.
Gildersleeve, Jessica. "Commemorating Forgetting: 1922 and Golden Age Detective Fiction." *Modernism/Modernity*, December 13, 2022, 290.
Hall, Lucy, and Gill Plain. "Unspeakable Heroism: The Second World War and the End of the Hero," in B. Korte and S. Lethbridge, eds., *Heroes and Heroism in British Fiction Since 1800* (Cham: Palgrave Macmillan, 2017). https://doi.org/10.1007/978-3-319-33557-5_7.
Hoffman, Megan. *Gender and Representation in British 'Golden Age' Crime Fiction* (London: Palgrave, 2016).

Larkin, Philip. "Poem about Oxford: For Monica." *Collected Poems* (Boston: The Marvell Press and Faber & Faber, 1988).

Martin, Sarah. "Psychogeography and the Flapper Sleuth." In Mary Anna Evans and J.C. Bernthal, eds., *The Bloomsbury Handbook to Agatha Christie* (London: Bloomsbury Academic, 2023), pp. 139–54.

Norton-Taylor, Richard. "Agatha Christie was investigated by MI5 over Bletchley Park mystery." *The Guardian*, February 4, 2013. Accessed February 24, 2024, https://www.theguardian.com/books/2013/feb/04/agatha-christie-mi5-bletchley.

Pugh, Martin. *'Hurrah for the blackshirts!' Fascists and Fascism in Britain Between the Wars* (London: Pimlico, 2006).

Scowcroft, Philip. "The Woman Detective in Fiction: Sayers' Contribution." *Sidelights on Sayers*, vol. 35, June 1991, pp. 12–17.

Shakespeare, William. *Troilus, and Criseyde Book II*. The City University of New York. Accessed March 5, 2024, http://academic.brooklyn.cuny.edu › troilus2.

Suh, Judy. "Rerouting Wartime Paranoia in Agatha Christie's N or M?" *Journal of Modern Literature*, vol. 46 no. 2, 2023, pp. 140–156.

Vipond, M. (Mary). "Agatha Christie's Women." *International Fiction Review*, vol. 8, no. 2, Summer 1981, pp. 119–23.

6

Deep Egypt

Death Comes as the End

Because she spent so much time (1930 to 1958) as a member of her husband's team when he went on his archaeological digs in the Middle East, Christie became increasingly interested in the history of this region, "travelled yearly to archaeological sites in Iraq" (Melman 189) and became an expert on Mesopotamian archaeology. As Billie Melman shows, Christie's work was a key part of what Melman describes as the modern rediscovery of the ancient Near East. She set several of her novels in the Middle East and in Egypt. She also wrote a play, *Akhnaton*, set an era later in Egyptian history than *Death Comes as the End*. What Edmund P. Cueva says about *Akhnaton*, that it sees the Eighteenth Dynasty heretic Pharoah as a figure of "ancient modernity" (Cueva 38) and that Christie's interest in him is traceable to a post–Enlightenment icon of a "Romantic Egypt" (Cueva 50), is also true, mutatis mutandis, of *Death Comes as the End*.

This novel is Christie's only historical mystery and was foundational in the now-proliferating historical mystery form as such. There had been mysteries referring to ancient Egypt, such as S.S. Van Dine's *The Scarab Murder Case* (1930), but this was a novel set in modern times and did not make the leap to understanding that using rational investigative procedures of the sort needed to solve murder cases would work in societies that believed in complex metaphysical systems very different from our own perspectives. Notably, though, whereas the historical mystery genre as it flourishes today foregrounds atmosphere and provides a vivid sense of the period over plot and character, Christie's novel is a psychological crime story that just happens to be set in a different period. Though certainly doing more worldbuilding in the book than in her modern mysteries, Christie does not let the worldbuilding overwhelm plot and key characters. This is still a Christie mystery.

"As Jesper Gulddal says of Christie's *Appointment in Death* set in modern Palestine, Christie in *Death Comes as the End* was able to relocate an English murder mystery" to a Middle East "rife with cultural and mythical meanings" (Gulddal 1803).

Death Comes as the End was the product of Christie's new research as well as the extensive background knowledge on her part. Her story is one she derived from actual letters found in Egypt and were translated by the Oxford Egyptology professor Battiscombe Gunn, which tell of a farmer and mortuary priest named Heqanakhte who lived at the end of the Eleventh Dynasty, around 2134 BCE. The letters contain "intimate aspects" (Melman 295) and complain about his family and their treatment of his concubine.

Christie's setting includes a depiction of an Egyptian household of the time, although, like the art of the time, this depiction is slightly abstracted and geometric in presentation. Christie also emphasizes the agricultural calendar, which had three seasons that ran from July to July. The year in this novel ends just before the next inundation, when the fields would be once again planted. Christie threads into the novel a sense of how "the ancient Egyptian mind-set" was "deeply rooted in their distinctive geographical surroundings" where the Nile could "both create life and destroy it" (Wilkinson 25).

More than usual in Christie's fiction, the Nile and its valley play a role in the structure of the book. It is as if only in a distant past, where her social context was absent, could Christie gesture to the non-human agency of the riparian infrastructure. Moreover, in ancient Egypt, water was not just backdrop, but power. As Sina Marx asserts, "irrigation has always been closely related to the formation of states and the exercise of power over its citizens" (Marx 47). Christie states that "it so happened that the inspiration of both characters and plot was derived from two or three Egyptian letters of the XI Dynasty" (Foreword n.p.). Another way of saying this is that Christie found in those archival sources a story with the elasticity to seem as if it could have happened anywhere, not weighed down by potential linkages to other stories (like the Bible) or by extraneous historical detail.

As John Curran shows, Christie mooted having there be a "modern parallel running along the historical" plot (Curran 235), foreshadowing something like an ancient Egyptian version of A.S. Byatt's *Possession*, but refrained from doing this, adding to the general sense of restraint and proportion in the book's conception, without relinquishing any modern applicability. The story is transposable, even as it derives from a certain set of cultural conditions that can be read as specific literal conditions; Christie constructs a story that is meant to speak to the present. What Christie is doing is what all historical novels do, which is write to readers who will always be in a historical present, will be in their own moment in time.

6. Deep Egypt

All historical novels are written to speak to the present, and Renisenb's story is one that Christie inflects with modern resonance. More must be said about the setting of the novel: not so much that it is in ancient Egypt (even though Christie could have been said to have initiated the idea of setting detective stories in the deep or ancient past) but that it is in Egypt rather than Mesopotamia. It is also significant that *Death Comes as the End* is in early Middle Kingdom Egypt rather than a later time that could plausibly be linked to Biblical settings. Even in her play *Akhnaton*, set at a time and context often linked by other novelists to the Bible (Joseph, the Exodus, monotheism), Christie keeps to a rigorously intra–Egyptian context and centers her plot on Egypt itself as if Egypt alone were more than enough of a world.

It is interesting to realize how fascinated Christie was by Egypt, a locale producing the famous modern-set novel *Death on the Nile* as well as the ancient *Akhnaton* and *Death Comes as the End*. Her relationship to Egypt was a deeply personal one. Max Mallowan was a specialist in Mesopotamia and Syria, rather than Egypt. But Agatha Christie visited Egypt long before she married Mallowan or Archibald Christie for that matter. Her first visit was as a 17-year-old in 1907, when she saw the great pyramids and other sites of ancient Egyptian culture. Egypt, though in political terms never formally a colony of Britain, was a "veiled protectorate" (Deane 183) of Britain and was, practically, under British occupation for many decades. Indeed, Egypt was the area in the Middle East that was most fundamentally important to the British Empire, far more so than Iraq—the modern name for Mesopotamia—which was under British sway only as a post–Ottoman Empire League of Nations Mandate.

One might say that Egypt appealed to Christie at a more atavistic level because she had been there earlier, and that is why she set a historical novel there, as opposed to the two contemporary novels *They Came to Baghdad* and *Murder in Mesopotamia*, and her underrated portrait of Mandate Palestine in *Appointment with Death*. One could also say that ancient Egypt was, as a setting, more deeply ingrained in the British imagination. One can equally say that in writing about ancient Egypt, not ancient Mesopotamia, Chrystie was working on an area adjacent to, but not the same as, the academic specialty of Max Mallowan.

One could also say that ancient Egypt was, as a setting, more deeply ingrained in the Anglophone imagination than ancient Mesopotamia, particularly since the latter was only known in any detail after 19th-century archaeological excavations. Additionally, Britain's colonial involvement with Egypt and such discoveries as the Carver/Carnarvon expedition's finding of Tutankhamun's tomb made Egypt both iconic and accessible to Christie's reading public.

But the choice of where temporally to set the novel within ancient Egyptian history also gives a clue as to why Christie chose Egypt rather than the Fertile Crescent, which was her spouse's archaeological expertise.

The early Middle Kingdom of 2000 BCE goes so far back as to be before Abraham, Jacob, and Joseph and certainly before Moses (using the dating of these individuals that late-Victorian British people assumed, along with assumptions of their historicity). A setting, certainly in the New Kingdom, and even in the latter stages of the Middle Kingdom, would have required Christie to consider what other historical novelists of the late periods of ancient Egypt have also to consider: whether and to what extent to include or allude to Hebrew or Biblical personages. Because of this early setting, her characters are purely Egyptian. And, given the basic framing of their alterity, the characters are then pulled forward into the reader's orbit by an assumption of common humanity.

Christie was specifically asked to write this novel by Stephen Glanville, an Egyptologist who was a colleague of Mallowan's and was a good friend of the Christie family. As Waltraud Guglielmi has shown, Glanville introduced Christie to the Hekanakhte texts which heavily influenced her in the writing of her novel. Glanville is prominently mentioned in Laura Thompson and Lucy Worsley's recent biographies of Christie, and Lisa Hopkins speaks of his "guidance" (Hopkins 36) of Christie's approach to Egypt. Glanville's assistance enabled her to depict the sort of well-off but not the sort of politically important or super-wealthy family that she tended to depict in her modern-set novels. For instance, the name "Imhotep," used as the patriarch of the family in the book, clearly refers to that of the Third Dynasty architect and scientist who is one of the few famous figures in Egyptian history who was not a Pharaoh or a Pharaoh's wife.

Christie's reliance on Gunn and Glanville as sources is notable because both men were of a younger generation than the most prominent British Egyptologist of the 20th century, Sir William Flinders Petrie. Petrie, as the recent work of Debbie Challis has noted, was a noted racist. He was, indeed, perhaps the most virulent racist of any English-speaking humanist of his time. Petrie persistently saw the more Northern peoples as superior to the ancient Egyptians. Yet Gunn and Glanville avoided racialized conceptions of the ancient Egyptians or ones that characterized them as inferior to less dark-skinned and more northern peoples. The younger generation was less exclusively interested in archaeology, political history, and language decryption than was Petrie, and broadened their approaches to include sociological, anthropological, and cultural modes of inquiry.

Indeed, there is a sense in which *Death Comes as the End* is a fictional and ancient-set equivalent to Christie's nonfiction book about modern Iraq, *Come, Tell Me How You Live*. Both have a similar relationship both to her own fictional oeuvre and to Mallowan's archaeological work. *Come, Tell Me How You Live*'s interest in the lives of women and of ordinary life is contrasted with Mallowan's interest in edifices and inscriptions of the past that were largely authored by men and were there to serve the purposes of what by then had become a patriarchal society. Similarly, *Death Comes as the End* focuses on the daily life of the past more than wars, dynasties, and upheavals. Nonetheless, the way the novel ends portends a new order in Egypt, and concomitant with the revelation of previously suppressed truths, stresses domestic revitalization, and documents this change within larger Egyptian society.

Any writer who uses a formula, as Christie does in many of her plots, will want to test that formula by seeing whether it can be applied to other places and times. Indeed, this sort of application is part of a formulaic writer's attempt to show that being formulaic does not make one merely repetitive. If formulas are transposable across time, place, and culture, they become less stereotypical and more abstract templates whose application to specific contexts reveal those contexts. The formulae—of plots, suspects, murders, denouements—are grounded in circumstance while giving the literary figurations of these formulae a certain immunity from the constraints of the specific. Christie drives this point home when she says: "Both places and time are incidental to the story. Any other place at any other time would have served as well" (Foreword, n. p.). The initial reviews mentioned that Christie had evoked her setting with tact and had done so "delicately." These words hint at Christie's eschewing of any large-scale historiographical points. Instead, we see Renisenb, an ordinary woman, returning to her family after the death of her husband, but soon finding the insularity of the family suffocating. That this is a family prison of its own making means that we wonder if it is not possible for Renisenb to simply open the door and walk out, rather like Nora in Ibsen's *A Doll's House*. Instead, the family circle is weakened through attrition—through murder.

Like *And Then There Were None*, this is a mystery in which it is impossible to find a true detective, although Renisenb, Esa and Hori can be said to share this function. Using a first-person point-of-view suggests that Renisenb is this novel's major character, but she is less a detective who discovers the solution to the crimes than a central consciousness whose discoveries move beyond solving the mystery into issues of self-knowledge and personal change. The mysterious crimes do, however, shape Renisenb's circumstances. She begins as a widow, which initiates an aura of melancholy that pervades the entire novel. This is intensified by the family feuds and mounting losses, which also add a layer of bitterness. And, in addition to the depiction of a house not only divided but decimated, Christie adds a hint of the uncanny; for some characters it is the vengeful spirit of the deceased Nofret that is responsible for everything going so wrong.

The father Imhotep's new companion Nofret is the first victim. There are even more murder victims, however—two of them are Renisenb's brothers, Sobek and Ipy; one Renisenb's Miss Marplish grandmother, Esa; another Satipy, the wife of the murdering brother Yahmose; and two servants. These are, in other words, what Hercule Poirot would call classic *crimes intimes*. Esa and Henet are interesting here as they are superfluous women; they are women who are not defined by their reproductivity, or their sexuality. Esa is older and more upper class and is part of the main family—a valued grandmother as was Christie's own. Henet is younger and a servant, but she is not part of a marriage plot, or a family plot. Unlike Nofret, Imhotep's newly introduced concubine, Esa and Henet are insiders, but although they cannot be said to be "players in the game," they nevertheless are taken out by the evil Yahmose.

The concentration on the family unit, on domestic jealousy, personal rivalry, and eventually on individual psychological pathologies is juxtaposed to the specific historical setting in ways that prevent the historical atmosphere from suffocating the plot; the reader soon concentrates on the characters and their family tensions—while always remaining aware of the ancient Egyptian setting, the story comes first. The major source of tension in the story is the new companion of Renisenb's father Imhotep. This would be Nofret, who stirs everything up from the beginning and who, after her death, is still a prominent figure. It is rare for an initial murder victim to be so thoroughly presented to the reader in a Christie mystery.

Like Lady Camilla Tressilian in *Towards Zero*, Nofret remains alive for nearly half the book; and, although in both cases the plot is rife with people with motives to kill her, she does not die until her character, and relationships with the other people in the household, are fully articulated. Unlike Lady Tressilian, though, who is thoroughly at the center of the household, Nofret is the newcomer, the outsider, the woman who not only threatens to upset the apple cart in terms of the sons' inheritance but represents, in her assertiveness and willfulness, a challenge to accustomed ways. Her murder proves to be the catalyst for a more fundamental crisis in the existing order. Notably, Nofret is slightly "raced" in the novel as she is from the North, from Memphis, and thus is an outsider to the Theban domestic community of Imhotep.

Moreover, Nofret has traveled outside Egypt. She speaks of voyaging to "Byblos beyond the gazelle's nose," and sailing "on a big ship in the wide seas" (46). In other words, she has left Egypt and gone to the lands of the eastern Mediterranean littoral, taking the course of such real-life male Egyptian travelers as Sinuhe and Wenamon. Christie is well aware that Nofret's Northern exposure is the inverse of a character from Southern Europe appearing in a very English family milieu, somewhat like Pilar Estravados in *Hercule Poirot's Christmas*, to which Robert Barnard (see Worthington 133) famously compared *Death Comes as the End*.

As Toby Wilkinson puts it, the ancient Egyptians had, to European eyes, an "unorthodox view of the world" (Wilkinson 18), in which "south lay at the top of their mental map, the north at the bottom." In Egypt the strange and othered is Northern and not Southern, enabling Christie to comment on the relativistic and arbitrary nature of racialized differences that had been presumed to be essential. Moreover, whereas racist Egyptologists such as Petrie saw the North as more vigorous and advanced than Egypt, the Imhotep family, if anything, sees Nofret as culturally inferior. Christie experiments with and upends the European ideas of the other, portraying Nofret as an outsider who is somehow also a center, who will both change the lives of the insiders and affect them in a way that will reveal their true character.

In keeping with Egyptian beliefs in the afterlife, it is only Nofret, the first victim, who continues to be a suspect even after her death. Indeed, the felt presence of Nofret's ghost not only speaks to Egyptian ideas of the supernatural—and perhaps a sense of haunting that Christie would have employed more in her modern mysteries had she not felt it would disrupt their verisimilitude. The surviving spirit of Nofret shows how she has changed the Imhotep clan's view of itself. Hori, a fellow scribe, points out to Renisenb that Nofret changed things by bringing to light the evil concealed within the hearts of the family, evils that had been previously suppressed and concealed systemically.

But while the other family members fear and loathe Nofret, Renisenb herself cannot help but admire her as a dissident, perhaps the dissident she herself wants to be. There is an affiliation with Nofret that goes against what she may believe are the better angels of her nature, represented here by her brother Sobek's wife Kait. While Renisenb is mysteriously drawn to Nofret she is increasingly critical of women like Kait. She thinks: "Is that all to a woman's life, Kait? To busy myself in the back of the house, to have children, to spend afternoons with them by the lake under the sycamore trees?" (133). Renisenb does not quite approve of the way Kait has found complete fulfillment in motherhood, or, at least, does not think this is something that would make her as content as it does Kait. Kait, however is not quite what she seems—although gentle, submissive, and seemingly not very bright, Kait somewhat resembles Gerda Christow in *The Hollow*, who when crossed or threatened, can call on reserves of ruthless strength. In this psychology, she anticipates the later analysis of the murderer, Yahmose.

Yahmose is dismissed throughout the novel as somewhat cautious, almost unmanly, someone who when compared with his father and his younger brothers is insinuating rather than decisive. That it is Yahmose who commits sundry murders and ends up butchering nearly his entire family, except Renisenb, Imhotep, and Kait, is surprising not just because empirically, Yahmose has himself been poisoned and recovers (a rather standard Christie trope of the murderer appearing to be the victim) but it is surprising because Yahmose seemed, in effect, too boring and predictable to be a murderer. Yahmose, as with other of Christie's criminals, had a very active evil inner life. His timid surface concealed a psychologically active but terrible interior which was at considerable distance from his visible persona, almost to a Jekyll/Hyde level. On the one hand, Yahmose is a compelling portrait of a psychopath who keeps his murderous insanity wrapped under a veneer of studied mediocrity. He has left a trail of dead bodies in his wake, although this spectacle may have been subtly diminished by our understanding that all the characters in the story are, temporally speaking, already dead.

Perhaps their loss is less wrenching as a result for the reader—although certainly not the characters themselves. And insofar as the reader is immersed in the narrative, we find ourselves in a place where very terrible things have happened to this family—this gives the novel a feeling at once suspenseful, desolate, and morbid. The novel does end with the marriage plot of Renisenb and Hori, but with such a mass of deaths the marriage plot conclusion is less reassuring than it would have been otherwise. It is almost as if Philip Lombard and Vera Claythorne had married each other as the last two survivors of *And Then They Were None*.

That so great a portion of the characters die in this novel could be an indication that, as Tony Sandset argued in his article on the necropolitics of Covid-19, black and brown lives are racialized as more disposable. Certainly whatever Christie's empathy for Egyptians ancient and modern, the scale of death in the novel can be interpreted as valuing non-European, and non-contemporary lives in a lesser way.

Another way to read the number of deaths is as a reflection of the wartime conditions and the context in which the novel was written. Indeed, and especially compared to the rather chipper *N or M?*, *Death Comes as the End*, is a dark book, a book about sundry deaths in a dead civilization, which might reflect not specific fears of Britain losing the war, which by 1944 were far less pervasive, but a sense of Christie's own present day situation in which she believes she herself is living in a civilization that could well one day be dead. One might indeed say that *Death Comes as the End* expresses a very British anxiety about the fate of its own empire. There is a slight resonance of Naguib Mahfouz's Cairo trilogy in this regard, with the proviso that Christie's is a far earlier Egypt, and that wartime is not in the world of the book but only in the back of the mind of the author.

As with other of Christie's murderers, the detection of Yahmose not only involves the mechanics of the crime but is also a matter of psychology. It is Hori who suggests that the introduction of Nofret into the household activated something lying dormant in Yahmose, who appears to be meek and submissive while a violent alternative identity seethed in his unconscious, feeding on the resentment and frustration of the conscious self. Although she is reminded by her grandmother Esa that the life inside tells us a story that is different from what appears to be the life outside, Renisenb has never considered the possibility that people may create "false doors" that deceive as to their true nature, aspects that may be concealed but that come to the surface with the catalyst of danger or insecurity. She understands eventually that the power Yahmose wields as a murderer, then, is a compensation for the suppression of any autonomy and initiative in his outward personality—constructed to please only one person—his overbearing father.

The dissociation was such that the more propitiatory and timid he appears to his family, the greater a hidden or even split-off inner sense of power and entitlement grew against his surface identity. This can be said to be something of a lesson or even a warning for Renisenb regarding the dangers of making choices that end in compliance and deference, but unlike Renisenb, the arc of the narrative for Yahmose is that of deterioration; even though his assertion of sadistic power has made him feel a conquering hero, these killings are dismantling the integrity of his personality and leading to disaster. What happened to Yahmose is described as a personality "too shut in, too folded back on itself," once again an image of blockage and imprisonment that derives from power struggles within a family constellation—his is the story of the worm who turns; Renisenb remembers that the time one of his brother beat the head of Yahmose against the ground, only to be mysteriously poisoned the next day, pointing to a compliance on the one hand on the part of Yahmose, and vengeful retaliation on the other.

It is Hori, the theorist of Yahmose, who constructs his psychological profile. For a time, it appears that Esa will be our detective, but ultimately this role belongs to Hori, Imhotep's scribe and estate manager. Like an archeologist, Hori believes that one must dig up evidence for oneself. Like Esa, he is also an older wisdom figure, and as such is the kind of detective Christie has always preferred. Additionally, like Esa, Hori acts as a counselor or even therapist to Renisenb. His name derives from Horus, the sky God, depicted as a falcon who hovers above or over the earthly world. One of the reasons Renisenb chooses the prudent Hori over the more romantic

Kameni is that Hori's sense of discernment and calculation make him not only a more durable partner for the long term but somewhat of a "sane Yahmose."

Similarly, one of the reasons she does not chose Kameni is that he is too much like Nofret—young, charismatic, physically attractive and from the North. That both Hori and Kameni are scribes not only reflect the importance of the profession in ancient Egyptian society but reminds the reader that ancient Egypt, however remote in time, was a literate culture. These two scribes invoke the prospect of Renisenb choosing between two authors or author-equivalents. She chooses Hori, as the author who inverts, in a positive way, Yahmose's surface traits of caution and canniness.

There is a certain "slow time" to this novel, especially its setting in winter. Renisenb herself slows down enough to think things through, and certainly the time she has spent pondering all that has happened prove to be very useful to her. And one might feel that to some extent the reflective solitude of Renisenb is emphasized at the expense of the plot but is part of her rather modern capacity to think for herself and to her development as an individual, not as a member of the larger group. This reflective solitude does pull the mystery out of its expected shape, something Christie is always likely to do, but Renisenb doesn't spend more than a cycle of seasons doing this—in this regard she is, like Nofret, working faster than is usual for the society.

Hori is also critical of a society that is going too slow, suggesting a conservatism that can prevent healthy changes. Ancient Egypt was a particularly rigid society, a good foil for the way Renisenb is established as something of a rebel. Christie's idea here is that the need to hold on to past patterns can lead to a fear of change that, as Hori suggests, can stifle not only Renisenb but an entire society.

The narrative brings Renisenb into a mood in which winter has been overcome; there is a fresh spring that brings life and not death. Renisenb and Yahmose—the reflective detecting consciousness and the hidden killer—undergo the most dramatic transformations. As Renisenb literally reaches higher ground at the end, Yahmose has degenerated into a kind of monster. But Renisenb's narrative does not end in death; instead, she imagines her future as unpredictable, bringing new things into her life. If she disagrees with the Egyptian concept of the afterlife, it is because her idea of life after death is more transformative, more of a change or advance. Her attention, however, is not to an afterlife, but to her worry that she is living the wrong life in the world, is false to herself.

Nofret is crucial here—she is a kind of spiritual force or energy that Renisenb can appreciate. Nofret shakes things up—she is something new, in a world that wants to assimilate everything to the familiar. If there was ever going to be a time when England felt some of that same morbidity, however, it would be at this time, at the end of World War II, with its massive quota of deaths both military and civilian. But Renisenb's task is to find a way out of this death-haunted world, not remain within it.

Just as Esa tells Renisenb that there is a "life within," Hori introduces a larger outward perspective to Renisenb, represented by their meeting on high ground, nearer the sky. It is when she is on higher ground, looking down at the family compound below that she feels she has risen above the confusions and feuds and quarrels of earthly things. The mystery has produced in Renisenb and Hori its romantic couple, which is what they become in the last paragraphs of the novel, high on that hill that so much speaks of the wider liberty Hori represents.

The ending contradicts the title, finessing the idea of death-as-terminus; death may come as the end of many people and things, but it does not come as the end of this novel. Renisenb's final recognition involves both the choice of Hori and a conviction that this choice transcends the reality of death and dying: it is possible, then, to apply this title to many things—the effect of Nofret on those around her, to Renisenb's "til death do us part" love story, to the metaphysics of ancient Egypt, and to a family or a society's decline and fall—or more simply to the way death quite literally ends the lives of so many characters in this novel. The final lines contradict the title, affirming various kinds of ongoingness, including love and good sociality, and particularly memory-through-love, a remembering that includes her first husband and the other family members she had lost. This last type of ongoingness is very much a piece with the Egyptian religion, which, much more than the Greek/Hebrew religion, places greater emphasis on those who had passed away.

One point Agatha Christie makes in her autobiography is that she let Glanville persuade her to alter a part of the dénouement. He had been her trusted advisor on all things Egyptian during the writing of the novel, and she allowed him to influence the ending, presumably to choose Hori as the new mate for Renisenb rather than have the book end with Yahmose's confession in a more "Dostoyevskian" style. She afterward regretted this and said it was the only time she had allowed herself to be influenced in this way. But although she suggested it would be more dramatic, Christie did not describe her alternative ending. This would suggest that the ending did mirror the title more accurately, with Yahmose himself, say, falling to his death off the precipice of the hill—his death coming as the end of his own murder spree.

But it could also be that the ending would have made Renisenb's choice of Kameni equally dramatic. Kameni was also an outsider and a scribe as well, albeit identified as "from the North" which gives him a greater sense of distance from her family of origin. And as said before, this allies him not just with Nofret but with a more marginal sense of Egypt stemming from the delta not the center of Thebes. The more dashing Kameni is the younger of the suitors, the one closer generationally to Renisenb herself; but as was true in *Third Girl*, Renisenb has opted for an older, therapeutic personality, who, it is suggested, is as much a faithful friend as he is a lover.

Renisenb tells Hori that she will share his life with him "for good or evil, until death comes" (158). But that Hori is "a song in her heart forever" paradoxically means that "there is no more death" (158). When faced between the more and less reliable option (as with Lynn Marchmont in *There Is a Tide*) Christie usually has her female protagonist choose the safer candidate, and that when there is truly mutual passion among her lovers it often leads to an anti-marriage plot as occurs with Vera Claythorne and Philip Lombard in *And Then They Were None*. Of the two, Hori is the "higher ground" option, who will lift her up and out of the world below. That Hori is the more spiritual figure may be responsible for the conclusion which confirms that, to quote Philip Larkin, what survives of us is love (Larkin 110).

This is moving precisely because there have been so many deaths in the previous pages that the landscape is virtually unpeopled. But these words also convey a personalized idea of the afterlife that is less of any ancient religion than of a modern, secular idea of the afterlife as stemming from subjectivity and affect. Moreover, Renisenb's choice of the older Hori over the more conventionally romantic Kameni is redolent both of Emma and Mr. Knightley in Jane Austen and Jerry Burton and Megan Hunter in *The Moving Finger*, which Christie published just two years before *Death Comes as the End*. In both cases, Christie sanctions an older man–younger woman marriage plot that the usual dynamics of the marriage-plot, including those in many of her other books, would forswear. This is because in both cases there is a sense of crisis, with the older man's wisdom more sustainable, another instance of the invisible presence of World War II in both *The Moving Finger* and *Death Comes as the End*. Even though the war is not mentioned in *The Moving Finger* and is distanced by the span of four millennia in *Death Comes as the End*, it is nevertheless indelibly and undeniably present.

The title, referenced by the grandmother, Esa, can be illuminated by learning that the Egyptian source reads specifically: "Men are made fools by their gleaming limbs of carnelian. A trifle, a little, the likeness of a dream, and death comes as the end of knowing her" (25). This use of the "death comes as the end" phrase references an unhappy love story, in which a woman with "limbs of carnelian" is very much a femme fatale or is perhaps the victim of a spurned lover. The quote also indicates that the ancient Egyptians even this far back had their own sense of a past, a repertoire of classic literary quotes from which they could draw. One can to a certain extent assign this quote to the "other woman," Nofret, but Renisenb's marriage to Khay is also a love story that ends in death—as in the ancient quote, death comes as the end of love.

The number of victims in this novel remind us constantly of death and dying. The level of dead bodies is almost Shakespearean in its extravagance; that this household is headed by a mortuary priest, concerned with the rituals of death and burial also adds to the morbidity. It has often been said that the conversion of this household into a killing field may also in a subtle way reference the wartime in which this novel was written, and the way in which all the fatalities in this story marked the end of an entire era.

Death also is indicated by the way Christie indicates the presence of the sacred sycamore tree, often included in Egyptian mythology and art, and interpreted magically in the Egyptian Book of the Dead. Sycamores were often planted near tombs; the sacred aspect of the tree pointed not to death, but to a maternal tree goddess to whom the soul was returned. Near the end, Renisenb and Hori promise honesty under the sycamore tree as a reference to this sacred aspect of their relationship. At the same time, Hori denounces his own religion as too unimaginatively and materialistically devoted to a cult of the dead, suggesting that their conception of the gods is limited and unsatisfactory, and that he does not like the way the established belief system can only conceive of a next world as a continuation of this one.

So, even as the title reflects on the finality of death, and features a great deal of death, there is also a sense of new life. And for Renisenb that new life requires a disengaging from her old family. Even though she was happy to return to the safety and comfort of home, we see this is a world she is outgrowing; that she is on a higher ground with the wisdom-figure Hori on the hilltop brings the sense of a beginning—there returns a sense of spring and love that was ended by the death of Renisenb's husband. The title can suggest death is the end of the life we know on earth, breaking the circle of life indicated by the seasons, and yet Renisenb also reflects on the way the seasons create the renewing of life, as the waters sweep away the old and prepared the soil for the new crops. She concludes that her own daughter, Teti, is one of these "new crops."

The narrative follows the Egyptian seasons, ending with the winter years endured and with a return of summer; it is as if the winter season mirrors the family's tragedies, but that cyclical season change mirrors the changes in Renisenb's life. There is an anticipation of spring that mirrors

Renisenb's new situation as well as Hori's hope for a better world, suggesting personal and social change in tandem.

Hori, in the bitter tone that is characteristic of so many of the voices in this novel, complains that Egypt is obsessed with death in a way that has produced a culture that is overly conservative and trapped in fear-based rituals and traditions that create sameness and prevent change. He is the character who opens the door to the future, and not only for the two of them—he introduces the big picture: "Look, Renisenb. Look out from here across the valley to the river and beyond. That is Egypt, our land. Broken by war and strife for many long years, divided into petty kingdoms, but now—very soon—to come together and form once more a united land—Upper and Lower Egypt once again welded into one—I hope and believe to recover her former greatness! In those days, Egypt will need men and women of heart and courage—women such as you are, Renisenb" (164).

Here Hori anticipates a rebirth of the Egyptian culture, an end to division and a return of greatness, in specific terms the rise of the Middle Kingdom after the decline of the Old Kingdom. His welcoming of change and anticipating that he and Renisenb will be among those bringing out a better future is very much at odds with the conventional wisdom about Christie's mysteries, which so often are characterized as a kind of staged Edwardianism, always looking backward, holding on to the past. It also indicates that the novel's seeming renunciation of political history in favor of domestic and psychological issues as a bit of a tease, as the novel's ending is not just one of domestic salvage but of social renewal. This surely resonates with a wartime England that, even if victory seemed more likely in 1943 than it did earlier, still understood that massive changes would be coming after the war.

If anything, Christie's investment in depicting how things were changing in England, and the importance of these changes, becomes more important and more intense during and after World War II. Christie herself noted the difference between her earliest and later work in an oft-quoted remark, she says: "When I re-read those first [detective stories I wrote], I'm amazed at the number of servants drifting about. And nobody is really doing any work, they're always having tea on the lawn" (Christie, "Agatha's Quotes").

Death Comes as the End, on the other hand, was not composed as if set in the long afternoon of the British Empire; it was composed in 1943, just after the battle of El Alamein which turned the tide of the war in North Africa. Until Montgomery's victory at El Alamein, Germany was sweeping through the north of Africa, and it seemed possible (as glimpsed for instance in Olivia Manning's Levant trilogy) that the Nazis could conquer Egypt. Egypt, as a referent, was hardly timeless. As in other of Christie's wartime-era novels, such as *An Overdose of Death*, Christie shows how a superficial challenge to a society, such as that of Nofret and Mr. Raikes, is far less dangerous than a hidden, more fundamental challenge—that of Yahmose and Sir Alistair Blunt.

While not anachronistic or tendentious, her depiction of Ancient Egypt establishes an awareness of resemblances to later times. Her comments that the Egyptian cult of death is all about making money, and her specific delineation of the sources of Imhotep's economic prosperity, show that greed was a motive long before the explicit rise of capitalism. That she was thinking in general of the workings of greed in precapitalist economies is shown in her notes, in which she likens the *ka*-priests such as Imhotep to Catholic priests in the Middle Ages, receiving money for praying for people's souls moving from Purgatory to Heaven.

Christie could not have set a novel in pre–Reformation England without taking a religious position; but she could deal more objectively with analogous issues in faraway ancient Egypt. Equally, the unholy crimes to *Death Comes as the End*, as well as the theme of the imported concubine, reminds us of Greek tragedy, a form that Christie (as, for instance, in her references to it in *Towards Zero*) knew well. But Egypt, with its far fewer cultural associations in the Western mind, was a more abstract tableau for Christie to deploy her elastic formulae than would have been Greece, so that she successfully combines the seemingly contrary themes of a deeply different past society with a civilization on the curve of changeover.

Any sense of a timeless Egyptian realm, living cyclically and peacefully through the change of seasons, was never really the case. Even at the start, this novel depicts the dismantling of one old school family, through exposure of both its fragility and through literal demise, which builds to a larger sense of a world that has died and disappeared, has come to an end. Christie did not end this novel, however, with the sense of an ending the title appeared to promise; and indeed there is no death at the end of this story. Instead there is a sense of a portal, an entrance, a threshold. In characteristic Christie fashion, the dying of this world is not showing us how things end, but how things change.

Chapter References

Challis, Debbie. *The Archaeology of Race: The Eugenic Ideas of Francis Galton and Flinders Petrie* (London: Bloomsbury, 2013).

Christie, Agatha. Agatha's Quotes. "Hercule Poirot Central," http://www.poirot.us/quotes.php#:~:text=%22When%20I%20re%2Dread%20those,think%20of%20the%20next%20one.%22

Cueva, Edmund P. "Ancient Modernity in Agatha Christie's *Akhnaton*," in Nizar Zouidi, ed., *The Monarch and the (Non)-Human in Literature and Cinema* (New York: Routledge, 2023), pp. 38–58.

Curran, John. *Agatha Christie's Secret Notebooks: Fifty Years of Mysteries in the Making* (London: HarperCollins, 2010).
Deane, Bradley. *Masculinity and the New Imperialism: Rewriting Manhood in British Popular Literature, 1870–1914* (Cambridge: Cambridge University Press, 2013).
Guglielmi, Waltraud. "Agatha Christie and Her Use of Ancient Egyptian Sources," in Charlotte Trümpler, ed., *Agatha Christie and Archaeology* (London: British Museum Press, 2001), pp. 351–390.
Gulddal, Jesper. "'That deep underground savage instinct': Narratives of Sacrifice and Retribution in Agatha Christie's *Appointment with Death*." *Textual Practice*, vol. 34, no. 11, 2019, pp. 1803–1821.
Hopkins, Lisa. *Burial Plots in British Detective Fiction* (Basingstoke: Palgrave Macmillan, 2021).
Larkin, Philip. "An Arundel Tomb." *Collected Poems* (Boston: The Marvell Press and Faber & Faber, 1988).
Marx, Sinaz. "Political Ecology in the Anthropocene: A Case Study of Irrigation Management in the Blue Nile Basin" in Jason M. Kelly, ed., *Rivers of the Anthropocene* (Berkeley: University of California Press, 2017), pp. 43–55.
Melman, Billie. *Empires of Antiquities: Modernity and the Rediscovery of the Ancient near East, 1914–1950* (Oxford: Oxford University Press, 2020).
Sandset, Tony. "The Necropolitics of COVID-19: Race, Class and Slow Death in an Ongoing Pandemic." *Global Public Health*, vol. 16, no. 8–9, 2021, pp. 1411–1423.
Wilkinson, Toby. *The Rise and Fall of Ancient Egypt* (New York: Random House, 2011).
Worthington, Heather. *Key Concepts in Crime Fiction* (Basingstoke: Palgrave Macmillan, 2011).

7

Flight from the Enchanter

Towards Zero

The setting of this novel is an estate in Cornwall, a setting that Mark Aldridge notes is associated with the "romantic" (*Agatha Christie's Marple* 20), and is situated on a darkly romantic menacing steep cliff called Stark Head, which overhangs a freshwater/seawater coastal river—an augur of danger and of the wider liberty of nature. While much takes place inside the seaside home of Camilla, Lady Tressilian at Gull's Point, the cliff and the river are also central to both the mystery and its message.

In addition to the disruptive potential of cliff and river, and the geographically extreme location, in English terms, of the setting on the Cornish peninsula, Christie also immediately creates the expectation that something terrible is going to happen—but as the outcome of this narrative, rather than at its outset. The tension derives from our understanding that it is only a matter of time before a diabolically clever crime will have been committed. She suggests through her title and the comments of two characters—the elderly lawyer Mr. Treves and the detective Superintendent Battle—that things are all going "towards zero," that is, towards the point at which a murderer's twisted plan has been completely realized. Since we know we are in a countdown, the suspense accumulates—the closer we come to the end of the novel, the closer we will come to Zero Hour.

That sense of time being of the essence is notable in the novel; the same sense of time is also visible in the very loose sequel to *Towards Zero*, *The Clocks* (a sequel because it also features a child of Superintendent Battle's named, pseudonymously, Colin Lamb). That the timeline of the plot is on a schedule and is devised by the criminal bring a sense of the ominous. Mr. Treves describes the atmosphere Christie creates perfectly when he says, "There is gunpowder about. The explosion may come at any moment. There is, I feel sure, a focal point" (85).

Much of the novel's fascination comes from waiting to discover who will be the murder victim, and who will prove to be the mastermind. Like *And Then There Were None*, there is an inexorability—but the difference is that in *Towards Zero* Christie introduces countervailing forces that disrupt the final part of the plans. Although this creates, as Brittain Bright has commented, a "less noticeably radical" (Bright 47) mystery in terms of poetic justice, *Towards Zero* introduces once again concepts of luck and chance that are surprisingly disruptive.

This story is also disruptive in that it begins with several different fragments, from old Mr. Treves at his club to a young Angus MacWhirter in hospital, to the fatherly Superintendent Battle's visit to his daughter Sylvia's school, to an unnamed malevolent consciousness planning to destroy someone he/she sees as his/her enemy, to the conversation of the dashing tennis star Nevile with his new wife about his wish to make peace with his ex-wife Audrey when they meet at Gull's Head. These narrative lines are highly dispersed and deliberately disconnected, and only at the end do we understand the relationship between a Scotsman's failed suicide attempt, a wrongful accusation of theft against a young schoolgirl, and the love life of a prestigious tennis player.

As the mention of Superintendent Battle suggests, this is not a mystery featuring either of Christie's most famous detectives, Hercule Poirot and Miss Marple, although Poirot, sometimes a colleague of Battle's, is evoked as a kind of guiding spirit. It is interesting that although Poirot is never present, he is somehow nevertheless mentoring Battle in this case—one might wonder why, then, not have it be a Poirot case in the first place? Battle has appeared previously in some earlier mysteries. He is comfortably English, and a capable detective—but Christie does not give him Poirot's magic. It may be that the magic of Poirot must be evoked, but kept at a distance, so the presence of the unremarkable Battle is less likely to interfere with the atmosphere of danger created by our knowledge that a fanatic mastermind is at work and by our participation in his victim Audrey's continuous state of dread.

Additionally, this mystery features a murderer considered one of Christie's irredeemably evil figures, one whom Poirot could not have brought himself to help escape the dreaded justice system and one for whom Poirot could find no opportunity to introduce a "Papa Poirot" lesson. Since he can be said to truly be one of Christie's damned, he requires the cool detachment of a Superintendent Battle.

One of the other reasons Battle is the detective is that he recognizes the victim Audrey's false confession as like his daughter Sylvia's experience at boarding school when she had made the same sort of confession for a crime she did not commit. Sylvia, then, has the same psychology as the murderer's victim, Audrey—each can be said to somehow be complicit in their own victimhood. For the detective to father a child exactly like the victim, one cannot have either Poirot or Miss Marple, detectives who never married nor had children and whose non-reproductivity was part of their percipience as detectives. Additionally, to have a child with similar psychology to the victim may open the question of flaws or failings of parenthood that would shake our confidence in our two Great Detectives.

Battle, on the other hand, is what one could call an ordinary bloke, and is indeed able to solve the crime partially through his experience as a father. It is a very different subject-position from Christie's usual detectives who succor marriage-plot and social self-realization from outside modern British society—Battle is an insider to such an extent that the manifestation of an "Audrey" type of daughter is perhaps not all that surprising. The novel is also the last to feature Superintendent Battle. It is almost as if *Towards Zero* is his *Curtain*, the novel in which he, like Poirot, also violates an ethical commandment.

The reader is at first convinced that the professional tennis star Nevile Strange, Lady Tressilian's ward and beneficiary, cannot possibly have murdered her because he has framed himself for the murder so thoroughly. Nevile is counting on the police, however, to see through this staged incrimination and exonerate him; his real mission is to successfully pin the murder of Lady Tressilian on his ex-wife Audrey. The reader also begins to suspect Audrey not only through the investigation of the detective, but also because Thomas Royde, the self-effacing, reticent cousin from Malaya (and therefore coded as a second-rank, relegated, "colonial" figure), happens to know that Audrey had an affair with Thomas's more charismatic deceased brother, Adrian, and that this is the true cause of Audrey's breakup with Nevile. Royde concludes that Audrey and Nevile agreed that Nevile would take the blame for the breakup of the marriage out of gallantry and to protect a lady's reputation, something consistent with his arranging it to look as if he is, at first, taking the blame for murdering Lady Tressilian.

The death of Audrey's lover Adrian, and his replacement by his lesser brother Thomas, is an interesting detail of this story. Were Adrian to have survived, it is likely he, unlike Thomas, would be competition for her eventual suitor Angus; indeed, had Adrian survived it may not have been possible for Nevile to execute his plan at all. Audrey Strange may have become Mrs. Adrian Royde. As it is, the death of Adrian allows Nevile to continue to promulgate the myth that it was he who had left Audrey for the younger and more alluring Kay. That he has staged an identity as the one at fault is an essential part of his plan—this means he has no motive to exact revenge against Audrey. If anything, it is she who would want to exact revenge against him.

The hidden Nevile shows himself as remorselessly indifferent to human life. Even though she has done nothing but support and care for him, Lady Tressilian becomes his murder victim because it is a convenient crime with which to frame Audrey (Lady Tressilian has not altered the terms of her will and has left half her estate to Audrey even after she is no longer Nevile's wife). He murders poor old Mr. Treves, a nonagenarian retired solicitor, in a similarly cold and ruthless way—Mr. Treves dies for being, as Maria Voždová puts it, a "guardian of the truth," having known Nevile as a child murderer who may murder again. And though he has remarried a beautiful woman in Kay, Nevile's motive here can also be put in the category of "nothing personal"—his fixation on Audrey suggests that he does not really love Kay, who serves him simply as a trophy.

Nevile is not fixated on Audrey in the wistful way Kay envies but in a retributive, recriminative way. Indeed, the true nature of Nevile's evil makes us in the end reevaluate the brassy Kay. Although she can be shallow and opportunistic, she is also a woman who has been manipulated by a man who does not love her. But this mystery is not simply about the toxic love story of Nevile and Audrey; Christie begins to establish the possibility of wholesome love through the romantic stories of ancillary male characters. Kay's would-be lover Ted Latimer is the only man who truly cares for her; his continuing devoted presence in Kay's life offers respite from her entrapment in an essentially staged marriage.

Similarly, Thomas Royde, who seems a hapless wallflower who has passively let himself be relegated to friend status by Audrey for decades, is given unexpected heroic status when he practices the advice of Robert Lowell, and chooses to "say what happened," revealing the crucial truth about Audrey and Adrian. John Curran reveals (332) that Thomas Royde's and Ted Latimer's names were established by Christie even before she settled on "Nevile Strange" for the culprit, suggesting a ground against which the later "strange" characters establish their deviance.

That Thomas and Ted are the ones who escort Mr. Treves back home shows us that, unlike Nevile, they are gentlemen and good men, despite their flaws and limitations (Latimer is overly brash, and Thomas is overly passive). The next day the two are appalled to learn of the death of Mr. Treves, demonstrating a decency and sanity that acts as a dramatic contrast to the character of Nevile.

The central decent man who is a countervailing force to Nevile is Angus MacWhirter, who has been introduced at the beginning of the story, when he is recovering from a suicide attempt; a year later he returns to Gull's Head as a form of therapy—revisit the very place where he had attempted to take his own life. This means that MacWhirter is unconnected to the gallery of suspects at Gull's Head and is not a member of their upper-class social circle. After Nevile's exposure, there is every expectation that Audrey will turn to Thomas Royde, her "true Thomas" (241) who has carried a torch for her since childhood and who is also the brother of Adrian, her true flame. Instead, Audrey turns to MacWhirter who has been where she is currently—in a state of emotional collapse and on the verge of suicide.

Notably, Angus can be said to be a version of Adrian—Angus and Adrian are similar as names, and like Audrey, they begin with A. But it is important that Angus be completely new, dissociated from anything to do with circles in which Nevile moved. Although we have seen the affinity between Audrey and Sylvia Battle in the way they are falsely accused and yet take responsibility, for crimes they did not commit, Audrey and MacWhirter have an even deeper affinity. Each felt life was not worth living, but at the very last moment backed away from the brink and towards a sense of a new life. Interestingly, in a novel awash with flagrantly Norman names—Tressilian, Strange, Latimer—MacWhirter has a stolidly Scots surname, as if Audrey needed above all to turn from the set who surround her and choose instead a sturdy Scotsman.

The emerging romance of Angus and Audrey, however, takes place within the spider's web Nevile has woven for his ex-wife. Battle is confident he can work out the pure mechanics of Nevile's masterminding of the murder of Lady Tressilian on a practical level, which involves a secret weapon, and a secret swim across the river to a resort in Easterhead Bay and back again. This is a crime that Christie encourages us to detect by including a map of the river, on which one side of the river is the resort and the other is Lady Tressilian's house. But the arrest of Nevile will require psychology as well as mechanics.

Although Superintendent Battle dismisses the entire idea of psychology when proffered by the headmistress at his daughter's school, he is nevertheless this novel's resident psychologist. For instance, although he does find some tangible clues, he ultimately relies on his ability to psych out the suspect, Nevile. Battle approvingly refers to Hercule Poirot in this regard, when he says, "No—the real genuine article—knowing just what makes the wheels go round. Keep a murderer talking—that's one of his lines. Says everyone is bound to speak what's true sooner or later—because in the end it's easier than telling lies" (160). This is what Battle does at the end of the novel with Nevile. His talk therapy is deployed in significant ways—it not only entraps the villainous Nevile but also uses his therapeutic tactics to counsel Nevile's ex-wife Audrey.

Both Nevile and his wife are investigated almost as psychological case studies. The presenting personality of Nevile is one in which he impresses as a very good sporting type of athlete, lighthearted, and happily married to a beautiful woman. But we learn that a different Nevile is lurking under the surface—someone Battle himself senses is in some way twisted. Christie wants us to consider Nevile's identity—the psychological make-up of a man obsessively dedicated to the destruction of his ex-wife but who can also cleverly conceal his true arrogant and vindictive nature. We eventually understand that it was Nevile who was the anonymous designer of a perfect crime introduced in the novel's first page, a plan he looks upon with the self-congratulatory pleasure of a job well done. He works his scheme out meticulously and believes that he considered every eventuality, and every possibility, with everyone's reaction anticipated, and everyone manipulated into unconsciously serving his plan.

But this novel is not about the smooth workings of Nevile's master plan—instead, the message is more in line with what one could call a "stuff happens" perspective. Mr. Treves introduces this sense of the unpredictable early when he and his legal colleagues speculate about crime and crime stories, and he suggests a plot in which an elderly victim has no idea he is reaching the zero hour of death more quickly than he had expected. Later, at Lady Tressilian's, Treves recalls a crime case in which a young boy planned a perfect crime with a bow-and-arrow down to the tiniest detail. But he also mentions an imperfection in the boy-killer—there were peculiarities in the length of his little fingers. This oddity echoes other small physical imperfections noted in various characters—Audrey Strange has a scar on her ear, Mary Aldin has a lock of white hair, Thomas Royde has a stiff right arm, Ted Latimer has an odd-shaped skull: as if the physical bodies of the gallery of suspects have not conformed to a systemic pattern of perfection.

Martin Priestman notes (158) that the array of minor deformities in the novel's characters is a symbol of the way Lady Tressilian is "screening out pariahs" from her homogenous social gathering, although it is indeed that gathering that Christie is herself making a point of disrupting, within her larger critique of the controlling and preposterously utopian planning of Nevile Strange; and indeed the many physical and psychological imperfections of the guests at Lady Tressilian's house party are such that to cull them from an imagined perfection would leave its population significantly reduced.

Treves himself is unwittingly imperfect when he makes a mistake by calling attention to the boy's fingers in the story in the presence of that boy (Nevile) himself. Later, an "out of order" sign is placed on an elevator so that an aging Mr. Treves would have to climb flights of stairs, exacerbating his heart condition and leading to his death. This death was not part of Nevile's plan. It is the first but not the last time Neville's well-laid plans are disrupted by the unexpected—or, as Christie is suggesting, disrupted by the way the world actually works.

Although Nevile is an arrogant perfectionist, his mastermind psychology is a consequence of a massive narcissistic injury he endured when Audrey ended their marriage through her affair with Adrian, producing a sense of grievance and injustice so powerful that he is driven to retaliate. Bolstered by cool composure he has acquired as a successful tennis player, he delivers a carefully calibrated performance, in which he appears to have behaved with the utmost chivalry to Audrey, and, playing the perfect gentleman, has assumed the blame for the marriage's failure. But he does not stop there—he has written a script in which he assigns a vindictive nature to Audrey that is so intense that she has arranged to implicate him in the murder of Lady Tressilian she herself has committed. The presence of a piece of sports equipment with his prints on the handle, and bloodstains on his coat have led Battle to conclude that suspicion has been thrown deliberately on Nevile as "a suitable victim" (181) by someone who hates him. The suggestion is that it is Audrey who has a "fine Italian hand" (153), a phrase associated with Machiavellian political skullduggery.

One of the interesting twists in this story is that Nevile has murdered two elderly people who likely did not have all that long to live—Mr. Treves and Lady Tressilian. Although neither of them is the end point of the murderer's plan, and although neither is a target of his animosity, that they become Nevile's victims tells us he evaluates them as easily disposable.

The improvised murder of old Mr. Treves is especially important to Christie's narrative strategy here; he is an echo of Lady Tressilian's "nothing personal" disposability but is the first example of something that has come out of the blue to require Nevile to deviate from his master plan. Indeed, there is a slight difference between how the plot of *Towards Zero* is organized and the typical Christie plot, in which a relatively closed circle of suspects all know each other or are adjacent to each other—found in its purest form in *And Then They Were None* or *Cards on the Table*. In *Towards Zero*, though, part of the mystery lies in how Mr. Treves and Angus MacWhirter, introduced at the very beginning of the book, will enter the main plot centering around the entourage attached to Lady Tressilian at Gull's Point. The accidental presence of Treves and MacWhirter makes the point that while Nevile may have a master scheme to bring about his desired outcome, there are other forces at play that Nevile has not expected.

The tension between the random and the freely-willed pervades the novel to such an extent that, when Superintendent Battle suggests to Audrey that Adrian's death was not an accidental one, but was yet another of Nevile's murders, we never quite know if this is the case—Christie also suggests it may have been simply a random road accident. Another example of chance over intent is that although Nevile may murder Mr. Treves by hanging the "Out of Service" placard on the elevator door and forcing the nonagenarian man to climb the stairs and die, he is not at all responsible for what has brought Mr. Treves to this area in the first place—it was just that his usual summer resort spot closed for renovations.

Equally, there is no way Nevile would have anticipated MacWhirter arriving to save the day for Audrey. But Nevile himself believes implicitly in the power of his own will, and his ability to use people as pawns on his chessboard. The pale and wraith-like Audrey is placed in a situation not dissimilar to Mr. Cust's in *The ABC Murders*—she is meant to take the fall for the murderer, who stands at a distance as a cool, controlled intelligence.

This means that Nevile has not only depended on the mechanics of his crime—the secret weapon, the secret swim—but also on his knowledge of his ex-wife's psychology. Far from being a Machiavellian murderer, it is as if Audrey is Nevile's defeated rival, who can never possibly win a match against him. While never perceived as a ruthless competitor on the court, in his life he will brook no opposition; considered a very good sportsman, we learn that a different Nevile is lurking under the surface. The key is the amount of difference between surface and depth in Nevile, in which the strain of playing the part of an even-tempered good sportsman pushed his darker impulses into a psychological netherworld in which they grew more twisted in the shadows.

It is interesting in this regard to consider the name "Nevile" which contains the word "evil," in apposition to his last name, "Strange." This name would seem to positively draw a big red circle around Nevile as a suspect, and yet Christie was sure her readers would not single him out as the sociopathic murderer because he is a celebrity, a presumed gentleman, and (in terms of the tacit rules of the detective genre) the so-very-obvious suspect. In addition, although all the evidence points to Nevile, he did not seem to have the opportunity to commit the crime.

There is a certain double bluff operative in *Towards Zero*, as one can find also in Lawrence Redding and Anne Protheroe in *The Murder at the Vicarage*. Similarly, an innocent person is set up to take the blame for the crime in each novel—and in each case, the intended innocent victim is driven to suicide. Additionally, Nevile has created a perfect mask—he covers his tracks so well that there is nothing to hold against him. As Audrey says, "I began to be afraid of Nevile soon after we were married. But the awful thing is, you see, that I didn't know why. I began to think that I was mad" (236).

Here Christie once again introduces her reading of criminality, in which the less Nevile's role is connected with his reality, the more the reality may prove to deliver unpleasant surprises. The irony is that although he is perhaps even too much the gentleman in his life as a professional sportsman, too much of a good loser to go for the brass ring, in his relationship with Audrey he is motivated by a need for vindictive triumph. And he has spent years anticipating a day of reckoning that will punish his enemy Audrey. Battle suggests that murder can be a long time coming and is the culmination of something that had its commencement in childhood. Battle wonders if the boy with the bow-and-arrow, for instance, may have sustained his childish murderer's heart over time, and which, combined with Nevile's sense of grievance against Audrey, began to distort his character in such a way that he himself may be beginning to believe that Audrey is indeed persecuting him.

The blow that Audrey dealt Nevile by leaving him, it is suggested, festered beneath a surface that was only apparently healed. Over time the brooding on his injury developed into a mission of revenge justified as a protection of his sense of self. Nevile's sense of certainty and his self-regard is such that it is not possible for him to imagine that Audrey is being punished beyond her fault.

As the title suggests, time is an important aspect of Nevile's crime, which is framed as a countdown. And in this narrative, everything seems to break Nevile's way, as he patiently, even luxuriously bides his time while his plan rolls inevitably towards the Zero Hour. But Nevile's master plan has been from the start a self-deceptive wish-fulfillment fantasy such that time brings not the fulfilling culmination he had anticipated, but an unraveling of his entire life.

Nevile's public presentation of self, however, is one of tolerance and forbearance—his charm and good manners conceal his lack of empathy, and although he may appear sophisticated, the suggestion is that he has barely entered the double digits in terms of emotional maturity.

Although essentially juvenile, his persona is that of well-deserved professional success, and his self-esteem requires recognition of that status. That it is Audrey who left him is a narcissistic injury but compounded by the sense that Nevile may be passing his prime, and that his athletic victories are behind him, requiring even greater investment in the illusion of easy and ongoing success. It is this false reality that Christie dismantles in this novel, a false reality in which Nevile appears certain of his invulnerability and ability to escape the accountability that would come with detection.

Nevile's second wife Kay is also someone who masks her own manipulative nature as well. Early on, Kay confesses it was not "fate" (51) that she and Nevile met, but careful planning on her part, making us briefly wonder if Kay is not the anonymous diabolical intelligence we witness at the beginning of the novel. But Kay is ultimately proven to have had no complicity in the murder and however manipulative and opportunistic she may be, she has none of Nevile's murderous malice. Nevile had always preferred the idea that he and Kay were fated to meet; he is terribly disappointed when she admits she had a human hand in it—that no higher power was in operation. On the other hand, when there is any evidence of mystic coincidence or the hand of fate intruding on Nevile's master plan regarding Audrey, it becomes a violation of his conviction that only he can make something happen in just the way he wants it to, with nothing to stand in his way, nothing left to chance.

Nevile's preference for a love story written in the stars is just one example of the way Christie is asking us to consider the phenomena of fate, luck, and free will. The idea of fate is introduced early in the person of the red-haired Scottish nurse, who is looking after Angus MacWhirter after his failed attempt at suicide. She suggests that everything happens for a reason—which means that MacWhirter was saved for a reason. She suggests to Angus that God may need him: "It may be just by being somewhere—not by doing anything—just be being at a certain place at a certain time—oh I can't say what I mean, but you might just—just walk along a street someday and just by doing that accomplish something terribly important—perhaps without even knowing what it was" (14).

The Scottish nurse is also described as coming from a family that had "the sight" (14). Darna Shealladh is the Gaelic name given to "second sight," and it was generally believed that the Scottish possess special psychic abilities, originating with the Celts of the Scottish Highlands, hence Christie's use of a Scotswoman to suggest the idea of psychic visions of the future. And early in the narrative MacWhirter's Scottish nurse envisions a picture of a man walking up a road on a night in September and thereby saving someone from a terrible death, a scenario that is realized at the end of the novel when MacWhirter prevents Audrey from throwing herself off Stark Head cliff.

MacWhirter however, does not wait for fate to take a hand when it comes to Audrey, but takes an active hand in fixing things, suggesting that he has freely used his own will to protect Audrey from being implicated in the murder of Lady Tressilian, even though at first, he really does not know if she is guilty or innocent. He deliberately lies anyway about seeing a man climbing a rope up into Lady Tressilian's bedroom, but then, providentially, manages to find the rope Nevile did use to climb up into that bedroom. Angus's "true lie" is far from the only lie in this story. The continuing depression from which unforeseen circumstances rescue Angus stems in part from the fact that he refused to lie for business success; to save Audrey, however, he is prepared to tamper with the truth. This presents a major change in Angus; he has categorically refused to lie at the

7. Flight from the Enchanter   127

beginning of the story but is perfectly prepared to do so at the end when what is at stake is not success but the welfare of the woman he loves.

Lying in this novel is not reserved simply for the evil Nevile or others who may have something to hide, and is not limited to Angus, who lies to save Audrey. Superintendent Battle also tells a lie as part of his tactics as a detective. Significantly, Battle stages an interrogation using Angus's lie about the rope and adding a lie in which he suggests Audrey is secretly laughing at Nevile in an infuriatingly superior way. This is hardly the case, but to even suggest that the joke is on Nevile is something Battle knows will push him over the edge.

The issue of lying is also raised with Battle's daughter Sylvia, whom he describes as "a very unusual type of liar" (21) whose lies are self-incriminatory. Sylvia Battle's false confession allows us to consider the psychology of false confession before it applies to Audrey. By making Sylvia an Audrey-type, Christie is suggesting that such false confessions are not an unusual phenomenon and that certain personalities can be manipulated by a dominant one. This subtle insight is one only Battle can recognize in Audrey because he has had a similar experience with his daughter's own suggestibility. And it is Audrey's psychology that makes Nevile confident that his bizarre plan will work.

But Angus MacWhirter and Superintendent Battle were not a part of Nevile's plan. MacWhirter is just simple bad luck for Nevile; similarly, if Superintendent Battle's daughter had not had the misfortune of being falsely accused of theft, he may have been less likely to recognize Audrey as in the same situation. These disruptions of Nevile's plans are yet another opportunity Christie gives us to reflect on issues of chance, probability, coincidence, and fate. These are issues that did not sufficiently interest Nevile—his egotism was such that he was certain he could manipulate the entire household of Gull's Head and intimidate Audrey into cooperating with his plan to destroy her. He failed to imagine unforeseen circumstances or situations beyond his control—or, even, the possibility that he is the one who will find himself entrapped at the Zero Hour.

On the surface, Nevile had happily remarried the vibrant Kay who serves as a dramatic contrast to the emotionally depleted, apprehensive Audrey. Audrey and Kay are described as opposites in this novel—they each take after one of the characters in the fairy tale "Snow White and Rose Red" (55) with the pale, wraith-like Audrey as the fairy tale character Snow White, and vivacious, auburn-haired Kay as Rose Red. It is significant also that this is a fairy tale about two sisters and only one prince between them, because the major love triangle in this novel consists of Nevile, Kay, and Audrey. Interestingly there are other love triangles involving Audrey. Here is Audrey, Thomas Royde, and Nevile; Audrey,

Thomas' brother Adrian, and Nevile; and Audrey, Thomas Royde, and Angus MacWhirter.

Indeed, for a woman so seemingly victimized by life, Audrey has at least four men interested in her—Thomas, the late Adrian, the psychotic Nevile, and the noble MacWhirter. Mary Aldin is, tacitly, left for Thomas to marry. Notably, John Curran reveals, in his study of Christie's notebooks, that Christie decided upon the essential names of Audrey and Adrian—and their alliteration—when she was still calling Nevile "Nevile Crane" (Curran 332–33), the alliteration suggesting not only affinity but that each is marked for death. But although the death of Adrian did not end in Audrey's twin death and instead found her free to choose a new life with Angus, without the Adrian–Audrey–Nevile love triangle, there is no plot at all.

The truly toxic love triangle of Kay-Audrey-Nevile, however, is the one continually nourished by both Nevile and his former wife. Nevile continues to have a wounding effect on Audrey such that she has agreed in a highly compliant way to spend her holiday at Gull's Head with her ex-husband and his new wife. Audrey still feels the need to propitiate Nevile and still finds it difficult to resist a strong imperious will who has duped her and made her the scapegoat. She herself admits: "But you don't know what it does to you being afraid for so long. It paralyzed you—you can't think—you can't plan—you must wait for something awful to happen" (237).

Audrey's sense that something terrible is about to happen pervades the entire novel, and Christie is careful not to interrupt that mood of fear and foreboding. Audrey has been so disempowered that she cannot imagine any way of escaping Nevile—he is described as a snake fascinating a bird so it cannot fly away. Nevile, like Iris Murdoch's many enchanters in her fiction, exerts a strange power over Audrey. Christie is here asking us to consider not only the psychology of the murderer but also the psychology of his perfect victim—which explains the "strange" surname, she shares with Nevile.

At this point, the suggestion is that only a miracle can save Audrey. Coincidence, on the other hand, governs MacWhirter's role in this story, he is not, and in social terms never would conceivably be, a guest of Lady Tressilian, but, as chance would have it, happens to be staying at the Easterhead Bay resort. And while Angus MacWhirter is prominent at the beginning; he is little present until the end. Here, he providentially returns to the scene of his own attempted suicide and, as a result, rescues Audrey, who, certain she will be arrested and hanged for the murder of Lady Tressilian, tries to throw herself off the same cliff. Angus identifies in Audrey the same sense of desperation, the same sense of being pursued by furies he felt when he had wanted to fling himself off the same cliff. This unexpected rescue of Audrey is meant to call to mind the red-haired nurse who has a vision of MacWhirter saving someone, but it also points out that Nevile's plans fail not so much because he has not thought of everything, but because he simply cannot do so—the world is full of too many coincidences and what poet Seamus Heaney called the uncanny "music of what happens."

The sudden whirlwind romance of Audrey and Angus ends this novel with something of a question, rather than an answer. This is yet another good example of the way Christie will in her mysteries suddenly stop short and leave things hanging in the air. Audrey's sudden decision to lark off to Chile with Angus is somewhat explained by the advice she gets from Battle to do the things she is most afraid of doing. Once again Battle, who appears to disdain psychology, is giving Audrey therapeutic advice. Audrey is described throughout the novel as ill, ghost-like, drained of energy, almost as if she were half dead—the idea is to get her to leap back into life. It is important especially for her to be fearless, since her relationship with Nevile was one that left her increasingly frightened and uncertain.

Taking up with Angus also suggests that she is going to regain her trust in love and marriage and that this is best done by leaping into the water, or getting back onto the horse, without reserve. Christie makes sure to impress upon us that Audrey is stepping off into the unknown, and in taking a risk, she is behaving almost out of character. But this is the first step in curing her of a timidity that could have ended in her becoming Nevile's victim. The radical step she takes in lighting out for Latin America suggests that she is not only changing her life but also changing her psychology, as if she will trust that the gods have arranged a good destiny for her.

There is something, loose and seemingly undisciplined about the ending, in contrast to the tight and oppressive sense of plot in the previous pages. Christie wanted to let into her last pages a sense of freedom and unpredictability as a contrast to Nevile's controlling plans, but it does catch us off guard and seems deliberately less plotted and planned than the rest of the book. But it has also been arranged that the two characters who had been in greatest despair in this novel are given a happy ending and are also given the novel's last words. There is a twinning of Angus and Audrey, through their names, their broken marriages, their mopey moods and manner, and through each one's determination to end it all at the very same menacing cliff.

When Angus providentially prevents Audrey from throwing herself off the cliff, their subsequent romance lifts his own depression and extricates Audrey from Nevile's diabolically clever plot. Christie makes room for this precipitous romance to lead readers to feel just a bit of fear—that by from throwing herself off one cliff into a bad marriage, she may be throwing herself off another, metaphorically speaking. In a way, then, the river and cliff are reinstated at the end, although with an emphasis on its message of wider liberty. What is important is that Audrey dispel the last traces of trepidation in the atmosphere, throw caution to the winds, take the plunge into the future in the spirit of a brave leap of faith. But there is no clairvoyant master plan, there are no ducks arranged all in a row, and no one can ever know what will happen next. In Christie's work, which seems so predicated on knowing the answers, there are times when a happy surprise requires a wait in the darkness.

Chapter References

Bright, Brittain. "Writing Through War: Narrative Structure and Authority," in Rebecca Mills and J.C. Bernthal, eds., *Agatha Christie Goes to War* (New York: Routledge, 2019), pp. 46–62.

Christie, Agatha. *Towards Zero* (New York: Dodd, Mead, 1944).

Curran, John. *Agatha Christie's Secret Notebooks: Fifty Years of Mystery in the Making* (London: HarperCollins, 2010).

Heaney, Seamus. Poem of the Week: 'Song' by Seamus Heaney. https://www.faber.co.uk/journal/poem-of-the-week-song-by-seamus-heaney/.

Lowell, Robert. "Epilogue." Accessed March 24, 2024, https://www.poetryfoundation.org/poems/47693/epilogue-56d22853c55c0.

Murdoch, Iris. *Flight from the Enchanter* (New York: Viking Press, 1956).

Priestman, Martin. *A Version of Pastoral, Detective Fiction Bibliography and Literature: The Figure in the Carpet* (London: Palgrave Macmillan, 1990).

Voždová, Marie. "Guardians of the Truth: The Elderly in Agatha Christie's Detective Fiction." *Polish Journal of English Studies*, vol. 9, no. 2, 2023, pp. 77–92.

8

The Artist Is Present

The Hollow

The country house known as The Hollow is in the words of Henry James a "great good place," presided over by the gracious Henry and Lucy Angkatell, whose house serves as a haven for such London guests as the poor relation Midge Hardcastle, artists like Henrietta Savernake, up-and-comers like Dr. John Christow, or fellow aristocrats. The Hollow is also the scene of a crime. Christie deploys a stanza from Alfred, Lord Tennyson's long poem *Maud* to suggest this dark side of the Angkatell house:

> I hate the dreadful hollow behind the little wood;
> Its lips in the field above are dabbled with blood-red heath,
> The red-ribb'd ledges drip with a silent horror of blood,
> An Echo there, whatever is ask'd her, answers "Death" [192].

What is important in this reference is not the presence of a literal hollow, but the way Christie also takes a pastoral scene and makes it a gothic one, stamped with the impress of murder. An echo of past crimes actually haunts the present in the Tennyson poem, and Tennyson's use of the word "echo" is also a significant point of connection with Christie's novel, which is also concerned with what one could call a decadent attachment to the past. Christie describes the Angkatell family as a hollow shell, an echo, a pale imitation of the venerable neighboring stately home called Ainswick, which was at least at one time the "real thing," a representation of what Henry James praised as the classic British "well-appointed, well-administered, well-filled country house."

As Evelyn Waugh suggests in *Brideshead Revisited*, the country house was admired as an actual artistic achievement—but, like Christie, he also shows us that the country house was doomed to decay. But although no longer playing any active social or political role in English society, Christie's authentic country house Ainswick is nevertheless constantly evoked, its tangible reality less important than its status as a nostalgic touchstone for an Edwardian era long past—a world that at an earlier time was, according to one of The Hollow's guests, "heaven on a plate" (253). Although an iconic English country house with all its traditions and perfections intact, Ainswick's status as only a golden memory calls into question the viability of The Hollow, its aspirational successor. The Hollow in many ways operates as what James Buzard calls an autoethnography—a look at home couched in the terms of the ways European ethnographers regarded "the other." Or, as Christie explores even more thoroughly in her later *At Bertram's Hotel*, this faux-Edwardianism is what Georgi Gospidinov describes as a dysfunctional "time shelter," a collective cultural denial of changing times.

The mistress of The Hollow, Lucy Angkatell, as a result is living in a fantasy world; like an echo, Lucy is not quite all there, which protects her from the actual realities of life in England in the wake of the Second World War. She lives in a dithery "elsewhere," with only her heroic butler Gudgeon—a relic from the Edwardian past—to hold the household together. As Richard York notes, Christie here exposes a world in which there is no longer any trusted community of the Edwardian kind in England. This novel, after all, was published in 1946, a year after the Second World War, a war of which all readers would have been highly aware, but which seems not to have happened in the insular world of The Hollow.

While often charming, Lucy's chilling insouciance can indicate a form of hollowness—an empty superficiality. Although accidentally placing a live lobster on her card tray can amuse through its Wonderland absurdity, other times there is a darker tone to her arrangements: when planning the wedding of two of the characters present at the scene of the crime, she muses on how nice it would be "in a way" (257) to keep the celebration to the same people who were at the house for the murder of John Christow, and all of whom were suspected of the crime. One can see in Lucy Angkatell something of William Empson's definition of the pastoral (Empson 53)—her trick is to simplify and limit her life by a near-hysterical insistence on "la belle vie" so that a recognition of her life's deficiencies or its hollowness is evaded.

Lucy's perspective not only finesses the tragic but doesn't seem to consider deep feeling at all; indeed, she hardly seems to apprehend the reality of loss; the whole business of personal relationships is solved and simplified by her conviction that "one shouldn't attach too much importance to anybody" (280). As fey as Lucy can be, the sense of an empty hole where her heart would be is exactly what encourages us to include her in our list of suspects. That Lucy herself becomes a murder suspect, and that her house becomes the site of a murder, returns us to the lines from the Tennyson poem, confirming Christie's emphasis not on Lucy's desired pastoral, but on menace, complexity and the inevitable passage of time.

That Angkatell is such an unusual name calls attention to the idiosyncrasies and troubles of the family itself, troubles which are intensified with respect to other Christie families, including those with more common names, such as the Lees in *Hercule Poirot's Christmas*. It is also apparently more consequential if the Angkatell line dies out than if the Lee line does, because there are many other Lee families, but few Angkatells. The Angkatells are a singular family not just in their quirkiness and their fixation on the occluded Ainswick but in their name. That sense of singularity speaks to the way there lingers throughout the novel a sense of deep investment in the fate of the Angkatell family, whose name reaches back to ancient times and had deep, primordial roots in England. The name "Ainswick" also has pastoral, nostalgic associations, recalling Painswick Hill in Gloucestershire and James Elroy Flecker's memorable lines on that vista; "Have I not sat on Painswick Hill, With a nymph upon my knees, And she as rosy as the dawn, And naked as the breeze?" (Hodgson 159).

Every character in the mystery is an Angkatell save the more modern couple, the Christows, and the modern actress Veronica Cray. Importantly, Henrietta Savernake and Midge Hardcastle are Angkatells by ancestry, but not in their surname, and thus in a way each is given a sort of independence and a future: Midge's in marriage, children, and as the chatelaine of what's left of Ainswick, and Henrietta's as an achieved artist (as discussed in Birns, "Agatha Christie's Portrait of the Artist"). The other Angkatells are blighted and depressed by their Angkatell identity. Edward Angkatell is perpetually in John's shadow, even though he is by far the doctor's superior in heritage and social class. As Lucy comments, "John Christow has always the most unfortunate effect on Edward. John, if you know what I mean, becomes so much more so and Edward becomes so much less so" (8).

This ineffectiveness of Edward places the Angkatell family in a crisis situation. Only Edward's suicide attempt and his rescue by Midge raise the family out of its crisis by making him less "less so" and more "more so," as, in the meantime, the overshadowing John Christow is no more. Lucy Angkatell is an eminently capable and robust Angkatell, who is far smarter than she looks, but her marriage to Sir Henry will bring no progeny. And despite his knighthood, Sir Henry is a pallid shadow of an Angkatell and unimportant in the family—their house, The Hollow, once again, is but an echo, a mournful ghost of Ainswick.

While Lucy plays a major role in the mystery plot, her husband Sir Henry remains a minor character. Despite his title (only an honorary knighthood, not an inherited title like a baronetcy) and despite not only having an air of distinction but (in a good qualification for an effective character in a murder mystery) possessing a large number of firearms, he is not key to the plot. Notably, though, he is described as the former colonial governor of the Hollowene Islands. There is no such place as the Hollowene Islands; Christie has made them up, but they obviously echo the name of The Hollow, as if the problems of home are the problems of empire returned and reflected. Or that the hollowness of British aristocratic life reflects the hollowness of a decaying and illusory sense of empire.

It is a small detail but, in a book published just as Indian independence would have been in the news, a telling one. The connection between the Hollowene Islands that Sir Henry formerly governed and its echo The Hollow where he now resides is, again, an autoethnographic one, a connection that applies the techniques used to observe other people's anthropologically back to one's own kind. Christie's novels of the late 1940s and early 1950s are not just a response to the rationing and hardship of the war and the social changes in England after the war; they register, however delicately, the loss of empire and the reexamination of home that loss of empire entails.

Into this Angkatell context comes John Christow, the novel's murder victim. He is competent, self-made, virile, robust, and outgoing, with none of the decadence of the aristocracy, but instead the vigor and health of the rising professional man. Christow, unfortunately, is married to the visibly neurotic, and ultimately homicidal, Gerda, who is not cut out to be a prominent man's wife and, out of her sense of inadequacy, retreats into her private neurosis. As Lucy Worsley notes, "Gerda is driven mad by her narrow life and her demanding, faithless husband."

Christie, precisely because of her own experience with Archibald Christie, knows how it feels when a woman's husband chooses an adulterous liaison with a more interesting woman over his devoted wife. Gerda's dowdiness and felt inadequacy are (despite her status as her husband's murderer) not condemned by the book; indeed, she is the object of measured sympathy. Many readers especially find their hearts go out to her when she manages to completely ruin the dinner she has served to her family—her desperation and her humiliation draw us with greater compassion to her character.

And yet it is Gerda who possesses and conceals the darkest of identities—an object of empathy, portrayed, as Silvia Rosivalova Baučekova puts it, in a "sympathetic fashion" (Baučekova 19), Gerda also murders her husband during an afternoon they were both guests at the gracious, well-appointed, Edwardian-style Angkatell house. In addition to exposing the Angkatell house as shallow, simple, and lacking in depth, Christie

8. The Artist Is Present

deploys the concept of a "hollow" to Greta's murder of John Christow as well. As Poirot tells Henrietta, he is led on a trail that deliberately ends in nothingness and hollowness.

Poirot's role in the novel begins when he fortuitously comes upon the scene of the crime, with Gerda holding a gun and standing over the body of her husband John. Poirot immediately understands that what he is seeing is something of a stage set; the guests at the Angkatell house are described as "actors" and he feels he is looking at "a highly artificial murder scene. By the side of the pool was the body, artistically arranged with an outflung arm and even some red paint dripping gently over the edge of the concrete into the pool. It was a spectacular body, that of a handsome fair-haired man. Standing over the body, revolver in hand, was a woman, a short, powerfully built, middle aged woman with a curiously blank expression" (110).

Prompted by the dying John, his devoted mistress Henrietta Savernake takes the gun from Gerda and throws it into the swimming pool. This is the first of a series of subterfuges adopted by Lucy and Henrietta calculated to block Poirot's investigation, even as they continue to enact their roles as innocent bystanders. Henrietta has planted false clues that indicate a different sort of murderer than the woman holding a gun over the dying body of the victim, clues that implicate almost anyone but that woman. Christie's strategy, as well, is to direct us away from Gerda and into various detours—in this regard, she too is protecting Gerda from exposure.

Gerda herself has staged the crime in such a way as to protect her from suspicion: she knows very well that she is holding a gun that is not the murder weapon, and she knows everyone sees her as vague and muddled—so that, in despite of the evidence, she cannot possibly be the murderer.

This is one of Christie's favorite narrative strategies, in which the obvious suspect is immediately considered and rejected as too discernible and detectable. Christie adds a twist to this strategy through Gerda's character—it has been established that Gerda does not possess the ability to imagine and plan such a sophisticated stratagem. She is portrayed as simple, whereas the crime becomes increasingly cluttered and complex. Gerda assumes the role of innocent victim who must be protected from false accusations, and who may have been set up by someone with brains and imagination; that is, someone like Henrietta. Christie realizes that her readers will respond to the picture of an innocent wrongly accused and scapegoated in a way that activates a sense of miscarried justice. That emotional response to perceived injustice, Christie suggests, will override an observer's more ratiocinative faculties.

As the reader is encouraged to rule Gerda out from the beginning, when she takes the gun Gerda is holding and throws it into the swimming pool, it is the clever, imaginative Henrietta who becomes the most-likely suspect. The victim John also appears to identify her as the murderer, rather than Gerda, who is not only perceived as lacking in competence, but whose worship of John makes it impossible for us to find a motive for his murder. We eventually learn John's dying wish was that Henrietta rescue Gerda; it is this unlikely teaming of the complex mistress and the simple wife that made solving the crime so difficult for Poirot.

The main narrative strategy then, is to juxtapose simplicity, an open-and-shut case that immediately implicates the most-likely suspect, with complexity, namely the machinations of Gerda's various enablers, which include first Henrietta but eventually also Lady Angkatell and Sir Henry. But Gerda is not quite as simple as she appears: the attentive reader will remember an early moment when she is still in her role as a defenseless victim, when she muses, "It was amusing to know more than they thought you knew. To be able to do a thing, but not let anyone know that you could do it" (4).

Gerda on one level is very like Cust in *The ABC Murders*, Audrey in *Towards Zero*, Norma Restarick in *Third Girl*, or Hawes in *The Murder at the Vicarage*—she is also an enfeebled victim deployed by a superior mastermind to take the blame for a violent crime. But in this case it is Gerda herself who is the mastermind, the one who is capable of murder. Gerda's appearance of guileless simplicity conceals a classic Christie criminal: that is, a controlling intellect who possesses a singleness of purpose and strength of will that is almost superhuman. Although Gerda appears to have hollowed herself out in order to become the self-effacing helpmeet of a powerful man, Christie hints quite early that Gerda may be concealing a capacity to commit a premeditated murder—that she is not as vacant as she seems. Like Christie's two famous detectives, Gerda also conceals her cleverness behind a persona that allows others to underestimate or discount her. Only on the surface is Gerda is an absence, a hollow, a disappearing woman.

Having created a crime that is both simple and complex, Christie layers yet another element into her novel. The odd minor character of the fortuneteller Zena introduces a different perspective on the crime. This is very much a pattern in Christie's mysteries—on the one hand we have a "mastermind" who plans and plots down to the tiniest detail; on the other, we have a seemingly clairvoyant counter-perspective that sees over, under, and around the machinations of the criminal.

In this case, this sense of oversight is articulated by Zena, whose dark prophecy of John's death correctly predicts the novel's actual turn of plot. This anticipatory prediction allows the reader to consider the possibility that tragedy was closer to the successful John Christow and the devoted Gerda than anyone knew; its sense of inevitability is confirmed by the mystical Zena. Christie assumed most readers would discount Zena as they do Gerda—nevertheless, the story does prove Zena right. Zena is not the most mystical of Christie's many seers and psychics; her readings have to do with intuitions of character, an issue of great importance in this novel. This mystery turns on the character and motive of victim, murderer, accomplices, and, indeed, the character of the detective Hercule Poirot himself.

The character of the murderer is the deep subject of this novel. Her victim, John Christow, has married a woman who was happy to shape her identity into that of the self-abnegating wife of an important doctor, requiring the effacement of her identity and the entire investment of her personality in that of her husband. But her husband is also, in his own way, hollow. One of Christie's interpretive tools in this regard is Henrik Ibsen's *Peer Gynt*, a play referenced by Henrietta. This reference to *Peer Gynt* is a good example of the way in which Christie will include a very literary reference to elaborate a point. In this case, she chose the encounter between Peer Gynt and a character known as the Button Moulder. Early in the novel, during a reverie in her art studio, Henrietta thinks about the clay of a failed project that she has returned to her bin: "That was the idea, wasn't it, of *Peer Gynt*? Back into the Button Moulder's ladle. Where am I, myself, the whole man, the true man?" (21). She then connects this sudden thought to her lover John Christow; anticipating his death, she wonders if it will mean he will be also cast back into an amorphous soup of unformed clay by a magical Button Moulder.

In *Peer Gynt*, this character will deliver an afterlife in which the individual who has failed to individuate or develop a true self will be consigned to a molten mass like that of a button maker's cauldron, to be completely reformed. In other words, the suggestion is that John Christow is hollow at the core, has failed, as the Irish would say, to "make his soul." Christie makes a point of this reference to *Peer Gynt* because she, like Henrietta, is suggesting that a lack or loss of authentic identity is a serious ethical and spiritual failure. Gerda has worshipped John as a kind of deity, presiding as he did over an emerging world of modern medical advance and social progress, a classic new man of the postwar world. Although there are inspirational aspects of John, he nevertheless takes his place in the long line of flawed doctors in Christie's work. He has been less heroic than comfortably materialistic; John as a physician is not a thing of the spirit that suggests a calling or vocation, but more an example of empty conventional success.

Like Peer Gynt, John suspects that he has lost his true self and has become almost literally undistinguished. Seen in this light, John's brisk, impatient demeanor is not simply that of a busy physician, but of an increasingly angry and alienated man who believes he has failed in an important life-task. The sudden reappearance of his old love Veronica Cray pushes John into a psychological crisis that confirms his suspicion that he has made a wrong turn. He had left the glamorous, successful Veronica for Gerda, whose name means "shelter" in Old Norse, and in whom John assumed he would find shelter and security. His meeting with Veronica, however, leads him to believe that his life has ground to a halt; that if he is to go forward, he must first go back and begin all over again.

Demoralized by his understanding that his marriage to Gerda has been a hollow one, John begins to wonder if his own personality has become hollow, or nothing more than the hollow idol that Gerda worshipped. He has become a man who has not fulfilled his earthly mission; quoting Ibsen, Henrietta suggests that John had ignored "God's mark" (21) upon his brow and abandoned any sense of higher purpose. It is almost as if John is prepared to die, just at the point at which Gerda is most prepared to kill him, the crime then the culmination of psycho-existential issues related to the meaning of work, love, and the purpose and point of the single self.

But Christie finds ways to delay and subvert the tragedy of John and Gerda and their hollow marriage, instead introducing other suspects, and in so doing allowing the novel to turn for a time into an exploration of the larger social issues concerning the decline of the aristocracy after World War II. Christow represents a modern world that is far from the old-fashioned enclave of Ainswick into which Edward has retreated. Once or twice, in fact, Christie suggests that even a deceased Christow still possesses more presence and vitality than does a living Edward; in conversation with Edward, fellow houseguest Midge Hardcastle quotes one of Ophelia's songs in *Hamlet*, which sings of someone "dead and gone" (275), but then notes that "John Christow was not dead and gone—for all that Edward wished him to be.... John Christow was still here at The Hollow" (275).

It is the living Edward who actually dead and gone (275) by representing a demographic whose pasts held more promise than do their futures. Edward seems to be the "ghost" in this novel, as if he has outlived his time and has no place in the postwar world. Despite his recessive character, however, Edward does carry out the romantic subplot that not only acts as a light counterpoint to the dark revelations that are at the heart of the story but also is a way to register some of the social changes facing England after the Second World War. For romance to come alive, and for romance to bring Edward back to the land of the living, Christie suggests that he must connect to a mid-20th-century world—the world of professionals

8. The Artist Is Present

like John Christow and of middle-class shopgirls like Midge Hardcastle. Despite having an Angkatell as a mother, Midge's upbringing was an ordinary, middle-class one—significantly, she grew up in the industrial Midlands, not in the aristocratic south of England. Although from different social stations, however, Midge and Edward both prefer the world of their childhood, in which Ainswick was still a vibrant center of British society. Economic exigencies have required Midge to face a real-world England— her work in a London boutique is far from the heavenly world she associates with her childhood summers at Ainswick.

It is in the Midge section of the novel that we find an example of a snobbish antisemitism that occasionally surfaced in Christie's work, in the person of a minor character Madame Alfrege, described by Midge to Edward as "a Whitechapel Jewess with dyed hair and a voice like a corncrake." The depiction of Madame Alfrege in *The Hollow* prompted a formal complaint by the Anti-Defamation League to Christie's publisher, marking it as the last of Christie's antisemitic references (*https://lib-archives. ex.ac.uk/Record.aspx?src=CalmView.Catalog&id=EUL+MS+99%2F1%2F1 947%2F1%2F39*). The social acceptability of the kind of parlor antisemitism found in this novel and in earlier ones was, Christie learned, no longer acceptable after the Holocaust.

One wonders, however, at the excessively unflattering depiction of Madame Alfrege, who owns the shop where Midge works as a salesgirl. The uncomplimentary description was evidently there to impress upon us the undesirability of Midge's current employment—to prove to us that she had good reason to feel terribly unhappy. But did Christie introduce Madame Alfrege as another misdirection, another way to keep us from thinking about Gerda? Christie is particularly eager to direct our attention away from Gerda, and as a result we spend considerable time in Madame Alfrege's shop. Is Madame Alfrege meant to entice some readers into considering her a suspect? To do that would play into a reader's suspicion of the foreign at the very least, if not actually playing into antisemitic prejudice. Is this a way to seduce readers into using their xenophobia against them, or to seduce the most guileless and gullible of Christie's readers down a real blind alley?

This is the persuasive opinion of Malcolm J. Turnball, in his *Victims or Villains: Jewish Images in Classic English Detective Fiction*. He suggests that Christie's depiction of the Jew is consciously in conformity with the routine views of the English middle classes at the time and deploys Jewish stereotypes as a form of red herring, misdirecting her readers by appealing to their own prejudices. In addition to Mme. Alfrege, other examples of this narrative strategy of misdirection are Herman Isaacstein in *The Secret of Chimneys* and Babe St. Maur in *The Seven Dials Mystery*.

Christie may deploy Mme. Alfrege as a red herring. But there is no doubt that she also uses her to draw attention to a familiar class signification. Christie's largely unattractive portrait allows her character Midge to prove her own superior social credentials. As Jane Arnold points out in her article "Detecting Social History: Jews in the Works of Agatha Christie," the antisemitism in *The Hollow* is typically Edwardian, and indicates how the upper classes of that time insulated themselves from those deemed their social inferiors. As Noël Coward put it, "The stately homes of England / How beautiful they stand, / To prove the upper classes / Have still the upper hand."

The role of Jewish referents in *The Hollow* is in a sense previewed by Christie's 1939 short story "The Regatta Mystery," featuring an alternate detective of hers, Parker Pyne (although an earlier version featured Poirot, bringing it even closer to *The Hollow*) and a jewelry dealer named Isaac Pointz, clearly marked as Jewish, whose precious diamond has been stolen by an American girl named Eve Leathern. Christie used an alternate version of the latter's surname, Leatheran, in 1936's *Murder in Mesopotamia*, set in Iraq, in the context of cultural encounter, which can be said to be so in this short story as well. Pointz, though not at all a Jewish surname (it is Norman and aristocratic)—as in Virginia Woolf's use of the name in *Between the Acts* does sound like German–Jewish names that end in "tz." In "The Regatta Mystery" the heist of their jewels serves to spur the Welshman Evan Llewelyn in his courtship of Mrs. Rustington.

The story ends with the American (of ultimately Italian background) arrested, the Jew leaves the scene as quickly as the jewels and only the Anglo-Welsh couple remains. This resembles how, in *The Hollow*, the Jew is in the plot only to suture the bolstering of the alliance of Hardcastle and Angkatell, to buttress a renewal that uses the cosmopolitan only as an agent to secure reconstituted autoethnographic domesticity. That Merja Makinen has placed *The Hollow* in dialogue with Virginia Woolf indicates that Christie is also dealing with themes of aestheticism, displacement, and adaptation, which juxtapose social change and experimentation with a residual attention to hierarchy.

This attention to hierarchy also surfaces when Edward Angkatell tells Midge he simply won't have her working at Mme. Alfrege's shop--an edict that can also be interpreted as a demonstration of aggression required for a necessary masculine presentation. This casual antisemitism was even after World War II a time-honored way for the English and European males to assert virility, which means that Edward was in something of automatic pilot in this regard, perhaps another demonstration of the way Christie may be suggesting that poor Edward has very likely not entertained an original thought in his entire lifetime. His rescue of Midge from

Madame Alfrege is an unfortunate corollary of something that in purely plot terms is read as salutary for Edward and Midge, but that raises the disturbing question of whether harmony can only emerge in one community if another must be denigrated. This last mention of Mme. Alfrege is in the context of Edward's suggestion that the two of them celebrate their engagement with a return to the shop with the intention of being rude to Madame Alfrege almost suggests something beyond snobbery.

The negative picture of Madame Alfrege, her shop, and her customers also helps explain not just Midge's current misery, but also the reasons for Midge's intense longing for Ainswick—given her present situation, she prefers to live in the dream of the long golden afternoon of the British Empire, secure within one of the stately homes of inherited aristocratic wealth which were understood to celebrate the achievements of British civilization. Her unhappiness with Madame Alfrege demonstrates that Midge is not finding a place for herself in modern, postwar England.

Midge resentfully notes the difference between her life and Edward's: "The fact that a working day of nine to six, with an hour off for lunch, cut a girl off from most of the pleasures and relaxations of a leisured class had simply not occurred to Edward. That Midge, unless she sacrificed her lunch hour, could not drop into a picture gallery, that she could not go to an afternoon concert, drive out of town on a fine summer's day, lunch in a leisurely way at a distant restaurant, but had instead to relegate her excursions into the country to Saturday afternoons and Sundays and to snatch her lunch in a crowded Lyons or a snack bar was a new and unwelcome discovery" (245).

Not only does Midge find her work unfulfilling, she does not do it well; unlike John or Henrietta, she hasn't secured work she finds meaningful. Her working life largely consists of fawning over customers who are not always well-mannered or good-natured. Despite Midge's nostalgia for the Ainswick of her girlhood, in her present situation she not only feels estranged from the Angkatells and their ilk, she looks at them with a critical eye that translates the personal into the political. When her sullen socialist cousin David Angkatell points out to her that the workers should have all the amenities of The Hollow, Midge heartily agrees. It is interesting to note the degree to which Christie does include the socialist revolutionary into her cast of characters—we will also find one in *Death on the Nile* and *A Murder Is Announced*, among others. Perhaps, however, Midge is suggesting that only she herself should have all the nice things associated with an upper-class life; certainly, once she and Edward get together, there is no further talk of revolution. One can, however, conclude that the introduction of David's ideas does prepare a context in which the impending marriage of Edward and Midge does have a political aspect to it. On a personal level, the marriage of Midge to Edward rescues her from selling luxury to the middle class, and has, instead, secured something more valuable—the safety of unassailable social status.

David Angkatell, himself another suspect and another guest at the Hollow, is depicted as a sullen Marxist, set against all that Ainswick represents, but ultimately has problems more in the realm of Doctor Freud than Mr. Marx. He is attached to his mother in such a way that ensures that he will never marry, which means that David is not providing a male heir for Ainswick. This is eventually redressed by Edward and Midge's marriage. One can slightly reverse this plot. Had David been a more conventional young man of the 1940s (Coldstream Guard, Jesus College Oxford, Brooks', South Kensington) it is likely Edward would simply have permitted himself to abandon the task of activating his hetero-progenitive impulses leading to marriage to Midge.

This may suggest that perhaps Midge is marrying a house more than a man, but Christie's emphasis is on how Midge can be useful at Ainswick, where she will not only humanize Edward, she will also resurrect him—she literally rescues Edward from attempted suicide, but she also revives his dead spirit. While his love for Henrietta represented Edward's attempt to repeal modern times and return to the old Edwardian aristocracy, Midge will provide the traditional British middle-class values of cozy home life, making Ainswick less a museum-piece and more a site of "daily companionship and love and laughter" (286).

Midge's ability to provide Edward the strength, warmth, and love that he lacks constitutes not only the novel's romantic happy ending but also solves Midge's difficulty in finding that purpose-driven life that is so much a subject of this mystery. Ainswick had become a lonely place whose point Edward can no longer recognize, but thanks to Midge the house will be resituated in a more middle-class present. As such it is Midge, the girl from the North Country, who represents the future of the stately home in this novel—and indeed the future of England itself. The celebration of the vitality of the middle and lower classes—represented by Midge, John Christow, and his patient Mrs. Crabtree—is not something associated with Christie, who is too often dismissed as a kind of Tory dinosaur, but it is something we can find in other of her novels as well, for instance *The ABC Murders* or *A Murder Is Announced*.

In the beginning, however, Midge and Edward both are living metaphorically in a heavenly past as an alternative to despair; their nostalgia for the golden age of Ainswick is an indication of their present dejection, signaled by the novel's melancholy autumnal season. There is indeed an autumnal aspect to this novel—a sense of an ending or a suggestion of a general melancholic crisis associated with the changed situation of

England after two world wars. It is despair that is more a subtext in the lives of a number of the characters in The Hollow—Midge and Edward are two examples; John had also begun to despair of the choices he has made in his life; similarly, an episode in Henrietta's studio involves the despairing destruction of her failed sculpture.

Additionally, David Angkatell spends the entire time fuming and sulking, while the actress Veronica Cray, the girl who has everything, is desperately trying and failing to win John Christow back. It is interesting that in Christie's own 1951 dramatization of *The Hollow*, Veronica Craye (as her surname is in the theatrical version) is a much more prominent character, as her movie-star charisma is far more viable in a dramatic rather than novelistic genre. Moreover, with Poirot absent in the play, replaced by the far more staid Inspector Colquhoun, Veronica Craye supplements some of the performative outlandishness left absent by Poirot's extraction.

In the novel, though, Veronica can make little impact on the pall that has been cast over The Hollow. Many of the Angkatells' guests cannot find any serenity even as they have escaped to a country place that as Vita Sackville West put it, promises "peace and permanence." But tellingly, it is only when Midge essentially reinvents Ainswick as a cozy middle-class domestic haven that both she and Edward can find a way into the future.

This classic Cinderella ending is however only one thread of Christie's story. The situation of Henrietta Savernake, Gerda's accomplice, turns this novel in quite a different direction. Henrietta had been the mistress of the modern, forward-looking John, and despite Edward's pleas, is not interested in either going back to Ainswick or, unlike Midge, providing Ainswick with a bridge into modernity. She is, instead, as devoted to the modern John in her own way as is Gerda. An important aspect of the narrative is Christie's exploration of the significant differences between John's wife Gerda and his mistress, but at the same time, it is important to note that Gerda and Henrietta can be said on one level to be as if two sides of the same dissociated personality.

It is significant, for instance, that Poirot finds this murder case difficult precisely because two women are involved in covering up the crime; Henrietta, at John's request, has conspired with the criminal, Gerda, and frustrated the course of justice. To fulfill her task, Henrietta introduces the drawing of the mythical, mystical Ygdrasil the sacred tree of life from Norse mythology (66), and also the name for the old oak tree at Ainswick. Henrietta plants her drawing Ygdrasil at the scene of the crime to confuse Poirot, but it also unwittingly references Gerda's obvious Nordic name, yet another way in which Gerda and Henrietta's identities are blended. The drawing is in this regard more of a confession of complicity, than an actual clue to the crime—as if Henrietta's drawing is telling Poirot that someone other than the murderer knows the truth, and that artistry has been involved in both the crime and its cover-up.

The concept of Ygdrasil itself is meant to connect everything in a grand design—it is a tree of life, a world tree which represents the cycle of life, and binds the divine and the earthly together. It is also sometimes associated with the tree of knowledge, and it is indeed Henrietta who possesses knowledge of the crime, as well as an intuition of a larger sense of cosmic design.* In that regard, the Tree of Life drawing is far from a misdirection—it is pointing at the existential issues that the triangle of John, Gerda, and Henrietta must face at this crisis point in each of their lives. That sense of a larger, if mysterious, metaphysical dimension beyond a socio-historical moment is one we will see elsewhere in Christie's work— in *The ABC Murders*, for instance, or in *Towards Zero*, or *Murder on the Orient Express*. This side of Christie's work cannot be safely ignored or discounted, and must be addressed if one is to see Christie clearly and see her whole.

One of the fascinating aspects of Henrietta, our artist who has depicted the Tree of Life, is that she is close to being the murderer, and initially seems identified as such by John. Not only has she placed a mantic drawing at the scene of the crime, Henrietta has also found the true murder weapon, which she buries in her sculpture of the Trojan Horse she has created for that purpose. The drawing immediately suggests the hand of the artist, but her dissembling is also something Poirot identifies with the creative mind: "We were contending against a mind capable of intricate and ingenious inventions, so that every time we seemed to be heading or the truth, we were being led on a trail that twisted away from the truth and led us to a point which—ended in nothingness" (260). The deliberate engineering of a hollow is, then, planned; as Poirot suggests, pointedly to Henrietta, "the mind that is plotting against us is a creative mind, Mademoiselle" (260).

Like Justice Wargrave in *And Then There Were None*, Henrietta deploys her artistic ingenuity for criminal purposes—in this case, covering up the identity of the murderer of John Christow. The Trojan Horse she created to conceal the gun Gerda used to kill John is a good example of Henrietta's inventive deceptions, and it is also hollow, likely another way of reminding us of the novel's title.

Henrietta is not simply complicit with the murderer, however; she

---

* One wonders also if Christie understood that this tree was also associated in mythology with a gallows. The tree would then be the gallows in which Odin sacrificially hung himself; Ygdrasill refers to the word Yggr, or terror, suggesting that the name means "tree of terror." Another interpretation suggests that Ygrdrasil derives from "yggia" or yew tree, associated with death and rebirth.

also is a detective. Ahead of Poirot, she has seen through Gerda's dissimulation, although cannot bring herself to expose the truth. In this regard, she ends up in a situation very similar to Poirot's. Lucy, for instance, presciently points out that once Poirot has learned the truth, he will be satisfied to keep that knowledge to himself. This is also true of Henrietta. What is complicated, however, is that to know the truth about Gerda, one must also come to know the truth of Henrietta. It is only when Poirot develops a special relationship with Henrietta that he understands that he is also drawing closer to the murderer.

The murderer and her accomplice, one holding a gun, the other hiding the real murder-weapon, are the victim's wife and mistress respectively, seeming adversaries, but at times twinned, as if doubles for each other—at one time each wears the same sweater, and we are not quite sure which one will drink the poison that Gerda has prepared for Henrietta. Although what is clear at this point, is that one of them must die. Gerda leaves the room briefly, and when she returns, she promptly drinks the poison tea meant for Henrietta. Although he is not sure if she is drinking from the poisoned cup, Poirot does not stop her—he stays his hand. What cup Gerda chooses is up to chance, or fate—but no one will know that it was Poirot who let it be. After Gerda dies, Poirot turns to Henrietta and provides an alibi for them both, suggesting that Gerda took her life while of "unsound mind" (300).

This is another good example of the way Poirot finds creative ways to solve the problem of what to do with a criminal once caught. Here, he personally manages to dispose of one member of the criminal team and draws the other member to his side. Like Gerda, Henrietta, too, will be protected from the justice system. Poirot, one must remember, is not a policeman. He is not from Scotland Yard or any other department of Justice. He has elected to solve the mystery without exposure of either Gerda or Henrietta, the surviving Henrietta moving from being the murderer Gerda's partner-in-crime to becoming the detective Poirot's partner-in-silence.

Like so many of Christie's mysteries, the question of innocence is left open—Poirot has secured Henrietta's freedom from any onerous association with Gerda, but Henrietta is nevertheless complicit. It is Henrietta who carries what Christie has always portrayed as the virtue of so many of her criminals—their inventive minds, their tenacity in executing their plans, their daring. One could call this the "good" in Christie's evil characters; certainly, Poirot admires Henrietta's masterful mind. But her protection and her enabling of the spiteful and unprincipled Gerda means that Henrietta's innocence can never quite be secured.

We do not conclude this novel with a scene of Midge and Edward's home life in Ainswick, which would be a conventional way of resolving the dilemma of the British country house. Instead, the heroine who emerges from this novel is the complicated and somewhat compromised Henrietta, who has established her independence from everything associated with traditional old country houses, whether Ainswick or its imitation, The Hollow.

It is an artful ending that demonstrates sympathy for Henrietta and secures the fragile Gerda from exposure and punishment. Instead of making Henrietta's complicity with Gerda known, Poirot immediately himself develops a collaborative relationship with Henrietta, as if they are a team. At the same time, Henrietta also draws him into the suspect circle: when Poirot asks Henrietta if she would like his fingerprints as part of the evidence she will submit to the authorities, she jokingly responds as if she were the detective, and he the prime suspect. And indeed, Poirot in his own way joins the conspiratorial circle that includes Henrietta and Lucy. It is a tribute to the way Christie has established the integrity of Poirot's character that it can survive the numerous shady choices and sketchy short cuts we so often observe when he is on the case. But it is nevertheless Poirot's moral agility, his moral realism and moral ingenuity as well as his sense of higher courts and higher powers, that have made him a premiere Great Detective.

A case in point is the death of Gerda, This is, strangely, a death supervised by Poirot, who must make some quick decisions in an ambiguous situation. Gerda seems once again to have dissolved into a puddle of incompetence—typically, has confused teacups, and has accidentally drunk the poison she had meant for the increasingly inconvenient Henrietta. But once again, there is a second, clever Gerda we know to exist, which leads to a leftover question—*did* Gerda know? Did Gerda simply blunder into drinking the wrong cup, or did she, on seeing Poirot sitting together with Henrietta, realize the game was up and decide to end it all then and there? One could argue that she must have known; seeing Poirot at the table, she must have known why he was there and knew that Poirot was giving her the chance to end it all.

This reading would suggest that, as with other of his murderers, Poirot has allowed Gerda to spare her family and herself the misery of a trial, imprisonment, and execution and has elected as a result to leave the crime officially unsolved in a somewhat untidy way. That sense of tacit understanding is something we have already seen between Poirot and Henrietta—it may also be operative with Gerda as well. This would also make Gerda more accountable for her own death, and Poirot, happily, less so.

Poirot is necessary to this story because it is he who identifies the ruthlessness in Gerda, and understands that Henrietta is in danger; he understands that Gerda is not as harmless as she appears, but that, on the contrary, she can be quite dangerous if she feels her back is to the wall.

But Poirot does not like to prosecute; he allows Gerda the opportunity to choose to avoid exposure as a criminal, even if, in a way, he becomes her executioner. Poirot also introduces the possibility that the cup was not chosen by chance, as if it may have been fate that led Gerda to the cup; or as if it may have been the agency of Gerda herself, accepting Poirot's merciful suggestion. Poirot has elected to stay his hand, serving some other agency, whether it be chance, fate or Gerda Christow, reminding us of the way Poirot has somehow manifested at The Hollow to facilitate not so much human justice, but to serve something higher and more mysterious.

There will be no trial, no punishment no execution—in fact there will not be an official closing of the case.

Poirot provides an uncomplicated narrative to explain the accidental death of Gerda, so that, except for Poirot and Henrietta, no one will ever know what really happened. Confessing that one day he will relent and tell Gerda's already inquisitive son Terence the truth, he advises Henrietta herself to pivot to the future, as does John Christow's former patient Mrs. Crabtree. The working class Mrs. Crabtree moves us far away from the world of Ainswick as possible, but towards a vitality that Ainswick no longer possesses. Henrietta notes a joyful acceptance of all of life in Mrs. Crabtree 's voice, and her pleasure in being live is interestingly, also somehow mysteriously related to the way she is thrilled by the unexpected murders she reads about in the newspaper—ironically she would relish hearing more about the murder mystery Henrietta herself is keen to leave behind.

Despite her guileless Cockney brogue and seemingly simple heart, Mrs. Crabtree has a sixth sense about Henrietta and her strange relationship to John and Gerda Christow, and earthy love of life, murders and all, are a breath of fresh air for Henrietta. She needs to hear just what Mrs. Crabtree tells her: "Don't fret, ducky—what's gorn's gorn. You can't 'ave it back" (306), advice that, while exactly what Hercule Poirot said in so many words, is expressing the same thought in language that oozes just the vitality she must recover for herself. Mrs. Crabtree's comments also slightly echo Ophelia's song in an uncanny way, "He is and gone, lady, / He is dead and gone, / At his head a grass-green turf, / At his heels a stone" (276), even as the phrase is recycled, repurposed, and made to open the door into a new life, far from the illusory world of The Hollow.

Christie returns to Henrietta's art at the end of the novel to further elucidate the way Henrietta has changed, but it is not until she creates a piece called "Grief" that she can free herself from a series of sculptures that are all strangely contaminated by the presence of the spirit of Gerda. For instance, Henrietta had taken Gerda as a model for a sculpture called

"The Worshipper," but realizes that the sculpture reveals nothing but idolatry—a worship that brings with it a desire to control, to possess to the point of suffocation. Some unlovely second personality, something ignoble coming from within herself but not unlike Gerda's, has ruined her sculptures.

It is only at the end that we see that these sculptures are part of Henrietta's journey to freedom from her "inner Gerda." This suggests that Henrietta cannot easily separate from the conniving, short-sighted Gerda, and indeed it takes the space of the entire novel for this sundering to occur, aided by Hercule Poirot, whose detection is increasingly not so much the apprehending of Gerda as it is the rescue of Henrietta. That sense of Christie mysteries involving rescue more than prosecution is one we will see very often in her work. And here Henrietta's rescue involved her needful separation from both John and John's wife Gerda, which will allow her to somehow reach for some higher purpose beyond herself, something associated with her artistic drive, which makes her its instrument.

Henrietta abandons her Gerda-influenced art, returning it to clay to be reformed into something better. This decision echoes *Peer Gynt's* Button Moulder, who returns mediocre selves back to a molten mass, but Poirot's solution of the crime permits Henrietta to complete her alabaster sculpture called "Grief," an expression of loss which release her buried emotions, bringing to this story a deep feeling that complements its ratiocinative plot. At this point, Hercule Poirot is nowhere to be seen—the novel has been handed over to Henrietta, who has grown into its major character.

This effacement of Poirot is what Christie later realized she wanted all along. She later complained in her autobiography that the presence of Poirot had "ruined" her novel, reflecting a general discontent with her famous detective at this point in her writing career (473). But did Poirot ruin this novel? Without him, this would be more completely Henrietta's story—even as it is, we are invited into Henrietta's consciousness in a way that excludes Poirot. He knows nothing of the revelatory thoughts in her head as she creates her sculptures. Poirot's complete absence, however, could mean that it is Henrietta who would stay her hand when Gerda chooses a teacup. This certainly darkens and complicates the character of Henrietta, who in the end becomes not Gerda's protector but Poirot's accomplice. It is Henrietta's relationship with Gerda that Michel Houellebecq was referencing when he discussed the novel as one of deep waters with powerful undercurrents" (Houellebecq 71).

And it could be that, without the intervening Poirot, the waters would be ever deeper, the undercurrents more powerful. Gerda, in the end, has planned to murder her guardian Henrietta, and, without Poirot, her guardian would have to do to Gerda what Poirot did—outdraw her. And without Poirot Henrietta would carry the death of Gerda with her as a shadow—a secret dark side. It is Poirot, who manifests as if from another dimension, who will keep Henrietta safe from any sense of new doubleness; he is on the wall, protecting her. This suggests that although Christie did not want him on that wall, she still needed him on that wall. Instead of a shadowed Henrietta, there is an exhilarating affirmation of Henrietta's creative power and an identity that is given its authenticity through service to that power.

We have come a long way from Ainswick and The Hollow; while the novel promised a country house whodunit, the deeper detection involves not the manners and morals of the mid-century British upper class, but the search for the true self. It should begin to be clear that on one level this is the depiction of the long, strange introspective journey on the part of Christie herself as she secures her own creative powers, free of all that is Gerda, free of all that was holding her back. The self-portrait that emerges in this narrative is there to tell us this: that the artist is present.

Chapter References

Abramovic, Marina, artist. *Marina Abramovic: The Artist Is Present*. New York, The Museum of Modern Art, 2010.
Arnold, Jane. "Detecting Social History: Jews in the Works of Agatha Christie." *Jewish Social Studies*, vol. 49, no. 3/4, Summer-Autumn 1987, pp. 275–282.
Baučekova, Silvia Rosivalova. "The Salt of the Earth or the Murderess: The Problem of Femininity in the Novels of Agatha Christie." *Prague Journal of English Studies*, vol. 10, no. 1, 2021, pp. 7–22.
Birns, Margaret Boe. "Agatha Christie's Portrait of the Artist." *Clues: A Journal of Detection*, vol. 1, no. 2, 1980, pp. 31–34.
Buzard, James. *Disorienting Fiction: The Autoethnographic Work of Nineteenth-Century British Novels* (Princeton: Princeton University Press, 2005).
Christie, Agatha. *An Autobiography* (London: Collins, 1977).
Christie, Agatha. *The Hollow* (New York: Berkley Books, 1984).
Christie, Agatha. *The Regatta Mystery and Other Stories* (New York: Dodd, Mead, 1939).
Coward, Noël. "The Stately Homes of England." https://lyricsplayground.com/alpha/songs/s/statelyhomesofengland.html.
Empson, William. *Some Versions of Pastoral* (New York: New Directions, 1974).
Girouard, Mark. *A Country House Companion* (New Haven: Yale University Press, 1987).
Gospidinov, Georgi. *Time Shelter* (New York: Liveright, 2024).
Hobsbawm, Eric, and Terence Ranger. *The Invention of Tradition* (Cambridge: Cambridge University Press, 1994).
Hodgson, Geraldine Emma. *The Life of James Elroy Flecker: From Letters and Materials Provided by His Mother* (Boston: Houghton Mifflin, 1925).
Houellebecq, Michel. *Platform* (New York: Knopf, 2003).
James, Henry. "The Country House and the English Novel." *The Guardian*, June 10, 2011. https://www.theguardian.com/books/2011/jun/11/country-house-novels-blake-morrison.
Makinen, Merja. "Agatha Christie in Dialogue with *To the Lighthouse*: The Modernist Artist," in J.C. Bernthal, ed., *The Ageless Agatha Christie: Essays on the Mysteries and the Legacy* (Jefferson: McFarland, 2016), pp. 11–28.

McClung, William Alexander. "The Country-House Arcadia." *Studies in the History of Art*, vol. 25, *Symposium Papers X: The Fashioning and Functioning of the British Country House* (1989), National Gallery of Art, pp. 277–287.

Sackville-West, Vita. *Knole and the Sackvilles*, Chapter one. https://www.gutenberg.org/files/65107/65107-h/65107-h.htm.

Tennyson, Alfred Lord. "Maud." https://www.gutenberg.org/files/56913/56913-h/56913-h.htm.

Turnbull, Malcolm J. *Victims or Villains: Jewish Images in Classic English Detective Fiction* (Bowling Green, OH: Popular Press, 1998).

Waugh, Evelyn. *Brideshead Revisited* (New York: Back Bay Books, 2012).

Worsley, Lucy. *Agatha Christie: An Elusive Woman* (New York: Pegasus, 2022), p. 255.

York, R.A. *Agatha Christie: Power and Illusion* (Crime Files) (New York: Palgrave Macmillan, 2007).

Zucker, A.E. "Goethe and Ibsen's Button-Moulder." *PMLA*, vol. 57, no. 4, 1942, pp. 1101–1107.

9

The Murder Game

A Murder Is Announced

The idea of the game is at the heart of mysteries, and especially mysteries such as Christie's, which foreground a problem or puzzle as if a game has been arranged between the reader and writer. On the level of a puzzle or game, the characters in a mystery are there to serve the riddle. In *A Murder Is Announced*, Christie is as usual on one level setting up a murder game with the reader, but here she is also using a Murder Game self-referentially in the plot itself; the popular pillar of the community Letty Blacklock is staging a murder game. This is the kind of party that rose in popularity in tandem with the rise of the whodunit in the 1920s, and here, even in the 1950s, it is considered good harmless fun. But that the game ends up becoming real—and that its victim is Rudi Scherz, a man with an indelibly German name, means that there has been a change augured by the Second World War and a consequent change in the whodunit. The days of the pure puzzle, uninflected by social or psychological factors, are over.

The entire idea of a murder game is comic and this novel's first chapters are also comic in tone, as if we are all being invited to a party. There are other comic/satiric touches in the novel as well. For instance, Bunch's cat, Tiglath Pileser, permits Miss Marple to put together a clue crucial to the solution of the mystery. Tiglath Pileser is the name of one of the most prominent, and authoritarian Assyrian emperors, "ferocious and furious" (Elayi 36), reflecting once again Christie's interest in archeology. But there is also some belief that the historical Tiglath Pileser usurped the throne from either his brother or his father. Since Lotty—Charlotte Blacklock—usurped the identity and high status of her sister Letty—Letitia—the name of Tiglath Pileser can be said to be a very abstruse clue to the identity of the murderer.

In the context of the depiction of Letty Blacklock's home and her clever party, the phrase, "a murder is announced" is simply amusing.

Letty's housekeeper Mitzi, too, is deployed for an almost constant series of broad comic turns. And Rudi Scherz, the victim who dies during the murder game, is told that the entire party will be for fun, a joke. But Rudi is the novel's first murder victim—it is Rudi who had innocently recognized Letty as her sister Lotty, having worked at the Swiss hospital where she had her surgery for goiter. Aside from his identity as a European immigrant, we know little about Rudi—but he was happy to come to the party and play his part. One great appeal of the party game is its social value; members of the community gather in a shared project. This kind of party is considered a good way to bring out what scientists call the neural synchrony that will develop when a group of people share a project, such as the playing of a murder game.

Community indeed is at the forefront of the mystery. *A Murder Is Announced* is framed by the various households of Chipping Cleghorn— the Swettenhams, the Easterbrooks, the Harmons, each receiving the local newspaper the *Gazette* and each reflecting on the recent events. The narrative as a result has an extraordinary amount of characters, and although the characters are partially there to be murder victims, such as Murgatroyd, or suspects, such as Julia Simmons and Philippa Haymes, the novel has enough characters to populate a Victorian multi-plot novel and are used for purposes beyond their role in the puzzle. That there is a backstory as well of Letitia Blacklock's life, and what happened to her, as well as an entire strand of the absent Goedler family, adds another layer to the story. Both immediate and extended community intercalate with a sense of game and play to provide both a ludic levity and a representational sobriety.

The book begins with Mrs. Swettenham, a very minor character, who is reading the *Gazette* and commenting on her local community—it is only through that fabric is the murder game introduced. Despite the spectacular deception practiced by Charlotte Blacklock, and the legerdemain with which Christie at once conceals and reveals clues to her spectacular deception, the novel concludes what that same sense of plural community—a quality reminiscent of the works of Elizabeth Gaskell or George Eliot. If *The Hollow* resembles a modern psychological novel, with mystery included, *A Murder Is Announced* possesses the seriocomic, satisfying multiplicity of a Victorian tome several times the actual length of Christie's actual novel.

One good example of the way Christie engages in both play and representation is the list of clues Miss Marple has collected after the death of the second victim, Dora: Miss Marple's train of thought and selection of clues is a brain teaser: "Lamp. Violets. Scherz. Where is bottle of aspirin? Delicious Death. Mitzi. Making enquiries. Severe affliction bravely borne.

Iodine. Pearls. Letty. Berne. Old Age Pension" (241). We begin with the first trio of lamp, violets and Scherz. Here, the violets and the lamp are especially important clues because they involve what Dora Bunner actually saw (Letty holding a vase of violets, the water of which she used to short the lamp) against what Letty said she held (a cigarette case).

We then reference the murder of Dora with aspirin, Mitzi's cake "Delicious Death" serving as that other comestible, a red herring. And then on to the sisters Letty and Lotty. This is a solvable riddle that invites us to play against the house, and sometimes a Christie reader will beat the house and solve the mystery—although not often.

But Dora Bunner, who helped her friend Letty arrange the murder game, had a sober moment at about the time of the presentation of this solvable riddle—suddenly the fun of competing in a game moved in her mind to the possibility of real aggression, from comedy to tragedy. Miss Marple reflects that Dora had at first thought it had been fun "getting the revolver out of Colonel Easterbrook's collar drawer. Taking along eggs, or jam—slipping upstairs in the empty house. It had been fun getting the second door in the drawing-room oiled, so that it would open and shut noiselessly. Fun suggesting the moving of the table outside the door so that Philippa's flower arrangements would show to better advantage. It may have all seemed like a game" (269).

But soon enough Dora becomes frightened, and soon enough the entire party atmosphere within the novel attenuates. But although the fun and games are counterpointed by a wider weft of representation, Christie's mystery itself will retain its identity as a game to the very end: the puzzle, which works to distance our fears, mingles with the novelist's goal to emotionally educate, to "teach the heart," bringing the same fears managed or deflected by the puzzle—loss, illness, mortality, rejection, dark impulses—into the light of day, to be faced.

In this mystery, the victims are victims are not only in a game but in a story, are not only impersonal markers in a logic problem but characters that elicit sympathy and concern. Each murder becomes increasingly an occasion for sympathetic concern; the murderer herself is an occasion for empathic interest, psychiatric interest, and even the pity and fear we associate with tragedy. Like other of Christie's villains, Lotty's mild-mannered persona conceals an inner rage at the way her needs have not been met, and the way her wishes and hopes were never realized. It is only when she reinvents herself as her sister Letty that she begins to live the life deserved, using her inner rage to attack anyone who would expose the duality of her identity.

At first, Lotty misdirects Miss Marple by setting herself up as the victim during her murder party. This is not simply a ruse, however, because

Lotty does see herself as a victim and has adopted her sister Letty's identity as a compensation for all she has suffered. Her sister Letitia or Letty, a highly capable secretary to financier Randall Goedler, had rescued Goedler from financial ruin, earning his eternal gratitude and inheriting his sizeable fortune. But when Letty died in Switzerland while sister Lotty was treated for thyroid illness, she takes on Letty's identity and will proceed to dispose of anyone who presents an obstacle to her new happiness, her good life.

Letty, however, is not simply a cold mastermind. "Bunch" Harmon, the wife of the Vicar in Chipping Cleghorn, and owner of the cat Tiglath-Pileser, is deployed to remind us of the humanity even of murderers. Miss Marple agrees that Lotty is to be pitied, even as she also notes how dangerous Lotty can be, precisely because a repressed woman like Lotty has no way of controlling the volcanic rage that would emerge if there were a threat to her new self, shaped to resemble her successful sister.

Miss Marple suggests that while Lotty took on Letty's sense of command, there is a major difference in terms of moral compass. While Letitia developed an adult conscience, Charlotte's illness and domination by her father culminated in an arrested development that left her without an adult sense of compunction. Instead, she felt entitled to her sister's money and her sister's life as a justifiable redress of grievances. Lotty saw herself as having been given a second chance, attempting to crowd a whole lifetime into the years that remained for her. Life itself, she presumes, owes her Letty's money and the happiness she has achieved in Chipping Cleghorn. Thus she can dissociate herself from any concept of wrongdoing or transgression.

Furthermore, her companion Bunny is considered highly disposable, not only because she has seen what she should not have seen but also because she is old and fragile. Lotty is determined to interpret the death of Bunny as a mercy killing to the point of giving her a special last birthday complete with delicious chocolate cake baked by the housekeeper Mitzi. While Letty puts Rudi's murder in the context of his participation in an enjoyable game, she puts Dora's murder in the context of a good action. The idea that even a kind and morally sensitive person can be capable of a murder perceived as a social good is one we will see explored at greater length in *Curtain*, arranged to be published some years after *A Murder Is Announced*, even though written some years before.

Bunny's longstanding deep friendship with Lotty makes her murder of a different order than the killing of Rudi. Bunny's death was designed to follow a celebration of her life—it comes at the end of a festive occasion. And since we know Bunny more than we knew Rudi, it is a death calculated to upset us even more when we realize Lotty mentally justified this murder by dint of her own superior status. Her crimes were to protect her identity as Letty, a false self that nevertheless secures money, respect, admiration, status. Her manor house is hardly major, but its name, Little Paddocks, references its bucolic past and its Georgian style situates it in "deep England."

Her sense of entitlement, however, is most prominently signaled by her very notable string of large pearls that she wears constantly—pearls that validate her sense of election, but which also conceal the thyroid scar that tells us she is the lowly Lotty. As the splendid Letty, her victims are all subaltern or marginal in some way—or considered as such by Chipping Cleghorn. They include the immigrants Rudi and Mitzi, the lesbian Murgatroyd and the superfluous old lady Dora. None of her victims are English men, or young women with an appeal on the marriage market. That Letty perceives Dora as possessing lesser or unstable status, is a classic rationale for treating her as disposable.

That Lotty was perfectly capable of creating a convincing impersonation of Letty tells us that in some ways, she was both Lotty and Letty at the same time—one side of her affectionate, sophisticated, and clever, the other side simple-minded, weak, and childlike. When the superior Letty, adept and expert, is exposed as the unsteady and all too human Lotty, this fall from grace moves her unmasking into a zone of tragic truths.

Thus this novel becomes a novel of deterioration—what we are seeing is that Lotty could not sustain her identity as a mastermind. We are not only witnessing a series of baffling murders, we are also witnessing Lotty's breakdown—the unraveling of Lotty, the dismantling of her identity and her world. Our emotional involvement then, is not only through her victims, Bunny and Murgatroyd, but through the pathos of Lotty herself.

Although to the outside world the pearls signal triumphant success and unquestionable insider status. Lotty's status is an illusion—the pearls conceal the scar that singles her out as the wounded Lotty, whose cunning murder party crime has led her to the brink of madness. For Lotty, *la commedia e finito*; after a crafty game and the whimsical party, the crude and artless nature of her murders express a core of limitless grievance and insatiable aspiration.

Christie creates a contrast between Lotty's bitter experience of illness and the illnesses of Belle Goedler, the wife of Randall Goedler, whose death will mean her husband's fortune will pass to Letitia Blacklock, the expert secretary whose skills had saved him from financial ruin. Belle's life has also been marked by illness and loss. She has become an invalid in her later years, but unlike Lotty she was grateful rather than sorry, and could fall back on her memories of a happy girlhood—whereas it was the lack of same in Lotty's life that made all the difference. We can conclude that Lotty simply never grew up but remained a twisted child. The murderer as fundamentally twisted child can be found in such killers as Gerda Christow or Nevile Strange, or even referenced in the nursery rhyme titles of novels such as *And Then There Were None*, *The ABC Murders*, *Hickory Dickery Death*, and *A Pocket Full of Rye*.

Interestingly the mystery with the nursery rhyme title of *Crooked House* does feature a literal child murderer. Lotty is, however, not a child, but a childish murderer. Her companion, Dora Bunner, known as Bunny, is even more childlike than is Lotty herself. That she and Lotty make their party into a game, and that she is later given something of a child's birthday party, makes the point that the two of them were always, in a way, little girls together. The murder game and the birthday party are murders syntonic with the fairy-tale life Lotty had built for herself and Dora. The death of Dora, however, is the death also of the dream of a childlike neverland.

If Facebook or Instagram existed in 1950, the plot of the novel would disintegrate—as it is, no one is able to find photos to verify Letitia Blacklock is actually her sister Charlotte in disguise (possibly generative AI could retro engineer images of a past Letitia that looks more like Charlotte). Christie, though, takes advantage of the way that, after the war, a previous sense of continuity is shattered, and unfamiliar faces and names begin to appear in British Villages. Furthermore, the crucial people, Dora and Belle, are either in on the secret, or are safely away in Scotland.

But certainly, this is a world where malefactors can, for a time, mask darker identities. Miss Marple herself particularly references darker realities as a counterpoise to the novels' early party atmosphere; she reminds us that she will always believe the worst. And when Miss Marple discusses the unmasking of Lotty, her voice is described as no longer "excited and pleased," but "quiet and remorseless"—Miss Marple herself is unmasked in a way that suggests she can be as remorseless as a detective as has been Lotty (279).

Like so very many characters in this mystery, Miss Marple is almost always part of a couple, whether it be Inspector Craddock, the Vicar's wife Bunch, or, finally, Letty's housekeeper and cook, Mitzi. It is the final teaming of the expressive European immigrant Mitzi and the reserved English Miss Marple that is the most significant. Mark Aldridge, while noting that Mitzi one of the novel's "least likable" (*Agatha Christie's Marple* 84) characters but has "the most sympathetic back-story," thinks Mitzi's connection to wartime trauma "falls flat" (*Agatha Christie's Marple* 84). But the key is how Mitzi's trajectory interacts with those of the other characters. It is significant, for instance, that both Mitzi and Miss Marple are outsiders, and that Mitzi and Miss Marple alliterate as well.

If one agrees with L.P. Hartley that "the past is a foreign country" and that "they do things differently there" (Hartley 21), one can characterize Miss Marple as someone who like Mitzi is a "stranger in a strange land" in the England of the 1950s. The partnership of the deracinated European and the similarly deracinated Edwardian is one in that somehow makes them particularly qualified to work together. It is not exactly that they represent an Archimedean point outside time, but the deracination creates a dispassion that allows them to take the liberty of disrupting the status quo through their staging of a trap for the pretender Lotty. In addition, Miss Marple coaches Mitzi by recounting and even inventing stories of heroism on the part of girls in the Resistance, introducing Mitzi's own historic context to produce a sense of requisite investment in her performance.

While Mitzi is playing the part of unsuspecting victim, Miss Marple deceives Lotty by impersonating the voice of Dora, a voice from the grave directed to Lotty herself, not her reinvention as Letty. Finally, the truth of Lotty's past returns to expose her deceptions and self-deceptions. Here Miss Marple surprises with her dramatic powers; she delivers a performance convincing enough to prevent Lotty from drowning Mitzi in a tub of dishwater. That Miss Marple is here something of an action heroine is unusual—usually she is associated with the armchair; it may be, however, that the even more dramatic and daring Mitzi provides her with a context that makes Marple's out-of-character episode perfectly acceptable.

It is through this act of heroism that Mitzi becomes not a suspect, or a classic "suspicious foreigner," but a heroine who will take her place as member in good standing in the Chipping Cleghorn community. Mitzi is happy to bask in her star turn as a heroine, and as such is the deliberate obverse of Marple—she can be said to be the hidden or suppressed shadow of Miss Marple as well as her confederate, her co-conspirator.

Mitzi had been a source of contention in Chipping Cleghorn. A refugee from Poland (although the name Mitzi sounds quite German), Mitzi is greeted with suspicion on the part of the denizens of the village, whose emotional reserve is affronted by her theatrical personality. This theatricality leads many of the English to believe she exaggerates or even lies. Her status is not high because she does not conform to the code of British reserve, and it is indeed her diminished status that marks her as someone Lotty can more readily dispatch.

Mitzi's high emotional register has often been interpreted as a consequence of the traumatic experiences she must have endured in Europe during the war; that she has a good example of what will come to be known as Post Traumatic Stress Disorder (PTSD). Her backstory can explain her emotional volatility. It can also point to the way she shares a readiness to do battle with evil that is similar to Miss Marple's. But the portrayal of Mitzi is not a subtle one—Christie certainly could have toned it down had she wanted to. Why does Christie move to exaggeration with Mitzi? Part of the reason is to throw suspicion on her, as if she is playing the part of a European and is not the real thing—or as if she confirms everything a xenophobic British person would assumes about anyone from the continent.

Mitzi not only challenges the more self-contained British characters in the novel, but she is also a challenge to the British reader as well. She is not someone who has assimilated into the English way of doing things. And the way her volatile, emotional nature may indicate trauma or injury can be said to push people out of their comfort zones. Mitzi is indeed an "over-the-top" portrayal of a European and certainly does play into the hands of those who stereotype the middle–European immigrant. It might be we are meant to see Mitzi as a kind of comic relief for much of the novel, and certainly she is often played for laughs. But excepting the murderer and Miss Marple, all the characters in the novel underestimate her, and it also may be, as was true especially of the early Poirot, that the stagy European persona is meant to trick us into misjudging her as a simple comic turn.

Christie includes Mitzi in the list of the novel's possible suspects, but also deploys her to reveal the shortcomings of her English characters, who will claim to prefer understated British puddings to Mitzi's dramatic culinary triumph, a confection that has been resourcefully created out of a society, Christie reminds us, that still must still conform to rationing laws. This means that Mitzi must rustle up her the raisins and chocolate she needs, including, significantly, butter from America, to produce the triumphant confection the character Patrick Simmons has decided to teasingly call "Delicious Death."

Patrick's term is lifted from a line from Handel's opera *Acis and Galatea*: "Love in her eyes sits playing/And sheds delicious death." Here the phrase has been repurposed—the title indicates the irresistible temptation of a rich and sugary cake. Mitzi does not care for the dark context in which her cake has been placed by Patrick—and indeed the phrase can be said to be an example of Patrick's continued persecution of Mitzi; he has also sent her a prank postcard warning her the Gestapo was on her track. This cake, imagined by Christie with no recipe attached, inspired actress Jane Asher to create such a recipe, translating the cake from "representation into actuality" (Yiannitsaros 117) and confirming one of the major missions for the character of Mitzi in Christie's novel—to show that Chipping Cleghorn has simply failed to appreciate her.

The cake does put Mitzi briefly under suspicion of the murder of Dora, but it is a banal and boring aspirin bottle that is the actual method, bringing the narrative just that much further from any party fun. Even without any atmosphere of party, however, the third murder—the one after

Bunny and the one before the attempt on Mitzi—comes about because one of the characters is still treating the situation as a kind of game. That Lotty's crimes are not a game, that the cake is, as Yiannitsaros says, "a metonymy of Miss Blacklock's murderous immorality" (Yiannitsoros 116), is very much at the heart of this novel—while it begins as a party game, the narrative becomes ever darker and begins to engage us not as a puzzle but as a story. But that the third murder retains the ghost of a game within it is exactly the problem.

Hinchcliffe continues to see the mystery exclusively in terms of a puzzle, thus misunderstanding the dangers in the situation to such an extent that her partner Murgatroyd becomes Lotty's third victim. Murgatroyd is murdered because of Hinchcliffe's determination to play the part of the town's Sherlock Holmes, which she does with "a game's afoot" brio. John Francis Kent Coffey contrasts Murgatroyd-Hinchcliffe as a dyad to Lotty-Dora as a dyad, saying the first are a "voluntary couple" (Coffey 46) but the second are a "necessitated couple." The murder of Murgatroyd is not in the context of a murder party, and although at first Hinchcliffe seems to make a game of it, the murder is a good example of the way the narrative is moving from comedy to tragedy, deployed in a crime that brings with it with the reality of loss, which will be intensified when Dora is murdered at her birthday party.

Hinchcliffe is especially inconsolable because she is haunted by the belief that in some way her assumption of the role of detective caused the death of her beloved. A same-sex couple who are never considered politically or sociologically, Hinchcliffe and Murgatroyd have simply chosen to live in their own way, have set up a perfectly respectable domestic life together, and have assimilated into the community. That the couple is there at all may cause talk—but only among the readership of the novel, not the village of Chipping Cleghorn itself. One could conclude, however, that for Lotty, who needs to seize every advantage, Hinchcliffe and Murgatroyd, like other victims, lack the prestige, the mark of approval, and the uncritical acceptance to which she is entitled; in this regard the victims Hinchcliffe and Murgatroyd, along with the enfeebled Bunny and the immigrants Rudi and Mitzi are more easily considered *outré* by Lotty.

There is an intriguing amount of same-sex female couples in the book. Not only are Hinchcliffe and Murgatroyd as explicitly lesbian a couple as one might find representable in the Anglophone novel in 1950, Dora's relationship with both Blacklock sisters is highly homosocial and her collusion with Lotty has slight overtones of sadomasochism. Moreover, Pip and Emma turn out to both be women—Pip is Philippa and not, as in Dickens's *Great Expectations*, Philip.

Also less conventional are Patrick and Julia Simmons, who pose as brother and sister, whereas the real Julia Simmons—who has no financial motive because Letitia's relatives never really have a prospect of inheritance—never appears. That brother and sister are not what they seem is a comment on the identity-switch between the Blacklock sisters and the sororal nature of the Blacklock sisters' relation to Dora. The Simmons siblings are also a good example of the way *A Murder Is Announced* is filled with people, and indeed entire sets of relationships, who do not fit in, are in disguise, unconventional, *outré*.

That *outré* aspect, especially in the person of the stagy Mitzi, also calls to mind Early Poirot. Mitzi's identity as someone whose foreign personality alarms the English, as Yiannitsoros argues, is in a liminal position between English and non–English, reminiscent of Early Poirot, who was similarly as confident of the power of his little gray cells as Mitzi is of her baking. Poirot's accent, his affectations, and his praise of his own powers were deliberate challenges to British xenophobia, deliberate misdirections, deliberate masking, inviting a patronizing underestimation on the part of the insiders, a standard group of Christie characters who one can also refer to as the usual suspects. Mitzi is a similar challenge.

Unlike Mitzi, however, the character of Philippa, another suspect, is that of a Perfect English Rose, a pretense assumed to conceal her connection to her European father Dmitri Stamfordis, his wife Sonia Goedler, and the originally European uncle, Randall. She is also the sister of the European-raised Emma Jocelyn Stamfordis who had worked in the resistance, and who, like Mitzi and Philippa, had also lost everything during the war. The insinuation of such names as Stamfordis (perhaps the most unlikely Greek name ever), Goedler, Scherz and Mitzi into the narrative is one way to reference a changing, more diverse England, and one can see this matrix as addressing Mark Aldridge's concerns (*Agatha Christie's Marple* 84) about the flatness of Mitzi's character.

Philippa Haymes was at one time Pip Stamfordis, one of the twin nieces of Randall Goedler who are also in line to inherit his fortune. There is much falsity in Philippa's identity—for instance, she sets herself up as the widow of a British air hero, when her husband was in reality a deserter from his regiment. Her mission to appear British, however, not only makes her false to herself, her surface persona is so generic and stereotypical that, like Mitzi, she is also an exaggeration, even a satire. This depiction of Philippa is, like Mitzi, another way to challenge English insularity—unlike Mitzi's provocative expressive personality, however, the rigidly conventional, inhibited, and stereotypically English Philippa represents the kind of insularity that led to the *aperçu* that, for the British, "Khartoum begins in Calais."

As with Lotty, Philippa's assumption of a perfect British identity is an upgrade in status, as if she is one who is above reproach. Letty's housekeeper and Polish refugee Mitzi complains that everyone will lend credulity to the words of the fair-haired, blue-eyed English girl because "—she is so British—so honest. So you believe her and not me. But I could tell you. Oh yes, I could tell you!" (113). That latter comment suggests that Mitzi has not been as deceived by Philippa's mask of English perfection or indeed the Nazi ideal of the blond and the blue-eyed with which she was already sadly familiar.

Once again in this regard she is similar to the way Poirot, the refugee from Belgium, is also never deceived by a performance of impeccable Englishness—from the perspective of Poirot, in fact, the performance of Englishness may appear as preposterous to him as his own calculated performance of his national identity appears to the English. Edmund, the novel's resident revolutionary communist, finds Philippa attractive, thinking at first that Philippa would make a fine Rosalind in *As You Like It*, but quickly amends this thought, realizing that the legendary Elizabethan sense of life and movement has somehow been quashed by a suppression of emotion that Philippa values as essentially English, an image of national character without a spark of mischief.

Interestingly, Christie named her daughter Rosalind, after the high-spirited and adventurous Shakespearean heroine, and so the notion that Philippa is no Rosalind can be said to be a particularly stinging critique. This is especially so since Christie's daughter would have been about the same age, in her early thirties, as Philippa. Philippa Haymes' impersonation of a stiff, proper English girl is one that Christie suggests not only prevents her from the kind of intimacy she could find with Edmund, but is a psychological prison as well. What Philippa is hiding are strong feelings of shame, grief, and panic—emotions that, ironically, would humanize her, make her both approachable socially, and offer her greater self-knowledge. Understanding this about Philippa mirrors the exposure of Lotty, who, while revealing feet of clay, is nevertheless more sympathetically human as well.

Edmund, in turn, also needs humanizing. We meet him at the novel's opening, a limousine socialist who lives in a comfortable English country cottage with his mother while subscribing to *The Daily Worker*—a subscription which, ironically, their cleaning woman, an actual worker and presumably true-blue Tory, resents. That Christie has Mrs. Swettenham rib her writer son for not working a day of his life is a bit of meta-commentary on the part of Christie. but Swettenham is a more socialized version of David Angkatell in *The Hollow*—dour, mother-obsessed, and untenably left-wing in political terms. That Edmund ends up becoming socialized through marriage to Philippa brings him into the heterosexual economy—an economy that might even be said, however, to have become a minority status in the book.

But, looked at another way, Edmund's radical politics do not interfere with his village sociality and his marital fulfillment reflects the Labour victory in the 1945 British election and the fact that, even in the Chipping Cleghorn part of the world, many people voted for Labour at that time. This is but a minor reflection of a major aspect of *A Murder Is Announced*—that it is not just set after the war in a changing England but that it misses no opportunity to telegraph to the reader that it is engaging in such representation. This might explain the profusion of characters in the book, who are there less for plot reasons than to be symptoms of a changing social landscape.

This landscape is featured even after the culprit who had pretended to be the victim has been exposed. After Lotty is exposed and her motives revealed, we return to comedy, and a comic-romantic ending featuring the marriage of Edmund and Philippa. The conversant Bunch is brought in to suggest a happy text for her husband Julian's next sermon, suggesting an off-the-cuff quote from the Song of Solomon, "For lo, Spring is here and the Voice of the Turtle is heard in the land" (265), although in its exultation perhaps verges on becoming yet another sarcasm. This not-quite celebratory quote does usher in the resolving of this mystery through a marriage plot, however—a resolution Christie does not overdo as perhaps Bunch has done with her quote from *The Song of Solomon*—there is no Voice of the Turtle for Patrick and Julia, for instance, who go their separate ways.

The woman Patrick hoped to take as his wife was with the French Resistance for eighteen months, and she dismisses him as a "soft young man"; in the light of his earlier derisive mockery of Mitzi, it is likely the reader may greet his romantic defeat as suitable. The festive quote from *The Song of Solomon*—deployed by Bunch with a certain qualified optimism—references, however, not simply the young couple, but England itself. England has, at last, come through. As has Philippa, who was not only a war widow, but her name also itself references war—her name and that of her sister is derived from the British military—"ack emma" for the A.M. and "pip emma" for the P.M. In the end Philippa is moving beyond her old nickname and her previous troubled marriage into a new more relaxed identity and a better marriage. As Miss Marple points out, Philippa had cut herself off too much from everyone around her with her overly retrained English persona, but once unmasked and married, her transformation marks the definitive end of the war. England is now in a new period of adjustment and transition, in which the country will find itself more diverse, more socially mobile, and more labile, and will also discover that, mysteriously, the hand of time has circled from age to youth.

If one understands that Charlotte was attempting to kill Mitzi when she was apprehended, two of her four intended victims were, respectively Eastern European and German. Furthermore, Belle Goedler, the widow, has a German last name. That Belle is in Scotland conveniently removes her from the possibility of recognizing Charlotte, both for Charlotte's purposes, but also puts her in a locale, Scotland, portrayed as very different from the south of England, as if itself something of a foreign country. Craddock's visit to Belle Goedler has a very different quality to it, one that is not cozy and English but with a different tone that registers a different infrastructure. In addition to the various iterations of "the foreign," Chipping Cleghorn is itself also not St. Mary Mead. Unlike the pastoral and ecclesiastical overtones of Miss Marple's hometown, Chipping Cleghorn contains the old English word for merchant and is a far more modern and egalitarian place.

While the young people in the novel are suspects and entertain less-than-pure motives for their presence in Chipping Cleghorn, they all eventually coalesce into an identity as an emerging generation whose ongoingness suggests that history has, indeed, turned a page.

The story ends on a note of community, which is where it began with the local newspaper, read faithfully by everyone and that, like the murder game, deepens bonds. Indeed, here one can bring in the considerable body of work on the festival, the pageant, and a renascent rural community in modern England. One can call to mind Virginia Woolf, in the pageant of Miss La Trobe (a character reminiscent of Letitia Blacklock, perhaps more the real one than the fake one) in *Between the Acts* and the Abinger Pageant written and staged by E.M. Forster.

In a more general way, Alexandra Harris in *Romantic Moderns* has written of how an interest in landscape, nature, and the region coexisted with the same modernist British aesthetics that *de jure* scorned such Romantic adhesions. Jed Esty has spoken of these local pageants and rural interests as "alternative public ceremonies to the corporatist rituals of fascist Europe" (17).

The murder game at Chipping Cleghorn is a dark inversion of these prewar pageants, and even if it had not claimed an actual victim in Rudi Scherz, its pageantry renders a darker scenario. As it transpires in the book, Rudi Scherz's death is not a theatrical enactment of rural reassurance but acts indexically towards a war that has disputed that sort of reassurance entirely.

During the investigation, Inspector Craddock also references the impact of the war, lamenting the way the new identity cards and ration books were without photos or fingerprints, making it impossible to know English who was and who was not, who was a friend and who foe, leading him to feel that the subtle links that had held English country life had fallen apart. As Richard York notes, Chipping Gleghorn has been in danger of *Gemeinschaft* giving way to *Gesellschaft*, in which the community becomes an anomic modern society (York 134). But the conclusion assimilates an obdurate Communist and a quiet European bride, consecrated by the blessing of the local newspaper *The Gazette*, which appears to manifest out of thin air to bless their union.

Although the flowers and the voice of the turtle may be an exaggeration, the worst is indeed over, and the ending concentrates on the hopes and dreams of the next generation. The rather irritable novelist Edmund Swettenham has turned over a new leaf and written a very successful farcical play titled *Elephants Do Forget*, a title that anticipates the last novel Christie wrote, 1972's *Elephants Can Remember*. This last novel also featured doubles and it's clear she decided to repurpose some of the motifs in this earlier novel, which also involves remembering and willed forgetfulness. The title of Edmund's play is also a way to reference memory issues within this novel—beginning with Rudi Scherz's memory of seeing Lotty in Switzerland and Dora's memory of the time when Lotty was her true self. In this novel, Christie may be suggesting that while Edmund's title reminds us that while elephants can forget, her mystery suggests that human consciousness can and will remember, and sometimes remember all too well.

Chapter References

Aldridge, Mark. *Agatha Christie's Marple: Expert on Mysteries* (London: HarperCollins, 2024).
Christie, Agatha. *A Murder Is Announced* (New York: Black Dog and Leventhal, 1978).
Coffey, John Francik Kent. "'Otherness in Agatha Christie': *The Moving Finger* and *A Murder Is Announced*." Master's Thesis, Binghamton University, 2024.
Elayi, Josette. *Tiglath-Pileser III, Founder of the Assyrian Empire* (Atlanta: SBL Press, 2022).
Esty, Jed. *A Shrinking Island: Modernism and National Culture in England* (Princeton: Princeton University Press, 2004).
Handel, George Frideric. *Acis and Galatea*. http://opera.stanford.edu/iu/libretti/acis.htm.
Hartley, L.P. *The Go-Between* (New York: NYRB Classics, 2002), p. 17.
Yiannitsaros, Christopher. "Delicious Death: Criminal Cake in and Beyond Agatha Christie's *A Murder Is Announced*." *Clues: A Journal of Detection*, vol. 39, no. 2, Fall 2021, pp. 107–118.
Yiannitsaros, Christopher. "Unhomely Counties: Gothic Surveillance and Incarceration in the Villages of Agatha Christie." *Gothic Studies*, vol. 23, no. 1, 2021, pp. 77–95.
York, R.A. *Agatha Christie: Power and Illusion* (Crime Files) (Palgrave Macmillan, 2007).

10

Time Shelter

At Bertram's Hotel

At Bertram's Hotel is Miss Marple's only visit to London. There are only two other books in which she is outside the English village, *A Caribbean Mystery* and *Nemesis* (where she is on a bus tour of southern England). This narrowness of venue could be viewed as emphasizing Miss Marple's irremediable provincialisms. But we should remember that Jane Austen, George Eliot, Elizabeth Gaskell, and Charlotte Brontë all used London minimally as a setting. The Miss Marple novels thus continued the rural emphasis of many major 19th-century English novelists, especially women writers. Miss Marple's visit to London in *Bertram's* is her most distinct engagement with an iconic image of the modern and urban world. Mark Aldridge, indeed, calls *Bertram's* "not a puzzle mystery" (*Agatha Christie's Marple* 194) and one of the "most fascinating" Marple books.

While the novel's setting is "very present in 1965" (Bernthal, *Agatha Christie* 68), the London of this book is in the middle of the era of the then-modern Kensington Air Station (1957–1974). *At Bertram's Hotel* does not intend to historicize itself—the novel intends only to be contemporary. But it has become historical. It was the Jet Age, the age of, in Harold Wilson's phrase, *White Heat*, of the scientific revolution, the time when the British people, in Harold Macmillan's words, *Never Had It So Good* (see Sandbrook, *White Heat, Never Had It So Good*). It is an era of London as a transnational city, albeit London even ten years later will be much more multilingual and multicultural. Whereas St. Mary Mead might preserve at least the appearance of consistency and continuity over two or three decades, a London hypersensitive to fads, fashions, and finance will not. At the time Christie wrote *At Bertram's Hotel*, it was intended and was mostly effective as a newsy, up-to-the-minute depiction of crime at a posh London hotel, a depiction that becomes something of an exposé.

Although the inspiration for Bertram's hotel is Brown's Hotel, established in 1839 and known for its Edwardian atmosphere, the time in this mystery is the 1960s and the hotel is now what Georgi Gospodinov in his novel of the same name would call a "time shelter" from the modern world. The hotel is a warm, inviting haven that escapes the stresses of the modern world. It is however in reality the site of a modern criminal gang, cynically using English types and traditions to conceal its nefarious activities. These two identities, one a pre-Edwardian identity and the other a post-World War II modern identity, very much compete in this novel. Readers are as likely to revel in the luxurious illusion as to be unsettled by the grim reality.

Miss Marple herself immediately senses the simulation of Edwardian times, the very Edwardian times she herself uses to both secure what one could call her verities, and to understand the present. Like Christie, Jane Marple's childhood was deeply Edwardian, but in this novel she is facing a changing England, even as she realizes that Bertram's Hotel's romantic reenactment of the past is purposed as therapeutic for a culture unsure of the future. In the staging of a resurrected past, Christie is in this mystery referencing a cultural phenomenon in which suddenly the old Edwardian world came to represent England's last golden age, the long golden afternoon of the British Empire.

After the war, Bertram's Hotel is presented as a miraculous survival of the good old English ways in the face of a new uncertain reality. As Gospodinov has put it, this is a logic that suggests that, if we live in a Dark Present, one solution is to return to a Bright Past. Christie is similarly aware that the hotel represents a false Utopia, a false hope—like Baudrillard's simulacrum, the hotel reflects Edwardian England only through caricature or cliché. The entire hotel is a stage setting, with its staff and its guests playing the role of stereotypical Edwardian. For instance, the face of what appears to be a country girl in service as a chambermaid appears to Miss Marple to be positively unreal: "A real chambermaid looking unreal, wearing a striped lavender print dress and a cap, a freshly laundered cap. A smiling, rosey, positively countrified face. Where did they find these people?" (35).

The hotel manager, Mr. Humphries, can glibly allow himself to be taken for the founder of the hotel because he can assume the role of the character actor he very likely truly is. These artful reconstructions cannot fool Miss Marple, who knows and remembers the real Edwardian era. Her suspicions are aroused by the way the hotel appears untouched by time, looking just as it did when she was a girl and had first visited the hotel. Miss Marple's unease and anxiety contrast with the cozy surface so that one is living in two realities—a faux Edwardian setting and an emerging reality, each of which tell us that, indeed, times have changed.

Marty S. Knepper, in her contribution to Phyllis M. Betz's anthology

10. Time Shelter

of essays on analysis of the subgenre of the cozy mystery, remarks that Christie's mysteries, often considered cozy, in fact stage "the illusion of coziness" as a structural effect, an illusion shattered by the eventual revelation of "the dark side." (Knepper 21) This effect is especially acute in the Marple novels, because Miss Marple herself, as a fictional character, appears to abide by this illusion. In *At Bertram's Hotel*, both the character of cozy Miss Marple and the setting of the allegedly impeccably preserved genteel hotel are constructed only to be shattered.

It might be argued that Christie was so good at creating, in Knepper's phrase, the illusion of coziness as to fool or even delude some of her readers into thinking she herself, as an author, was cozier than she was. Rather than living in a zone of timeless coziness, Christie herself was conversant with its major intellectual and cultural developments of her era, even if she did not necessarily like them, appreciate them, or feel completely *au fait* with them. Even if Christie is, understandably, not viewed as the central recorder of 20th-century Britain, it should not be automatically assumed that her work had nothing to do with the historical realities of the time. George Meredith, similarly, and equally understandably, is not named as the major writer of the 19th century, even though it never has to be pointed out that Meredith was, in fact, aware of the Crystal Palace, the Crimean War, the Spasmodic Poets, and positivism. Christie also, like Miss Marple, kept up—she did not close the door on The Sixties, but instead investigated the era.

The subject of this Marple novel is indeed modernity and is itself a modern novel. And Miss Marple, in *At Bertram's Hotel*, is surprisingly modern, using the term "Doppelgänger" (230), for instance, with ease and sophistication. Doppelganger is a word not every old lady in every English village might be expected to know, but that Miss Marple uses it insinuates that, despite her disinclination for the modernist aesthetic practice of her nephew Raymond West, she was not firmly opposed to *au courant* ideas.

The idea of the Doppelgänger is indeed central to the plot of *At Bertram's Hotel*. The duality of the hotel itself and the way so many guests are "doubles" for real people is also accompanied by a duality of plot. There are two criminals in this novel, who commit two separate crimes, even as our two villains are deeply connected as mother and daughter.

The first wrongdoer, the aristocratic Lady Bess Sedgwick, is the mastermind of a criminal syndicate that has used the hotel as its base of operations. Bess Sedgwick is responsible for the first crime—the assault and kidnapping of Canon Pennyfather. It is she who has masterminded the whole idea of creating criminal doubles of respectable people, which Canon Pennyfather has disrupted by accidentally meeting his Doppelgänger. As a result, he is attacked and kidnapped, and later found in a house recuperating from what is described as a car accident. The same night he disappeared, however, a man who resembles him has taken part in a train robbery.

Here it is not so much the kidnapping that is the central message of this episode—it is that Canon Pennyfather has a double, an imitation of the antiquated Edwardian cleric who is indeed the "real thing." This is the first clue to what will be exposed as a systemic replication of the world of Miss Marple's girlhood. Marple notes that she had not been at Bertram's since she was a girl, but then notes that it looked in 1955 as it did in 1939, suggesting that the change in Bertram's was a postwar one, or a change precipitated by the war and its aftermath. Later Marple notes that many London hotels were bombed during the war, another reference that secures the makeover of Bertram's was somehow a consequence of the war.

The ruthless and brilliant Lady Sedgwick is the brains behind this ambitious replication, complete with false vicars, judges, admirals. Chief Inspector Davy is impressed—her venal underworld operation and above ground Edwardian paradise is virtually a work of art. As is true of so many of Christie's masterminds, Lady Sedgwick is yet another artist of crime. An original and unexpected villain, the rebellious Bess has chosen to shun the conventions and lead a life that is that risky but exhilarating—she worked in the resistance during the war, flew airplanes, drove fast race cars, conducted a notorious love life, and although she is making a fortune with a simulation of a bygone England, she herself is quite the modern woman. Davy admires her, telling her: "You're a very interesting woman, you know. One of the few really interesting great criminals" (187).

Bess is yet another one of Christie's many unruly women, whose ingenuity even the law admires. She is also a woman who believes she is not meant to be a mother. While she did give birth to a daughter who has grown up and become The Honorable Elvira Blake, she provided her with a sheltered old-fashioned upbringing that had none of colorful risks of her own adventurous life. Because Bess, however, could not imagine a context in her postwar life in which she could successfully raise her daughter, she provided Elvira instead with a "time shelter," very like the one she provided for Bertram's Hotel.

Bess ends by feeling she was wrong to give Elvira a faux-Edwardian upbringing, which simply imposed on her daughter a false self, a false identity, and a hollow motherlessness for which her impersonal guardian Colonel Derek Luscombe could not compensate. Luscombe is so out of touch that when Elvira's lawyer alerts him about a possibly undesirable boyfriend, he refuses to believe it simply because something like this had ever before been brought to his attention. He will not hear of the unheard of.

In her presentation of the difference between modern mother and sheltered daughter, Christie rejects the conventional wisdom that suggests that Bess would be a bad influence on her daughter and that Elvira should be insulated from the modern world by an old-fashioned upbringing—if nothing else her upbringing in a modern, postwar context would have the virtue of being real. Christie also suggests that Elvira could have been able to learn from her mother's mistakes or benefited from her mother's street smarts. Elvira did not necessarily have to become her mother's dark double.

In both the raising of her daughter and in the context of her business, however, Bess was invested in sustaining the illusion of an Edwardian world. She trades in these traditions, and in her private life has elected to give her daughter an upbringing that is a mirror of her old-fashioned English hotel. Taken together, one can interpret the entire old-fashioned setting of Bertram's Hotel and the context of Elvira's upbringing as false goods, replications of a former England that has devolved into a series of unsustainable pretenses. Miss Marple, characteristically using analogy, unexpectedly compares the entire perpetuation of Olde England as like a garden invested by ground elder, a kind of weed: "It is like when you get ground elder badly in a border. There's nothing else you can do about it—except dig the whole thing up" (176).

One villain is, then, systemic—the evil is the "time shelter" in Elvira's life and the life of London as represented by Bertram's hotel. Christie well understands that the evil is a modern one; this longing to reinstate the past is a sign of new and stressful times. Certainly, in actual Edwardian times there would be no necessity for the society to attempt to replace itself. Elvira herself is like the hotel; a perfect replication of Edwardian values that conceals a darker reality. On the deepest level, there is a connection between the nature of the evils of Elvira (her name contains the letters "evil") and the nature of the evil of the hotel.

At first, Elvira presents herself as the innocent victim—someone has tried to shoot her, someone has tried to push her in front of a train, someone has sent her poisoned chocolates, someone sent her a note warning her that her life was in danger—but for Miss Marple to solve this crime, she must go beyond false appearances to unearth the true Elvira. Just as the hotel conceals a hidden underworld, the well-brought-up Elvira may appear compliant and the picture of good breeding, but underneath her docility is an intense obsessive will that is determined to maintain the waning interest of the playboy/race car driver Ladislaus Malinowski by murdering the gang member/ hotel doorman Micky Gorman.

Micky's brief marriage to her mother is what leads her to eliminate him so that she will be in line to inherit the family fortune that she believes

Malinowski will find irresistible. While the crimes of Bess were the crimes of a shady businesswoman seeking to sustain her successes, Elvira's murder of Gorman mirrored her turbulent emotional life, marked by a deep sense of lack and loss that fundamentally had nothing to do with money, even as she reasoned that it would be only through money that she would ever secure love.

It is the love problems of Elvira that inspire sympathy on the part of Miss Marple, who sees Elvira as not an overprotected and well-cared-for young woman but a lost girl in need of the guidance of a cooler head. Miss Marple's memories of her Edwardian childhood allow her to detect the falsity of Bess' simulacrum at Bertram's Hotel and her daughter's insulated Edwardian estate, but her memories of a dangerous romance of her own also lead her to detect the desperation behind the facsimile that is the Hon. Elvira Blake. Miss Marple can solve this mystery by recalling a time when she was as young as Elvira and attracted also to an exciting but irresponsible person who did not have her interests at heart.

The revelation that Miss Marple's heart, too, has had its chance is also another example of the way Christie suggests that her persona as a fluffy old maiden lady is a misdirection. Miss Marple's memory of her own heartbreaking love story makes her, in a novel of many doubles, briefly Elvira's double; Miss Marple has felt what Elvira felt. Even in what appears to the modern mind to be the safety of Edwardian times had among its population good-looking rogues who could turn the head of young, impressionable girls. It is somehow mystical and synchronistic that Miss Marple should find herself in hotel that looks as it did when she herself was a girl, and then finds in the hotel a young woman with a love story very like her own at that age.

Interestingly, when Bess and the victim Micky Gorman meet, both Miss Marple and Elvira are sitting in the lobby concealed in big Edwardian chairs when Micky tells Bess with meaningful innuendo that he has "not forgotten Ballygowlan" (38). Both Miss Marple and Elvira Blake are secretly listening to the same information crucial to the committing of the crime, as if twinned, as if each is a Doppelgänger of the other. The difference between them, Miss Marple believes, is that her mother helped her survive this damaging relationship so that she did not lose her head and go too far in some reckless way, whereas the neglected and motherless Elvira received no guidance; she is very much on her own and does become recklessly transgressive. This episode also tells us that our Miss Marple very well could have crossed a line and done a Very Bad Thing. That she knows what this urge to transgress is like. That she remembers.

But although we will never know if Bess could have made a good difference in her daughter's life, she remains a brave and ingenious mastermind and emerges as almost a heroine. Elvira cannot live up to her mother's legend. That is likely true of 1960s London when it looks to the elegance and quiet authority of Bertram's as well. As England itself felt its greatness was behind it, so too Elvira is a poor imitation of her brave and brilliant mother. But it must also be said that even if very different kinds, both mother and daughter in this mystery are its major criminals—it is they who are responsible for the novel's two crimes, kidnapping and murder. Just as Bess and Elvira are both criminals, the detectives Miss Marple and Chief Inspector Fred "Father" Davy are also paired as detectives. Father Davy has many of the same perceptions as Miss Marple; he also has a "grandpa" aspect, matching him well with the elderly Marple.

Father Davy appears more elderly than he is: "He had a comfortable spreading presence, and such a benign and kindly manner that many criminals had been disagreeably surprised to find him a less genial and gullible man than he had seemed to be" (30). Like Miss Marple, then, he has a persona that leads others to underestimate him; he isn't the addled old party he appears to be. His harmless elderly persona also suggests that he and Miss Marple mirror each other in significant ways, especially their shared belief in the existence of evil. Davy praises Miss Marple for possessing this psychological resource, saying: "Too many nice people who don't know anything about evil. Not like my old lady … she's had a long life experience in noticing evil, fancying evil, suspecting evil, and going forth to do battle with evil" (153). Similarly, he is skeptical of Bertram's lounge, whose perfect old-fashioned English afternoon tea activates his radar to the extent that he wonders whether anyone anywhere was ever what they seemed to be.

That Davy's nickname is "Father" is significant, especially in a situation where the major culprit is a fatherless child. That Elvira's guardian Derek Luscombe tries and is incapable of being a father figure to Elvira and that Elvira has never known her real father underscore this mystery's theme of fatherlessness. And we have in the story yet another father, Canon Pennyfather. Canon Pennyfather had gone to see a film called *The Walls of Jericho*, a postwar film that, in fact, had nothing to do with the biblical story Pennyfather had expected; but the biblical reference still stands and is placed as part of the narrative. As the walls of Jericho fell, indeed the façade Bess has erected in this story also comes tumbling down, although less literally. This interesting aside can be said to predict the outcome of one of the novel's mysteries, having to do with Bess overseeing a false reality that is dismantled.

The otherworldly Canon Pennyfather registers little of this. He is an unmarried, Anglo-Catholic, likely celibate, as much a scholar as a pastor. Like so many of Christie's priests, he reveals an interest in ancient Near

Eastern archaeology (in reading Christie one could be forgiven for thinking Assyriology is one of the major concerns of the Church of England). But whereas Canon Pennyfather, in his dithery, abstracted way might have forgiven Elvira, "Father" Davy is inclined to be more reprobative and to rigorously defend the moral order. Similarly, Miss Marple remarks that her uncle was Canon of Ely, and it is she who puts Elvira into a biblical and not legal context. Father Davy in the end stands for justice, but his identity as the long arm of the law can be said to compete with Miss Marple's more theological turn of thought; that the novel begins with Canon Pennyfather can be said to be a way of preparing us for Marple's concluding perspective.

At Bertram's Hotel's ending is an open one that mixes the punitive and the permissive and can be said to defy expectations. In addition, the atypical representation of Miss Marple in a changing London is so uncharacteristic of a customary Christie that it, too, should invite scrutiny. It is an unpredictable mystery, an example of the kind of mystery that was sometimes dismissed as a "dud" (as in Suanne Ngai's use of the term "aesthetic category") when in reality a mystery like *At Bertram's Hotel* reminds us that Christie was never content to write familiar, formulaic mysteries or mysteries that narrowly conformed to the genre.

The dénouement of the novel—with its generational switch, the daughter committing the crime we had thought was the work of the mother—itself stages a temporal shift. The reader is used to Christie opening her endings out to the new young generation—as in *The Murder at the Vicarage*—so that even when Elvira escapes capture, as if disappearing into new freedoms associated with the streets of London in the 1960s, she is not in any way a symbol of a generation that will create a good new future. As Laura Thompson indicates, Christie at different times portrayed the young people of the 1960s as redeemable and salvageable but at other times depraved and heartless; here one would have to conclude that Elvira trends into the depraved and heartless zone.

Her escape is also shocking because it has been enabled by her mother, Bess. Bess has had no role in her daughter's upbringing, and recognizes this by a gesture of atonement, giving herself up so that Elvira would be shielded. This quick substitution of the mother for the daughter as murderer may appear to suggest that once again the older generation is sacrificing to make room for the younger. But this outcome is twisted into something that is more an occasion for worry than celebration. Elvira, though 20, is indeed related in spirit to the child murderer of *Crooked House*, so that her mother's confession to the murder results in simply saving a cold, ruthless, and materialistic person who has gone to the bad. Elvira's response to the news that her mother confessed to the crime before she died is silence—she will let that false confession stand.

But even though Bess has sacrificed herself for her daughter, Father Davy is still determined to prosecute Elvira or somehow protect others from her. Davy concludes that Elvira's culpability and her danger to others cannot be pardonable simply on the strength of her mother's sacrifice. Elvira has, after all, coldly and cleverly murdered Micky Gorman, the lower-class Irishman who had been Bess Sedgwick's first husband, and whom Elvira believed stood in her way of all to which she felt entitled.

But although Father Davy vows to prosecute Elvira to the full extent of the law, a curious aspect of the ending is how Elvira seems to go free. We do not see Davy placing her under arrest, although he vows to make it his life's work to do so. But Miss Marple shakes his confidence when she goes on to say, "The law seems to go the principle now of allowing a dog to have one bite ... an experienced counsel could make great play with the sob stuff—so young a girl, unfortunately, upbringing—and she's beautiful, you know" (271). This suggests that a canny lawyer could use Elvira's youth and beauty to sway the sympathies of a jury.

Furthermore, Miss Marple introduces yet another perspective on Elvira, other than that of Bess or Father Davy, when she quotes a passage from one of the psalms in the Bible that suggests that Elvira is "one of the beautiful children of Lucifer" who "flourish like the green bay tree" (191), giving rise to visions of a generation of Elviras running free in the newly liberationist environment of the 1960s. Miss Marple concludes her comments by saying, "May God have Mercy on her soul" (180), indicating a higher authority than the law and suggesting that we may simply have to resign ourselves not to Father Davy's earthly justice but instead, in the words of the ghost of Hamlet's father, leave Elvira to heaven. This reflects what Sarah Hinlicky Wilson has called Christie's "very elusive" Christianity, which is seldom dogmatic or doctrinal but is often subtly present when analyzing the limits and possibilities of the human character.

As Aldridge puts it, *Bertram*'s ending is more "open" (*Agatha Christie's Marple* 195) than is usual in Christie, and "the reader does not get to witness the criminal being brought to justice" (*Agatha Christie's Marple* 196). Aldridge mentions that this perturbed *Good Housekeeping* magazine, who serialized the novel in the United States. This, then, is a Christie novel that does not end with a romantic couple emerging out of a maddening puzzle. If this novel is not only a struggle between good and evil, but a clash of youth and age, youth carries the day. But then, so does evil. That this untidy ending is not such a problem for either author or reader should remind us that mysteries are about comprehension and cognition, sorting out innocence from guilt, reality from appearance—and once that is done there is little interest in following the murderer to the gallows or prison. It is just not something built into the form.

When the guilty are identified and there is no danger of false accusation, we achieve true catharsis. It may be that Christie is suggesting the guilt belongs to the mother, Bess. Although Elvira would, like Bess, likely be a troublemaker no matter who raised her, the suggestion is that the kind of trouble she would make would be less dark and dire were she raised by Bess. Bess herself is a character who resists good girl/bad girl binaries, so we are meant to conclude that this might have been true of Elvira as well, had Bess been a role model. That, like Bess, she would have been an honest criminal—openly reckless, openly defiant of the rules but without the falsifications of her careful Edwardian upbringing, which created a level of dissociation that pushed the true Elvira into a damaging psychological hell.

With Miss Marple's "Children of Lucifer" remark, Christie seems to be warning that this new 1960s generation may be the kind of children that a liberal, permissive, or simply distracted culture will produce. A changing English society is a manifest concern of Bertram's. But although these changes may not all be good, and in fact may be alarming there is no going back. Bertram's hotel is exposed as an impersonation of a society that is dead and gone. As Miss Marple discovers that her old hotel doesn't exist except in the land of make-believe, she also notices other changes in London—hotels bombed during the war, townhouses converted into flats.

It may be surprising that the old-fashioned Miss Marple is sending the reader this message of inevitable change, but at the same time, Miss Marple is also suggesting that some things never change. She quotes the familiar French maxim, *Plus ça change, c'est la même chose*, but then she reverses the wording, suggesting that *Plus c'est la même chose, plus ça change* is also true. The trick, of course, is to discern what will endure from what must pass away. For instance, what endures, what is *le même chose*, is the memory of the passion that allows Miss Marple to see her youthful resemblance to Elvira. Whereas Edwardian-Victorian traditions do not necessarily survive into the existing present, what doesn't change is the human heart. The trick, however, is to discern what has endured (love problems) from what only appears to endure (Edwardian England), and it is her great old age and her excellent memory that allow Miss Marple to understand this.

On one level, Miss Marple has never been a part of the post–First World War modern England. One might feel that in this novel Miss Marple and Canon Pennyfather are the only authentic Edwardians, although at the same time, Britain is in the 1960s so overtaken with nostalgia for that world that it is trying to simulate it. There is a certain valedictory feeling here, as Jane herself acknowledges that she and those like her are the last of the "real thing." In a way she represents England's historical memory—she represents the very world that Bertram's Hotel is impersonating, one of the reasons she perceives its inauthenticity. Christie is suggesting that her society is hoping to find some sense of security or foundation in the fantasy world of Bertram's Hotel, but that this is possible is doubtful. Miss Marple's memory of the past, however, is altogether a different thing. It is her memory that creates continuity with what is often called deep England, and it is both her personal memory and her historical memory that is important. The idea here is that the past must be remembered, not relived; nostalgic simulations subvert actual historical memory. Miss Marple does not remember a utopian past or a beautiful dream of the past; her sharp mind remembers the dark side and can identify the evils of that time that are repeated in the present. It is Miss Marple's mediating consciousness, which moves between Edwardian past and the modern present, that gives her the wisdom and resources she requires to solve present-day mysteries.

The Christie of *At Bertram's Hotel* is conscious that the past cannot be restored and has irretrievably lapsed. In presenting England as a nostalgic, refined theme park that is a façade for a far more sordid and criminal world, Christie can be said to be correcting a misreading of her novels as a form of Edwardian nostalgia. She also is at pains to stress her own contemporaneity—she is a 75-year-old woman writing in the 1960s, and at a time when the literary culture was demanding the "relevant" writer who could come to terms with a changing "now." Christie was one of relatively few writers born in the 1890s even publishing in the 1960s, when the generation born in the 1900s was already the senior generation and, as in the case of Evelyn Waugh, was already dying; he passed away a year after *At Bertram's Hotel* was published.

As Ralph Poole notes, Christie featured hotels prominently in her stories of international travel; the focus on a London hotel brings this home autoethnographically, as something of a foreign country, in which Miss Marple has landed as a time traveler. Christie, so often accused of preserving Victorian conventions, was in the mid-1960s one of the few working novelists to remember both Victorian England, as Miss Marple did, and address the present day, as Miss Marple does. Miss Marple, even more steeped in the Victorian era than her creator, does in *At Bertram's Hotel* fully process the complexity and modernity of mid-century London. In looking at the lobby of Bertram's Hotel, Miss Marple is reminded that her purpose is to live in the present, which allows her to remember the past; one must not live in a restaged fantasy of the real thing.

What Christie brings to us in Miss Marple is the three-dimensional nature of her consciousness, which is made to contain not only what is past, but what is passing, and what is to come. The death of Bess suggests that her time shelter, with its façade of Edwardian elegance, will be left behind as well—that the future will go on without it. But Miss Marple has been saved to move on to future mysteries, future investigations into English life. The future will not leave Miss Marple behind.

At Bertram's Hotel has received serious critical consideration in the 21st century. Eloise Moss has focused on how the hotel is a place where "few among those present ... could truly be certain of one another's identities" (Moss in Mayhall and Prevost 188). Danny Nicol noted that the setting of the hotel underscores the resemblance of the "crime syndicate" (Nicol 7) to "normal business." These readings suggest that the hotel, in its juxtapositions of backward-looking signifiers and forward-looking indeterminacy, a yearning for identity whose capitalist configuration mandates the lack of any genuine identity, is a place that augurs quandaries and instabilities that have persisted in the sixty years since *Bertram's* publication.

Yet in its day, *At Bertram's Hotel* received no serious discussion of any kind. Even though certainly some highbrow readers of detective stories existed (Jacques Barzun, Edmund Wilson) and were also readers of high-modernist fiction albeit in a different mode, it cannot be denied that, in the 20th century, a class of readers emerged who read detective fiction avidly and expertly but who did not necessarily read mainstream literary fiction, especially as the latter trended towards experimentation. This distinction certainly does not apply to Christie herself. To deny contemporaneity to anyone is to provincialize and derogate them, and even if this practice is not invidious in the case of the bestselling millionaire Agatha Christie, it is not a good cultural habit to indulge, notwithstanding the comparative invulnerability of its target.

Today, critics are far more likely to apply practices of reading to many literary and cultural forms without proceeding from a previous ranking of cultural prestige or by cordoning off only a few select cultural artifacts as appropriate for close reading. Such a divide did exist in the high 20th century: a highly curated modernist canon of contemporary works deemed suitable for close reading and then a much broader canon of everything else that was published and deemed commercial and critically treatable by merely thematic summary. That this has very much changed now is because it is a change in the reading practices of the critic. Even today, people may read detective stories who read no highbrow literature.

But the readers of highbrow literature who read detective stories are not just highbrow readers at ease or off duty. They are readers manifesting a form of attention as they might with books in another genre: genre itself becoming much more permeable. The above comments especially speak to William Solomon's discussion of the detective story as a late modernist comedy, a characterization that can apply perfectly to much of Christie's later work, such as *At Bertram's Hotel*—albeit this latter novel features a surprisingly dark ending. But in her lifetime, Christie's readership, as the work of Light and Humble referenced in the introduction indicates, was deemed a non-highbrow readership, and this led to plausible assumptions that she and her readers either did not know or disliked modernism and modernity. This reality, however, should not lead us to be surprised that Agatha Christie herself was deeply invested in both modernity and modernism. *At Bertram's Hotel* addresses particular problems of modernity that are even more prevalent today, suggesting that Christie, far from falling behind the times, was ahead of the curve. Rather than return nostalgically to the Edwardian past, this is a novel in which Christie has, indeed, anticipated the future.

Chapter References

Aldridge, Mark. *Agatha Christie's Marple: Expert on Mysteries* (London: HarperCollins, 2024).

Bernthal, J.C. *Agatha Christie: A Companion to the Mystery Fiction* (Jefferson: McFarland, 2022).

Christie, Agatha. *At Bertram's Hotel* (London: Collins, 1969), p. 249.

Flaubert, Gustave. *Un Coeur Simple*, Chapter 2. https://www.gutenberg.org/cache/epub/26812/pg26812-images.html.

Gospodinov, Georgi. *Time Shelter* (New York: Liveright, 2022).

Knepper, Marty S. "'Contemporary Cozy Mysteries, Agatha Christie and the 1990s' Six Steps Towards a Definition," in Phyllis M. Betz, ed., *Reading The Cozy Mystery: Critical Essays on an Underappreciated Subgenre* (Jefferson: McFarland, 2021).

Moss, Eloise. "Death Haunts the Hotel," in Laura E. Nym Mayhall and Elizabeth E. Prevost, eds., *British Murder Mysteries 1880–1965: Facts and Fictions* (London: Palgrave Macmillan, 2022), pp. 187–210.

Nicol, Danny. "'Bad Business': Capitalism and Criminality in Agatha Christie's Novels." *Entertainment and Sports Law Journal*, vol. 17, no. 1, 2019, art. 6, pp. 1–10.

Poole, Ralph J. "Built for Europeans Who Came on the Orient Express: Queer Desires of Extravagant Strangers in Sinan Ünel's 'Pera Palas.'" *Amerikastudien / American Studies*, vol. 61, no. 2, 2016, pp. 159–80.

Sandbrook, Dominic. *Never Had It So Good: A History of Britain from Suez to the Beatles* (London: Little, Brown, 2005).

Sandbrook, Dominic. *White Heat: A History of Britain in the Swinging Sixties* (London: Little, Brown, 2006).

Solomon, William. "Crime, Comedy, and Late Modernism." *Studies in American Humor*, vol. 5, no. 2, 2019, pp. 309–29.

Thompson, Laura. *Agatha Christie: An English Mystery* (London: Hodder Headline, 2007).

Wilson, Sarah Hinlicky. "Agatha Christie: A Very Elusive Christian." Accessed March 4, 2024, https://mbird.com/the-magazine/agatha-christie-a-very-elusive-christian/.

11

Peacocks and Pretenders

Third Girl

Third Girl is famous as the book in which Agatha Christie determined to definitively come to terms with the "Swinging Sixties." The key figure in this attempt is a young man named David Baker. Baker is a painter who is presented as the boyfriend of Norma Restarick, the young woman in psychological distress who is the center of the plot. Although some of his social circle are scruffy, dirty, and unkempt, David Baker is a figure of great beauty; androgynous, stylish, reminiscent of a Van Dyck portrait. It is Poirot's new sidekick Ariadne Oliver who calls him the Peacock for his arty elegance, but his presence is more than aesthetic. He plays a very key role in the plot—the portrait he paints of the villainous Orwell disguised as the wealthy and powerful Andrew Restarick helps conceal the fact that Orwell is a fraud, and that to inherit the family fortune, he is sabotaging the mental health of Restarick's daughter Norma. Even more, it is David who becomes, quite surprisingly, the mystery's murder victim.

Although not always front and center in this novel, the artistic "peacock" David Baker adds an important complexity to his status as this novel's murder victim. Although he upsets the older generation, who would rather she find someone who does not represent the soul of London in The Sixties quite so much, it is obvious why Norma is attracted to The Peacock. He is the most colorful character in the novel, and the most charismatic. It is no accident that the first edition of the book in the UK, published by Collins, had on the cover a stylized image of a peacock. David represents what was considered a revolutionary identity that acted in opposition to conventional standards of masculinity, and in that regard his presentation of self is all about gender—the "new masculinity."

David adopts feminine fashions such as long hair, sumptuous fabrics, loud and lively patterns, bright colors—all of which made the men of the emerging "counterculture" generation more provocative and more attractive precisely because of the suggestion of effeminacy. As Ariadne Oliver notes, David's black coat, velvet waistcoat and long curly hair reverses the sober, puritanical dress that signified the masculine at the end of the 18th century, and which has been called the "Great Male Renunciation" in which male dress became clean and sober, trending to the utilitarian.

But we can see why the world of the novel wants so badly to believe in the beauty of the Peacock. The 1960s youth movement was a response to a humdrum world, and humdrum urban developments such as Borodene Mansions where Norma and her two flatmates live, "that great block that looks rather like Wormwood Scrubs prison" (13). Indeed, for all of *Third Girl's* surface emphasis on the Swinging Sixties and what Lucy Worsley calls the "rackety" atmosphere of that milieu, the novel is more deeply immersed in a kind of long mid-century, a post–1945 condition that is the sociological corollary to what Curtis Evans has described as the humdrum mystery, a subgenre which stressed "puzzle construction" (Evans 5) over style and characterization.

Evans emphasizes the routine aspect of this subgenre, which can also be slightly mirrored in the role the dull but assiduous Mr. Goby, who Poirot uses to investigate a character's background. Although David Baker is the obverse of the routine, many other characters in the book—both Claudia Reece-Holland and Mary's disguise as "Frances Cary" fall into this category. Also banal are country villages, such as Long Basing near the Restarick mansion, Crosshedges, where what had lately been the local grocer's is now a supermarket complete with "stacks of wire baskets and packaged materials of every cereal and clothing material" (21).

Long Basing is a town of no distinction or panache, "exhibiting length without breadth" (21). England, rebuilt from the war, is full of prosperity and progress, but all is utilitarian, with a conspicuous lack of beauty. This sense of the leaden can be said to completely explain the contrarywise manifestation of a David Baker. In this regard, the Peacock is less a threatening rebel than something almost wistful and nostalgic in its extravagance. "In a gold frame, wearing a lace collar, you would not then say the was effeminate or exotic" (27), as Poirot says to Mary Restarick. Mary, pretending to despise David, does not take in Poirot's comment; but in her other identity as Frances Cary, the art gallery employee, she would have understood that this was part of the appeal of the young painter. Indeed, Frances's other protégé, Peter Cardiff, is described as "positively reactionary," and "quite-quite—Burne-Jones sometimes" (143).

Christie is making two points here. One is that the Swinging Sixties may have played out, on one level, on a Right-Left axis—Restarick family member Sir Roderick is always referring to younger people as beatniks or Beatles. But on another level, David and Peter are registered on a more residual Roundhead–Cavalier axis, with a figure like the Peacock challenging a puritanical utilitarianism represented by the drab mid-century architecture of both town and country. Poirot himself notes that David's long hair and frilly cuffs and collars would make him perfectly at home in Regency-era England, which still sustained something of the fashions of the cavalier. Despite the romantic appeal of David, however, the exposure of pretense in his character is central to the narrative. He is revealed as indeed a rather cavalier young man in the current sense of the word, and while his youthful appearance and Regency affectations can be said to be a political statement, these things eventually are exposed as a form of masquerade, a way for someone not quite as young as he would have you believe to take advantage of the more credulous truly young.

Although an artistic bohemian, David is not highly regarded as an artist, and the one role his painting plays in the story is when he fraudulently passes off his own work as that of an artist named Lansberger, "a famous and exceedingly expensive portrait painter of twenty years ago" (25). By the 1960s, Lansberger is no longer highly regarded, derided for his scrupulous naturalism. Poirot suspects that in fact there was "a carefully concealed mockery" beneath Lansberger's facile portraits of corporate magnates. But certainly David, in forging his copy, is not responsive to this. Indeed, for all his lack of inventiveness, Lansberger clearly has an artistic flair that his copyist, looking only to achieve a viable similitude, cannot attain. Once again dissimulating, Peacock may look artistic, but his only artistic talents are technical and do not proceed from any actual creative vision—his painting is purely a business transaction.

David is on one level a perfect example of the beautiful new boys of a new generation but he (and Norma), in overturning established expectations of adult conduct, affect a youthful presentation of self that can be said to be almost willfully irresponsible and immature. For instance, when Poirot at one time observes David and Norma at a cafe, he notes a blithe David leaving a compliant Norma behind to pay the bill for his lavish breakfast. Norma's appearance expresses an even greater sense of the childlike—as Poirot notes: "there *was* something odd about Norma, certainly, but she might be odd in a different way to what she seemed." He remembered the picture she had made "slouching into his room, a girl of today, the modern type looking just as so many other girls looked, limp hair hanging on her shoulders, the characterless dress, a simple look about the knees—all to his old fashioned eyes looking like an adult girl pretending to be a child" (225).

Like Laura Franklin in Christie's Westmacott novel *The Burden*, Norma has never fully emerged from her cocoon because she is carrying the baggage of unresolved family relationships. Norma's childish identity is perceived as both very trendy and as one of her greatest vulnerabilities—especially since the childish persona leads to exploitative interest on the part of those who are her senior. This would include David himself; he is a pretender. There is a sense of theatricality to his dress, a sense of artifice that suggests performance, especially the performance of youth. David is actually described as rather older than one would suspect, and in this regard may call to mind the character of Arnold Friend in Joyce Carol Oates' story "Where Are You Going, Where Have You Been?", who is also older and more predatory than his assumed teenage persona would suggest.

Like Arnold Friend, Baker is taking advantage of the restless spirit of the rebellious era, even as simultaneously he is something of a throwback to earlier tropes of rakes, libertines, and heartless dandies. We suspect from the beginning that the family's suspicions are correct, that Baker does not really love Norma. By the middle we learn that the Peacock is accepting the cheques of Norma's father, who is paying him to stay away from his daughter. By the end of the story, he is murdered. His death elicits a cry of pity from Ariadne Oliver for the loss of a beautiful boy, but he was never what he seemed. Far from being a soulful aesthete at once modish yet with a touch of Cavalier dash, to facilitate an act of forgery and imposture, he has stooped to imitate the work of Lansberger, a man said to be the most pedestrian of mid-century portrait painters.

Even more, Norma's seemingly protective father is actually a man named Robert Orwell who has assumed the identity of her father, Andrew Restarick, long absent in Africa. Christie references the Victorian age's famous Tichborne case of an heir who disappeared into the wilds of Australia to make credible Orwell's scheme, which is to pretend to be a lost member of a prestigious British family to gain access to its mercantile wealth. His purpose in keeping David from courting Norma, however, has nothing to do with protecting his supposed daughter, but is the motive for the two murders in this novel, one happening before the story begins, offstage, but for the same motive—knowing too much.

While our first sight of Robert Orwell is when he is reprimanded by his new wife and Norma's brassy stepmother Mary, Mary and Robert are really co-conspirators and, in Mary's assumed identity as Norma's roommate Frances Cary, colleagues in a borderland where art and criminality meet. David may be young, but he is in the service of middle-aged greed, and when he eventually blackmails his patrons, we understand that his goals are financial. The Carnaby Street rebel is in the grasp of the socio-economic laws of the (fake) father. His theatrical identification with the counterculture has masked a core dedication to profit, little different from a conventional businessman. The message here is that there is no new radical present, just timeless greed assuming new guises.

In addition, as in *At Bertram's Hotel*, this novel associates the 1960s new business enterprises to organized crime—Mary's Wedderburn gallery, for instance, is described as employing young male artists in ways in which the law would not approve. In addition, David's participation in a drug trade that is both a stylish signifier of the counterculture and highly profitable at the same time is yet another revelatory look at the contradictions of his character. That David becomes this novel's major murder victim, however, tells us that both Norma and David were in over their heads in a society that, as is always the case in Christie's work, hides within it an underworld.

But Christie was out not only to guy the Swinging Sixties but to also grasp the problems of the current generation. She is also suggesting that even those, like Poirot, who appear "too old" to fully understand the present, are essential to its future. When Norma Restarick first comes to see Poirot, she is about to confide in him but ends by deciding that he is too old to help her; this motif of feeling sidelined by age haunts Poirot throughout the narrative. The book indeed uses the conceit of the aging great Detective to investigate the mores of a changing world, not unlike Ross Macdonald's 1963 novel *The Wycherly Woman* which does the same (and involves a similar dénouement of generational impersonation). But Christie deliberately makes dramatic the generation gap between Norma and Poirot from the start. Christie is giving the younger generation exactly what it wants: a depiction of the older generation as doddering and out of touch, as "irrelevant."

Poirot takes this comment of Norma's very much to heart, wondering if Norma is not right, and that he is indeed too old to know how to solve this new-generation case, amazing the psychiatrist Dr. Stillingfleet with his humility. Ariadne Oliver provides him with useful if unpleasant information in that regard—she notes that these days large numbers of people have never heard of him, especially the younger generation. She tells Poirot she was at a gathering at which she mentioned his name, and that no one knew who she was talking about. The mystery writer Ariadne Oliver, Christie's metafictive authorial stand-in, can be said to be imported to do some of this novel's legwork for the aging Poirot; in addition to her role as a kind of Watson, she can be said to also be something of a Special Lady in Poirot's life.

In that regard, Christie has done what her colleague Dorothy L. Sayers did with her characters Harriet Vane and Peter Wimsey: she writes herself into her stories as an author of mystery novels who becomes the object of her detective's affections. Ariadne Oliver, as has been widely commented, is a figure for Christie itself, complete with the pleasing matryoshka effect

11. Peacocks and Pretenders 183

of hating her detective, Sven Hjerson, much as Christie came to hate Poirot himself, putting him in her mysteries more often than she would have liked because of his immense popularity. Some of Norma Restarick thinking Poirot is too old to solve her case is meant to be seen as a false supposition—as Christie, of a similar case, is not too old to write *Third Girl*—but in other ways Norma's frustration with Poirot's self-manifestation mirrors Christie's own.

In fact, in *Mrs. McGinty's Dead* (1952), Christie has Ariadne consider posthumously publishing a novel in which she kills her despised detective, hinting thereby at the shape of things to come. Ariadne is especially important in *Third Girl* as the effort she makes to keep up with the times through her abundant if untidy hair extensions makes her less out of place when visiting the youthful art studio; her relative youth makes her more fit to negotiate its location in a sketchy part of London, and makes her also more likely to recover from the cosh to the head she receives while attempting to make her escape.

Even though he has acquired a somewhat distracting helpmeet in Ariadne, Poirot's character is developed in such a way that he deepens and enriches the mystery; this is a late work of Christie's in which his presence adds complexity. For one thing, just as Ariadne, as a character, is metatextual, so is Poirot. At the beginning of *Third Girl* he has just published a book praising the detective-story genre, denouncing "the romantic outpouring of Wilkie Collins" (1), (a comment with an even more metatextual valence, as "Collins" was Christie's UK publisher) and had lauded to the skies two American authors who he claims were practically unknown (1). One of these is most likely John Dickson Carr, later selected by Stephen Knight as the founder of the modern detective story (see Knight 174) or is meant to be perceived as such by the reader even though Carr was hardly unknown at the time.

Poirot, in other words, is not just a detective on one level and a character in a detective novel on another, he is also a critic of detective fiction on the third. *Third Girl* indeed is replete with tacit meta-genre references— that Andrew's dead brother is Simon Restarick evokes a similar situation of a returned lost brother replacing a "Simon" in Josephine Tey's *Brat Farrar* (1949). Poirot also reveals himself to be a man of rare discernment. Having just published a book—*Third Girl* explicitly refers to the project as a published book, replete with printer's errors—he makes no attempt to cultivate the many moneyed and privileged people he meets in the novel in order to promote the book, to get them to buy it, or, to use a late idiom, give it buzz. "Do a thing well and leave it alone" (1) is Poirot's gentlemanly, and to a 21st-century reader, refreshing artistic maxim.

One of the reasons Ariadne Oliver detests her own creation, Sven

Hjerson, is that he is a Finn (by the name, a Swedish Finn) and she knows nothing about Finland. Christie, incidentally, is also commenting on the fact that she made Poirot a Walloon. Poirot is a French-speaking Belgian, rather than presumably an even more austere and rigorous Fleming, just as Hjerson is a more familiar Swedish Finn rather than a more exotic Finnish Finn. Poirot, in this novel, passes himself off as a Frenchman to Sir Roderick Horsfield, demonstrating a valuable ability to fade into the more generic identity. Poirot lies and deceives people several times in the novel, forging a letter on Andrew Restarick's stationery, pretending to Sir Roderick to have served as a French intelligence officer in 1944 (which Sir Roderick half-perceives is untrue). That so much of the novel occurs outside of Poirot's point of view, and that Poirot himself is not above deception in the service of solving the crime, might have been a way for Christie to prepare the reader for *Curtain*, which she knew she had forthcoming.

Third Girl did not turn out to be the last-written Poirot mystery; there were two more, although given Christie's age she might have suspected that this was her last and wished to give the reader a less procedurally proper Poirot to prepare for the dénouement of his career in the posthumous novel. Poirot in his own way is also, like David, both a peacock and a pretender, and though morally differentiated from the criminals, there are ways in which he is a part of their milieu. He also is far from working alone in this novel. Like an elderly but still competent statesman, he knows how to delegate—as well as Ariadne, he has other helpers: his secretary Felicity Lemon, his footman George (sometimes called Georges by Poirot), the intelligence operative Mr. Goby, and the psychiatrist John Stillingfleet. These figures also are out and about more than is Poirot, even as Poirot makes most of the executive decisions.

As mentioned earlier, Poirot lies to Sir Roderick, saying they had worked together in intelligence during the war. He does this to obtain a pretext for visiting Crosshedges; his real reason is to investigate Norma and the Restaricks. In trying to convince Sir Roderick that they had indeed known each other, Poirot gathers some details about Sir Roderick and recites to the old man a battery of names, including such familiar figures from Christie's past novels as Colonel Race (another metatextual reference). If Norma thinks Poirot is too old, Poirot thinks with equal inaccuracy that Roderick is too old.

As it is, Sir Roderick does not see fully through Poirot's ruse but senses enough to remark to his assistant Sonia afterwards, "I don't think he knew I didn't remember him" (32). Later Sir Roderick calls Scotland Yard to try to find out Poirot's name. He had forgotten it, but remembered he claimed to be with the French during World War II. (Poirot, as a Belgian refugee who came to England during the First World War, emphatically would not have claimed to be French, but this is nevertheless what he told Sir Roderick, giving their first interview a certain Alice-in-Wonderland aspect.)

Poirot's strategic response to the issue of his age is to accept and admit it, to delegate when necessary, but to essentially rely on resources given to the elderly, such as experience, and, even more, the ability to become exceptionally reflective and contemplative. It is as if he has said "Very well then. I will be old." In this novel he literally becomes an "armchair" detective; Poirot sits alone in his room, in his chair in chapters that deliberately feel slow and unrushed: "Well, what are you doing? What have you done?" "I am sitting in this chair,'" said Poirot. "Thinking." he added. "Is that all?" said Mrs. Oliver. "It is the important thing," said Poirot. "Whether I shall have success in it or not I do not know." Poirot then relaxes into a flow of reflections that he is confident will lead him where he needs to go. He also recalls what are described as "three philosophic questions": "What do I know? What can I hope? What ought I to do? He was not sure he got them in the right order or indeed if they were quite the right questions, but he reflected upon them" (200).

That ability to "not know" or "not quite know" is what opens cognitive doors for Poirot; he does not make any effort to control the flow of his inner life. This part of the novel deliberately features Poirot's cognitive processes, in which he essentially goes into hibernation, becoming the opposite of a man of action. He closes his eyes and allows himself to relax, certain that in relaxing the pattern he needed would emerge. He is deliberately suggesting that from this point on, there was nothing he could learn from "outside," and that all the answers must come from within—that he, and the reader, have all the information they will need from the outside world. By implication he suggests that this is a point in the narrative in which the reader, too, should stop and think—just think and perhaps dream a little, especially with reference to the pervasive presence of the Restarick family, and to the way something about the Restarick family must not be known, is not allowed to be known.

Additionally, Poirot deploys the resources of age to become a fatherly figure to Norma, despite her rejection of him; he is portrayed as looking at her "through the eyes of someone old" (179), which leads him to rescue her from entrapment by Mary. Poirot also introduces her to the psychologist Dr. Stillingfleet, in hopes the two would marry, and they will. Although neither the word "psychologist" nor "psychiatrist" is mentioned in the book, Stillingfleet defines himself as a doctor who does not have a "surgery" (79) but a "consulting room" (79). As has been noted previously (N. Birns and M.B. Birns, "Agatha Christie: Modern and Modernist"), Stillingfleet presents a humane vision of psychiatry, unlike that demonized earlier in the 20th century in Virginia Woolf's *Mrs. Dalloway*.

This is Stillingfleet's third and last appearance in Christie's oeuvre: his first appearance was appropriately psychoanalytic in that he featured in a short story about a man haunted by a strange dream; the second appearance in *Sad Cypress* featured yet another vulnerable woman who, like Norma, must be remanded to a safe place. It is in his final appearance that Stillingfleet is at his most central. He provides a form of talk therapy and does not rely on prescription drugs, especially important because Norma has already been heavily drugged; indeed, he discerns and tries to redress the extent to which Norma has been drugged not just by the casual drug use in which many young women of that age participated but by a deliberate and malevolent administering of drugs to her by her supposed father and stepmother.

Stillingfleet heals Norma by believing in her, trusting her, and, in opposition to Poirot, allowing her the freedom she needs even if it places her in danger. Stillingfleet appears to be one of Poirot's helpers, like Goby, Ariadne, and Felicity Lemon, but then takes a far more active and independent role in the plot.

Norma ends up marrying the red-haired Stillingfleet, presumably about fifteen years older than she. This is a marriage fostered by Poirot, who in the final scene of the novel reveals he had chosen "this particular doctor on purpose" (198) to give Norma a happy ending. Stillingfleet—empathetic, caring, and above all confident in Norma's normalcy, autonomy, and agency—is the perfect foil to the Peacock, who represents the false dawn of a youth that is an imposture when it is not simply retro-Cavalier.

Stillingfleet saves Norma from being hit by a car, much like Angus MacWhirter saves Audrey Strange from suicide in *Towards Zero*; the only difference is that Stillingfleet is a professional and, in his own way, an authority figure. But Stillingfleet is also a modern man, humanistic, respectful of women, discerning and caring about people, patient and methodical in his attitude, believing in the potential for qualitative growth and above all nonjudgmental. Though he asserts his methodological independence from Poirot, the two are alike in that they are not simply bent on solving problems but, through their tactics, fostering an enlarged sense of the human condition. As previous criticism has noted (N. Birns and M.B. Birns, "Agatha Christie: Modern and Modernist"), Stillingfleet enables Norma to move from the extra wheel, the Third Girl, to be the First Girl, the heroine of her own story.

The novel ends in a harmonious and humane way. The wrongdoers are exposed, and we come to realize that Norma is a perfectly healthy young woman who has been drugged and deceived into thinking she was a criminal. Poirot even speaks to Norma's high school headmistress, Miss Battersby, to get a full impression of who Norma is. In another instance

11. Peacocks and Pretenders   187

of the novel's meta-awareness, it is mentioned by Frances (as it turns out, the villainess) that "Norma isn't normal" (20) while Miss Battersby later assures Poirot that Norma is a "normal girl" (155). This overt play on her name foregrounds the novel's hope that Norma will enjoy a happy ending and emphasizes the great extent to which Poirot goes to give her one.

We trust Norma will be happy with Stillingfleet. But there are two issues. The first is that Stillingfleet is marrying his patient, a woman, for all his relative youth, nearly a generation younger than himself. This would really raise a red flag in the 21st century, but even at the time orthodox Freudians would have spoken of countertransference as something to be avoided. The novel convinces us that the joyous Restarick/Stillingfleet love match is healthy and humane, but probably would not recommend such a therapist-patient relationship as standard practice—we in the 21st century absolutely would not.

The one exception to this issue is when Stillingfleet, who has, on Poirot's instruction, kept Norma under his care for ten days to protect her from those who would put her in danger, lets her walk away. Poirot is infuriated, but Stillingfleet reprimands him: "Your job and my job aren't the same. We are not out for the same thing" (167). Stillingfleet's goals, tacitly, are therapeutic, not investigative. His goal is to help Norma and to do so he has to offer her freedom of action, even if that freedom may put her at risk or muddle Poirot's attempt to solve the investigation. Still, Poirot's willingness to include in his army of helpers such an independent and conscientious figure as Stillingfleet speaks well of his ability to assemble and coordinate contrasting points of view. Poirot, in other words, may be too old, but he compensates for that by enlisting the meaningful aid of others.

The other issue is that Stillingfleet, even before he married Norma, was planning on moving to Australia. When he proposes to Norma, he says they will live in Australia, and that he will cable for her once he has made sure that the job prospect he thinks he has arranged is a sound one. This is unsettling in two ways. The first is that it is such a Victorian ending. In Anthony Trollope's *Lady Anna*, for instance, a couple too different in class background to viably live in England move to Australia because people there just did not care about those things as much. Australia was a different world from England then, a two months' sea voyage away; additionally, it was hard for people in the old world to follow those who settled there.

But in 1966, England and Australia are not very different. One need do no more than look at the novels of the Australian writer Elizabeth Harrower, whose *The Catherine Wheel* (1960), is set in England, and who presents a world affectively similar to her later *The Watch Tower*, published the same year as *Third Girl*, 1966. Australia is not a world away anymore, and although there is some mention of Norma's wanting to move away from people who will bother her for the Restarick money, by 1966 Australia was rife with money-grubbers to an extent equal to England. As in Arnold Bennett's *Anna of the Five Towns*, where the protagonist-couple leave for Australia at the end, Christie's is a Victorian ending, referencing a time when settler colonialism was a viable alternative to the predicaments of European whiteness. That it does not fit well in the British 1960s may very well be the point. Norma is not only leaving a place, She is leaving present time and sailing back to the safer past.

But, in a far more consequential way, the real issue is that England as depicted in the novel very much needs humane, generous, authentic people like the future Dr. and Mrs. Stillingfleet to help combat the pretenders and peacocks who are afoot in the novel. The plot, though, intends a happy ending for Norma, and the novel's dénouement is about how to bring about that happy ending rather than any attempt to wrap matters up in strictly puzzle terms. One might see this as a "Mary Westmacott" element of Christie creeping into her puzzle premise; but it can also, more simply, be interpreted as Christie's awareness that, even as she is writing a mystery novel that is highly conscious of its genre, she is also writing a novel.

That both Norma and Sonia marry older men can also be said to be a gesture that exacts a reparation of the 1960s generation gap. In these marriages, old and young have a synergetic relationship, similar to the triumphant concluding synergy between Leonard Clement and Griselda in *The Murder at the Vicarage* that took place decades earlier but with a similar generation gap. On the other hand, those who perform youth in a way associated with an adversarial youth generation of the 1960s—Mary Restarick in her persona as "dolly girl" Frances Cary, and David Baker in Carnaby costume as a young Restoration Fop—are respectively murderer and the victim, with concomitant fates.

Despite Norma's status as one of the young ones, however, it is this novel's mission is to see to it that she grows up, something true of Griselda in the earlier *Murder at the Vicarage* as well. Her maturation accelerates when she is reminded by Dr. Stillingfleet that, despite her confusion, she has proven that no one can make her do what she did not want to do, and that once she can see that someone is deliberately clouding her mind, she is perfectly capable of standing up for herself. And now that she has achieved some clarity, she can take responsibility for what she knows now are the actions and choices of a woman of sound mind. In her new sense of autonomy and initiative, one can see Norma moving from the Dolly Girl of the Sixties to the feminist of the Seventies.

Norma has been trapped in a false narrative, and is feeling false guilt, most often because there are times when she seems to go blank or black out. This dissociative fugue state is reminiscent of what may have happened to Christie herself, when she disappeared and lived in a state of amnesia for a few days. But Norma's own dissociative state is depicted as a sign of the times—she has taken LSD and other drugs associated with the 1960s culture and, it is suggested, has been culturally shaped into a preadolescent girl, rather than a womanly adult with a sense of her own sexual power. Or, as Poirot suggests she was "an Ophelia devoid of physical attraction" (8).

In the end it is the false Father Robert Orwell whose role in breaking down Norma's sanity has led Poirot to correct himself and call her an "Iphigenia," not an "Ophelia." That is, she has become her father's human sacrifice.

That Norma has been negotiated into the position of "useful idiot" is also suggested by the way the title is also referring to her. Ariadne Oliver identifies Norma Restarick as the third girl in a flat of three roommates, and, as a third girl, Norma's status would usually not be a friend nor someone the other two girls knew—she is simply there to usefully meet the demands of the rent. Being the "third girl" suggests someone who is something of a stranger, even a mystery. Norma is indeed a stranger to the two girls and the two girls are strangers to her; and as the newest roommate she is the odd girl out. There is also the well-known superstition of three on a match, or the superstition that bad luck comes in threes, which may beneath the level of notice also cast a cloud of suspicion on someone known as the Third Girl.

One of Norma's flat mates, Frances Cary, with her dual identity and dark depths, could also be called the novel's third girl. In her own way, Frances is as strange as is Norma. Her identity as Andrew's wife is as a capable woman with blond hair, a slight colonial accent, and a brisk way of talking, while in contrast her alter ego Frances Cary has a drawling husky voice, a face layered with black-and-white make-up, and whose black hair is cut in a fashionable 1960s way that conveniently shadows her face. Mary, with her forthright and capable manner, contrasts dramatically with the ghostly, gothic Frances, suggesting the kind of dissociation we identify as belonging to Norma, especially when paired with the way Frances too disappears into spaces of time for which she does not account.

Ariadne's description of Frances as (267) "the person who was not there" can apply as well to Norma, as if Frances is on one level a shadow-double. Poirot himself affirms that Frances, who was always a cipher because she spent so much of her time in her other identity as Mary Restarick, was the actual "Third Girl" of the novel, the odd girl out, the stranger. But unlike Norma, when Mary Restarick is "not there" as Frances, she is violent—it is she who hits Ariadne on the head as she makes her way home from the gallery; it is she who pushes the knows-too-much Louise to her death; and it is she who murders David Baker. It is also Frances who drugs Norma, gaslights her into believing in her own madness and guilt, and who stages the murder of David so that it is a dazed Norma who is holding the revolver and a quick-witted Frances who asks her what on earth she has done.

The revelation that Frances is the disguise of Mary Restarick should remind us of the pervasive presence of the Restarick family in this novel. In addition to Norma's place as the daughter of the False Andrew, the main tenant of the apartment shared by Frances and Norma is Claudia, secretary to the False Restarick. The murder of Louise Birell Charpentier, an aging party girl, is also connected to the Restarick family; she was the mistress of Norma's actual father. Her murder is a kind of rehearsal for the murder of David Baker at the end of the novel. Like David, she knows too much, and, as with David, her death is also an opportunity to implicate the innocent Norma. One could see Louise as another liminal third, since it was she who was Andrew Restarick's mistress—his "other woman" back when Norma was a child. This murder, however, is an improvised one. Louise has by chance taken a flat on a higher floor of Borodene Mansions. After Norma mentions that she has unexpectedly encountered her actual father's former mistress, Frances pushes Louise out the window of her 7th floor flat and then arranges to make Norma believe that she has committed the murder, or at least makes Norma fear that she did. This first crime was largely deemed an accident or the suicide of a troubled, lonely woman but in reality it served the purpose of eliminating someone with an inconvenient memory as well as preparing Norma psychologically so that she will allow herself to be framed for the crime of murdering David.

The murder of Louise is for much of the novel the one death that has visibly occurred in a mystery in which, as Poirot comments, there is bafflingly no visible murder. Louise Birell Charpentier is the one person who would know Orwell is not Restarick; all the others who might have seen through the disguise, it is carefully explained to the reader, were either too old or too young at the time of the real Andrew's leaving England. Thus, Louise must die, and this is the hastily improvised crime that is the major clue Poirot needs. But Louise not only has a French first name, by the time she is at the Borodene, the worse for wear and past her sexual prime, she also is Mrs. Charpentier.

Once that identity is established, though, the book refers to Louise Charpentier twice as "Carpenter," which could just have been a slip by an aging Christie but might plausibly reflect an English insistence on correcting Charpentier to the Anglo "Carpenter." In any event, although Louise's slightly foreign aura is concomitant with her sexual and behavioral

11. Peacocks and Pretenders

disrepute, she nevertheless can be said to be a victim more innocent than is the Peacock. The Peacock, on the other hand, is guilty of forgery, blackmail and a deceitful and damaging relationship with Norma, so that his death is more likely to fall into the category of just deserts. But although Louise can be said to be simply unlucky rather than complicit, she does fulfill Norma's wish that, as her father's "other woman," she be punished for causing her mother Grace much distress.

The other foreign woman in the book is Sonia, the half–au pair girl, half-secretary to the aging Sir Roderick Horsefield. To fully understand Sonia's role in the novel, we must first understand a bit more about Sir Roderick than the book clearly states or that past critics have observed. Sir Roderick is an uncle of Norma's mother Grace, thus no blood relation to the Restaricks. The family of Norma's mother thought less of the Restaricks for being in trade—another reason in addition to her husband's infidelity that perhaps explains Grace's bitterness and her retreat into a penitential form of high Anglicanism. Because Sir Roderick has never known Andrew and Simon well, Andrew is able to falsely present himself as Sir Roderick not so much because Sir Roderick is, as is frequently observed in the novel, "gaga" (37, 38, 121, 139) but because Sir Roderick had never really known Andrew in the first place.

Sir Roderick is old and forgetful. But he has not in fact lost his faculties. This matters with respect to Sonia, who is also not what most people take her to be. Visibly foreign (though never given any specific nationality), it is believed that Sonia is an opportunist who wants to inveigle money from Sir Roderick. She has also been sighted at Kew Gardens engaging in what could be espionage. But Sonia is given a happy ending, marrying Sir Roderick, and doing no more (it is implied) than stealing his papers not for any malevolent purpose but because she could then find them and play the heroine in a way that would encourage him to propose to her. Despite the age difference, it is demonstrable at the end that Sonia and Sir Roderick want to be happy in the same way as the other happy couple in the novel, Norma and John Stillingfleet. The novel does not completely free Sonia of guilt, however—she notably is said to have exchanged material at Kew Gardens with someone from the Hertzogovian Embassy. The Christie reader immediately thinks of Herzoslovakia, the Ruritanian imaginary country in Christie's 1925 *The Secret of Chimneys*.

But Hertzogovinia, although not at that time an independent country, is a real place. Christie is here gently decolonizing her vision of Eastern Europe, which conforms to the way Sonia is decolonized, recognized as a positive and forward-looking human being in tacit contradistinction to the returned English colonizers, the pseudo–Restaricks, whose Englishness is a front for their fraudulence. Everybody, including Felicity Lemon, is suspicious of Sonia because she is a foreigner, but, in classic Christie fashion, the people they should have suspected were the more-English than the English pseudo-Restaricks. Sonia is an example of how the dismantling of xenophobia can enable a more plural and capacious culture, a culture that can appreciate and include as many people as possible, something that is more a theme in Christie's work than is often appreciated.

Sonia's acceptance into English life is concomitant with the exposure of the false Mary Restarick. Sir Roderick (in another instance of his underrated acuity) has noticed that his alleged nephew's wife wears a wig but has accepted her explanation that "she lost her hair in a fever when she was eighteen" (107). Poirot finds Frances's "Mary" wig in her luggage at Norma's flat, when, in her identity as "Frances Cary," Mary has arranged to have Norma look as if she has killed the Peacock. Poirot exposes her not by stripping her of her wig, but by making her wear it. He forces it on her head, thereby exposing both her crimes and Orwell's.

There is a correlation between the exposure of Mary's English countrywoman pretense and Sonia's integration into English life. The same moment that exposes the fraudulence of Orwell and his wig-wearing consort also enables Sonia to be granted entry into English life as the wife of the aged Sir Roderick. The foreigner who appears to meld seamlessly into English life is an imposter; and Sonia, suspected of working as a spy and as too obtrusively foreign, becomes a welcome addition to her new country. Poirot's foreignness also contextualizes the novel's other foreign characters as well as the novel's understanding of xenophobia in England, and its construction of the foreign.

The year 1966 is not just a postwar but a postcolonial one, and one of the unsaid, though obvious, reasons Robert Orwell has had to return from Africa and pretend to be Andrew Restarick is that the financial pickings are slimmer in post-independence Africa than they were in the days of high colonialism. He comes to England in the company of Mary Restarick—a South African grifter pretending to be a traditional English country lady. In this regard, Mary is behind the times—Christie in this novel is pointing out the way the English have become more cosmopolitan. For instance, Poirot tells Mary that the great virtue of the English is that their gardens are perfectly made for French *potager*. Elsewhere, Stillingfleet asks Norma if she wants "a good solid old-fashioned English cup of tea?" (80) and when she says yes, then asks, "Indian or China?" And when Felicity Lemon preposterously informs the foreign-born employer Poirot that "it's better to know where you are when you are employing someone and buy British" (13), Christie is visibly noting an English insularity that is simply out of date.

On the other hand, one of the most redoubtably English characters in

11. Peacocks and Pretenders

this novel can also be considered the novel's "third girl." Unlike the other two girls in Flat #67 in the Borodene Mansions, Claudia Reece-Holland is neither the murderer nor the victim in this mystery. Because she has no real role in the mystery plot, she can certainly be considered the odd girl out. It is because she has no central role in the mystery or its solution, one might call her the real "third girl" in the novel. She may be considered in a light way the suspect, and is, like many of the others in this story, attached to the Restarick family, in this case as the ruthlessly competent secretary to Andrew. Although Claudia can also be said to be the "first girl" since it was she who was in original possession of the flat, her possible status as "third girl" is because the other two girls, are even more deeply connected to the Restarick family; Norma is the daughter of the real Andrew, and Frances has clearly been placed in the flat because she is in reality Mary Restarick, the false Andrew's wife. An interesting second connection to the Restarick mystery is that she is the daughter of the MP Emyln Reece-Holland, who (in what is perhaps an echo of the Profumo scandal) was engaged in a scandalous affair with the notorious Louise Charpentier (or Birell or Carpenter).

Although set in the hullabaloo of swinging London in the 1960s, this mystery fundamentally is one involving a single family—namely the patrician Restarick family, to whom all the characters are attached in one way or another. That Restarick is not just a Cornish name but that the novel explicitly states that it is a Cornish name (11), may activate an interest in thinking about the significance of names in the novel; as we have argued in the Introduction, names are something which critics of Christie should always consider. Christie liked to use Cornish names; *Third Girl* also mentions the Cornish name Trefusis which Christie used as the name of the heroine in *Murder at Hazelmoor*. She had previously used Restarick in *Murder with Mirrors*; *Third Girl* gave Christie the chance to use the name more prominently.

But that Restarick is a Cornish name, Orwell a place name in Suffolk (in the southeast of England) and Stillingfleet a name of a town in Yorkshire (in the North of England) renders the men in Norma's life in a kind of onomastic-territorial triangle, with Restarick and Orwell at the base, Stillingfleet at the apex. Although *Third Girl* can be called a "condition of England" novel, the name Orwell is not any reference to George Orwell, who took his pen name from the same Suffolk town, but instead draws us back to Orwell as a place-name parallel to the Restaricks of Cornwall in the southwest. Stillingfleet is at the apex because he can at once reframe the lost memory of Norma's real father and redress the false imposture of her fake father, who has established himself as the long-lost Andrew, hiring David to paint new family portraits of him that make him twenty years younger, and assigning his wife Mary the job of preparing Norma to become their victim.

In the end the integrity of the Restarick family is restored. But the positive ending of Sir Roderick and Sonia is left to bear the future of England alone, and Sir Roderick's great age, though not really impairing his mental acuity, suggests that the union will not last for long. There is perhaps a pinch of cultural pessimism at the novel's end about the future of England itself. What would otherwise be a tale of hope and enfranchisement for young Norma—who given how she was swindled by two unscrupulous people in middle age would be wise to, in the idiom of that age, not trust anyone over thirty (excepting, perhaps her 35-year-old psychiatrist)—becomes more bittersweet.

And despite the happy ending for Norma and Stillingfleet, the death of David, the "Peacock" is also bittersweet, in that he appeared to stand for the miraculous development of a social, musical, and artistic renewal of England free of war and deprivation. But although David represented the romantic ideals of the new, young generation, he is betrayed by his capitulation to greedy older figures and is exposed as a young man who has come under the influence of those who were considered his generation's enemies. As a result, it is one of the tasks of this novel to take David out of the picture—while Norma can be saved, nothing can be done for David, who had unwittingly been an agent of Norma's intended destruction.

Despite the depiction of a lamentable older, evil couple taking advantage of a younger 1960s couple, *Third Girl* nevertheless once again sends one of Christie's essential messages—it is the real task of the older generation to bring young people like Norma safely to shore. Poirot especially takes ownership of his status as one of the Old Ones. Despite the immense pressure of the era to remain forever young, Poirot is here deliberately made unquestionably old. He will not be the cool grandad. Poirot's goal is to educate Norma in the nature of "what absolute evil means," which, Poirot says, "will armor her against what life can do to her" (215).

During his earlier crisis of confidence, Poirot reminds us that although this novel is set in a newly romantic and renewed London, a Christie mystery is always going to detect the dark side. The danger and the harm evil brings, then, is found in the heart of the new "flower power" generation, which has been corrupted in the person of David by an infiltration of the very self-interested economic motives it appeared to oppose. Norma puts it this way when she discusses her states of dissociation, in which "they start with one thing, a party or something and suddenly you find you're in a jungle or somewhere quite different—and it's all sinister" (129).

The thrill of the novel is the solution of the mystery—and Christie concocted one of her most ingenious and satisfying puzzles in *Third Girl*—but there is interest beyond the mystery. *Third Girl* offers a crucial example of how we need to come to grips with a Christie text in its entirety to be able to read it well. *Third Girl* thus comes to terms with a host of sociological and psychological issues afflicting the England of its time. What Jessica Gildersleeve says of Christie's following two Poirot novels, *Hallowe'en Party* and *Elephants Can Remember*—that they "enact a social and cultural anxiety arising from the problems of modernity" (Gildersleeve 36)—is also true of *Third Girl*. In each novel, Christie continues to recruit an aging Poirot for the purposes of demonstrating that modernity, despite its utopian ideations, must still encounter the darknesses in the human heart.

Chapter References

Birns, Nicholas, and Margaret Boe Birns. "Agatha Christie: Modern and Modernist," in Ronald G. Walker and June Frazer, eds., *The Cunning Craft: Original Essays on Detective Fiction* (Essays in Literature) (Macomb: Western Illinois University, 1990).

Christie, Agatha. *Third Girl* (New York: Putnam, 1990).

Evans, Curtis. *Masters of the "Humdrum" Mystery: Cecil John Charles Street, Freeman Wills Crofts, Alfred Walter Stewart, and the British Detective Novel, 1920–1961* (Jefferson: McFarland, 2012).

"Ex fan des sixties." https://en.wikipedia.org/wiki/Ex_fan_des_sixties.

Gildersleeve, Jessica. "Nowadays: Trauma and Modernity in Agatha Christie's Late Poirot Novels." *Clues: A Journal of Detection*, vol. 34, no. 1, 2016.

Knight, Stephen. *The Killing of Justice Godfrey: An Investigation into England's Most Remarkable Unsolved Murder* (London: Granada, 1984).

Westmacott, Mary. *The Burden* (Harmondsworth: Penguin, 1988).

Worsley, Lucy. *Agatha Christie: An Elusive Woman* (London: Pegasus, 2022).

12

No More Murders

Curtain

By writing *Curtain* decades before it was published, Agatha Christie created a built-in problem: that of preventing the novel from dating by the time of publication. Christie was in a different situation from a writer who simply does not finish a work which is then published posthumously, or from writers whose work is never really published in their lifetime but rediscovered after their death. Christie wrote her last two published books in late midcareer, fully aware that not only would they be published afterward but also that they would have considerable commercial potential.

"Distant reading," in Franco Moretti's term, can supplement close reading here. Here, Christie's awareness of the sheer aggregate magnitude of her reading public both reassured her that Poirot's final adventure would have an audience and gave her as well a sense of the context into which she was writing, even if she would not be physically present for that context when it materialized. Technically, only *Sleeping Murder* (1976) was published posthumously, since *Curtain* was published a few months before Christie died in 1975—but it was published after she ceased writing and was very near to her death. It was traditionally thought that *Sleeping Murder* was, like *Curtain*, written during the war in the early 1940s, but John Curran (254) has shown that the novel had to have been written at the earliest just after 1947. Though published in 1975, *Curtain* was not only written long before the preceding published Poirot book, *Elephants Can Remember*, but even before *Cat Among the Pigeons* or *The Clocks*, published in the 1950s and early 1960s, or even before *The Hollow*, published in 1946.

Curtain was composed early in World War II, possibly just before or just after *N or M?* and after another mystery, *An Overdose of Death*, a mystery in which Poirot also must negotiate individual responsibility and the general good. Her problem was how to prevent the book from being too redolent of the 1940s to be a satisfying chronicle of Poirot's last case. In *Sleeping Murder*, the problem was solved more easily. Not only did Miss Marple not die, making it less of a conclusion, but that the important character Gwenda Halliday Reed was from New Zealand served as a counterpoint to any datedness in the novel: New Zealand, a country of the future, a new nation, a country which Christie could have counted still looking fresh and new (from an Anglo-American standpoint) in the 1970s.

The New Zealand referent, by taking the world of Miss Marple at the end into a more global context, takes care of any sense of the residual the novel might have suggested in 1976. *Curtain* presented a harder task. It hovered, as Alastair Rolls put it, "in limbo" during all of Poirot's subsequently composed adventures. Any writer in this situation knows how to take out concrete references: fashions, music, and politics of any given day. Where Christie fumbled a bit is with the colonial references in the novel, not so much concerning Sir William Boyd Carrington as an Indian provincial governor, and other references to the Indian Civil Service, but concerning Dr. Franklin's research among "West African tribes and cultures" (65).

If the book had been written or set in the 1970s, Christie would have recognized—as indeed she had much earlier in *Hickory Dickory Death*—that these African countries were now independent and that their people should be referred to as citizens of a given nation, not tribes or natives. The point here is not about Christie's inhabiting colonial mental structures but a simple question of probability—in the early 1940s people rarely imagined future African independence, whereas Indian independence was already a well-mooted possibility. Despite the emphasis on the tribal, however, Christie's African references were less colonialist than anthropological, and Judith Hastings' travel to Africa with Franklin does provide a kind of colonial happy marriage plot that echoes the original one of Captain Hastings and his "Cinderella" in Argentina and mirrors as well the Reeds' New Zealand connections in *Sleeping Murder*.

Additionally, that the Calabar bean is said to have been used by African societies to prove innocence or guilt, and that Poirot even speculates that the Calabar bean might have discerned the difference between Barbara Franklin and her husband in terms of malicious intent, affirms a sense of justice as well as criminological ingenuity to her African tribe. Beyond the colonial assumptions in the novel, the way Africa is represented in *Curtain* suggests that Africa would become more important in the future, another guess that gives *Curtain* an air of postwar modernity despite its wartime date of composition.

A book that is to be published posthumously, after some time, must take account of futurity and the gap of time between writing and its issuance into the world. This makes it, in Rolls' phrase, a "ghost story." The same sort of detail that would make a book published at the time seem up-to-date and contemporary would make a book of the same era stale and archival were it saved for posthumous publication. Christie's surest device for making sure the novel did not date was precisely to tie it to the past in her oeuvre. By having the novel take place at Styles, now no longer a stately home but a guest house for the genteel, operated by Colonel Luttrell, Christie could make any sense of anachronism seem latent in the place itself. Styles in this novel is both the Old Styles Edwardian house and the New Styles modern hotel, now subject to, as Rolls puts it, "decay and change."

The changing identity of the house and the use to which it was put after the war was something Christie may have foreseen—which made Styles au courant when published. By having her beginning also be her end, Christie raises the specter of completion, a circle from Styles to Styles that will make it an advance over *Hallowe'en Party* or *Elephants Can Remember*. *Curtain* is both set in an anticipated postwar world and in a place that evokes that other country of the past, giving this novel a sense of closure, a fitting end. One can take this sense of an ending into narratological permutations, as Rolls does in his chapter on the book. Although the book's series of permutations and reversals lends itself to these vertiginous narratological readings, it is hard to rival the narratological uncertainties wrought by time: when she wrote the book, Christie had no way of knowing what the future would hold for her, her life, or her literary career. But our reading, while noting the particular textual status conferred not so much by its killing-off of Poirot but the effects of its belated publication, will treat the story in concrete thematic, formal, and psychological terms.

Hastings reflects on his first time at Styles upon his return and mentions as well how things turned out for the characters at the end of the first Styles novel—rare in Christie's oeuvre, which has her detectives continue from book to book, but whose stories are largely stand-alone. *Nemesis* reuses a character from *A Caribbean Mystery*, and is also, intriguingly, a sort of "last book," as it was the last-written Marple. One wonders how much, in the Poirot novels written after *Curtain*, Christie kept in mind that she had this book in the vault. For the most part, one would have to say that she largely put it out of her mind, as if it were a novel still in her future.

Gerda Christow in *The Hollow*, however, has a touch of the *Curtain* character Barbara's resentment of her husband's devotion to medicine (and potentially other women), and as we will see there can be said to be a resemblance between Christie's Ancient Egyptian murderer in *Death Comes as the End*, and her modern *Curtain* killer. In *Third Girl*, not only is Poirot's increasing age mentioned more than once, but also present is the murder-by-persuasion plot—Andrew and Frances try to convince

Norma she has murdered somebody she has not. Additionally, there is the everything-old-is-new-again dynamic that allows Christie's key reference to an Edwardian play to avoid appearing incredibly dated. Though *Curtain* is hardly a series finale, in the sense that it is the sequel only to *Styles*, not to the whole run of Poirot novels, the frequent mentions of Hastings's last wife—whom he met, courted, and married in *Murder on the Links*—makes *Curtain* a sequel to that not-particularly-heralded novel as well. But *Curtain* can hardly be said to be the culmination of a series of linear narratives.

The return of Poirot and Hastings to the site of her first mystery, published in 1920 and set in the Essex country house called Styles Court, is, indeed, a circle as much as a line. Their reunion leads Hastings to recall his first meeting at Styles with Poirot, whom he had first met in Belgium. But Styles is no longer what it was in the first years of the 20th century, and one might also feel Poirot himself is no longer the detective we met in his first mystery. Poirot's famous "Watson," Captain Arthur Hastings, is also not quite the same man either.

In mourning for his wife, Hastings feels strongly that he has reached the end of the road, with his life behind him rather than ahead of him. As a result of the murder decades ago, Styles has also become, it is suggested, a place of regrets that would naturally somehow summon Christie's final twisted mastermind to its chambers, drawing in consequence Poirot and his most well-known biographer and helpmeet. But although Hastings is always identified as Poirot's "Watson," he appeared in only eight of Christie's novels; this novel marks his final appearance, even though Christie will go on to write more Hercule Poirot mysteries until she publishes the final *Curtain*. Hastings returns in no postwar Poirot novels, as if writing this novel during the war somehow led Christie herself to a turning point in which she no longer cared to have Poirot accompanied by his old friend—or as if in the new era after the war, a new Hastings-free Poirot also needed to emerge. It may be, however, that Christie may have taken the long view, electing to save Hastings to convincingly involve him, as we will see, in a series of surprise changes to a life that somehow had ground to a halt; until then he is placed in storage.

Despite Hastings's often mechanical and purely narrative role, the small number of Poirot's cases in which he is involved contain certain idiosyncrasies. In *Thirteen at Dinner* (1933) the person who hires Poirot turns out to be the culprit. In *Dumb Witness* (1937) the person who hires Poirot dies. There is, adjacent to Hastings, a certain instability of criminal and victim, guilty and innocent, which his stolid and unflappable status as on the right side of the law does not instance, but somehow solicits. This becomes even more true in *Curtain*, where Poirot not only becomes the criminal but also confides his crime to Hastings. Hastings, predictable in himself, generates unpredictability.

And indeed, this novel does put Hastings in unexpected situations. Although Hastings is always portrayed as the upright British gentleman, here he behaves unexpectedly by attempting to commit murder himself. He has been worked into a frenzy about his daughter Judith's seeming relationship with the rakish Major Allerton, encouraged to do so by a nondescript and colorless fellow guest Stephen Norton, who is the mastermind Poirot is seeking to detect. Hastings is desperate to rescue Judith from the caddish Major, feverishly planning to poison him. As a result of a sleeping potion Poirot has secretly introduced into his evening hot chocolate, Hastings falls asleep before he can execute his crime, but when he guiltily confesses his plan to Poirot later, Poirot's response is to point out that there are circumstances under which even the decent Hastings would not be above an attempted murder.

And indeed, this is the premise for the entire novel. Christie's mysteries do give us characters all of whom are deemed capable of murder, but here the potential murderers especially appear to undergo a surprising transformation of character to be capable of such an act. For instance, Hastings seems to become another person, as if undergoing a kind of dissociation in which an emerging unknown self is split off from the familiar one and prosecutes its own agenda.

Although Poirot prevents Hastings from carrying out the murder of Allerton, it is Poirot who later suggests to Hastings that he has been the agent of the death of another guest at Styles, the invalid Barbara Franklin. Hastings had unwittingly turned a table around in a way that led Barbara to drink the poisoned coffee cup she had intended for her husband John. This means our previously above-reproach Hastings has first planned a murder, and then, in another instance, accidentally facilitated one. The way Hastings is now associated with causing or wishing to cause death can be said to be a preparation for the even more shocking murder that Poirot himself commits. It is Poirot who murders the mastermind Stephen Norton, finally exposed as the character of "X" Poirot has been seeking. He arranges it so that it appears that "X" has once again caused a murder, which the reader knows means that, ironically, Norton has made himself his own victim. Norton has not been murdered by his own dark double, "X," but by our detective, who, interestingly, also commits the crime as another self, having taken on the appearance of his victim.

The murderous X, then, has been masquerading as the nondescript, colorless guest named Stephen Norton, but the criminal mastermind in this mystery does not actually murder anyone. He leads others to murder using emotional or cognitive manipulation. A classic serial killer, his method is one that completely defeats Poirot—there is no way Poirot can prove that it was Norton's power of persuasion that led various figures to act as his murderous proxy. Norton is a prime example of the way a powerful, coercive intelligence would be able to cloud the mind of his chosen victim, persuading his surrogate subliminally to commit murder. When the ability to operate by proxy is introduced, the sheer field of possibilities for motive and behavior multiplies vertiginously.

An early example of this is when the character Elizabeth Cole points to the strange story of her sister, who murders their tyrannical invalid father. She says that the idea that her sister Maggie would murder her father is "inconceivable—unbelievable. I know that she went to the police, that she gave herself up, that she confessed. But I still sometimes can't believe it! I feel somehow that it wasn't true—that it didn't—that it could have happened like she said it did. It just wasn't *Maggie*" (88). As Norton has persuaded Maggie to behave in a way that was not herself, so he similarly can influence the owner of Styles, Colonel Toby Luttrell, to such an extent that, after quarreling with his wife, he attempts to shoot her after he has psychologically demoted or dehumanized her to the status of a rabbit. Poirot speculates that Norton had the amazing ability to penetrate the concealed thoughts or wishes of the people around him and could then select those vulnerable to his homicidal insinuations.

Although what Norton said might seem insignificant, they were words that would have spoken to impulses Luttrell was concealing even from himself. Norton's conversation sends a hidden message that has been unconsciously received by Luttrell, or by the dark side of Luttrell's psyche. That Norton's words insinuate themselves into the inner life of Luttrell may express Christie's anxiety that her mysteries might indeed provoke homicidal copycats out in the world—her words also find their way into the inner lives of her readers. This kinship between Norton and the author is a good example of aspects of Christie's work that are "not supposed to be there," but points once again to that transgressive layer of Christie's writing—a transgressive layer that is demonstrated in more ways than one in this, Poirot's last case.

One can see in Norton some of the same bullying we saw in villainous masterminds such as Nevile Strange in *Towards Zero*, and Franklin Clarke in *The ABC Murders*. But as was true with the bullying Judge Wargrave (whose sense of justice and indifference to life is almost a midpoint between Poirot and Norton in *Curtain*) these villains did not outsource their crimes. As Poirot says, although Norton himself did nothing, he could make people do things they didn't want to do—as Poirot quickly amends, he could make people do things they thought they did not want to do.

Norton's weapon of choice, then, is psychology—reading the thoughts or wishes of the people around him, he can then select those vulnerable to subtle suggestions. Norton can subtly break down a stressed or fragile figure's ordinary resistance, so that out-of-character desperate steps are taken. Christie introduces the cautionary lines by the poet William Cowper in which the poet warns of taking desperate steps, since "the darkest day, live till tomorrow, will have passed away" (141) as an example of the way time will helpfully attenuate a dire state of consciousness. But Norton, creates such a sense of urgency and anxiety that any possibility of sleeping on it is eliminated.

Norton's immense psychological power is a given. Although a seemingly weak and recessive man, he can nevertheless put a strange psychological pressure on others, so that his murderous impulses surface inside the consciousness of his chosen target. The colorlessness of Norton is significant in this regard because the colorlessness is remarkable—he appears harmless, recessive, even a cipher. He is not like Christie's charismatic masterminds, but closer to someone like the serial killer Yahmose in *Death Comes as the End*. Yahmose also has an overbearing parent who limited his sense of autonomy and initiative, and similarly presented a "he-wouldn't-hurt-a-fly" persona—but he dissociates from his familiar bland and inhibited identity, compensating for it through his secret crimes.

It is perhaps significant in this regard that Poirot has just come back from Egypt as *Curtain* begins. A sense of emasculation or attenuated masculinity we associate with Yahmose can also be found in Norton. The blowhard Boyd Carrington, the self-absorbed researcher Franklin, and the sexually manipulative Allerton are all very traditional models of masculinity. But others in the novel are more like the inconspicuous Norton. The genteel Hastings and the vain and cerebral Poirot are also all outside this circle of trite masculinity, and Poirot and Norton are likened by both being short of stature and thus not conforming to associations of masculinity using height.

The name "Allerton" was previously used in *Death on the Nile*, which in that novel had pertained to a pusillanimous mama's boy, but in *Curtain*'s spectrum of masculinities becomes the name of the macho Lothario Hastings loathes. On the other hand, Norton presents as a mild-mannered, intellectual—a birdwatcher, not a man of might or war. He, too, represents a revised model of masculinity personified by Poirot, even as the moral polarities divide them.

Another possibility, however, is that Norton's persona does not truly reflect his identity—that his presenting self is not an alter ego, but a brilliant disguise, enabling him to enjoy what he likes best, which is to invade the psychic space of the vulnerable. Unlike the other murderers in Christie's mysteries, Norton deploys proxies—but unlike Norton, these proxies later feel regret or guilt. Norton can feel his hands are clean—any accusations against him would not be considered actual evidence. It is essential, then, for Norton to secure his own innocence, to eliminate any possibility of convicting him—a lawyer, for instance could place Norton's conversation with his victims within the context of free speech. Added to this frustration is our understanding that he finds the crimes he arranged as gratifying as did the sadistic Justice Wargrave. Indeed, just as Christie assigned the "mark of Cain" to Wargrave in *And Then There Were None*, so she assigns that mark to Norton as well.

Is it possible for Norton to have such control over the minds of others that they will commit murder? Christie does suggest that Norton cannot have influenced anyone who was truly innocent of a dark side—but then in Christie's view, there is no such person. But she does tell us that Norton must select a stressed or otherwise fragile psyche, people who are already not quite in their right minds. In other words, there must first be some breaking down of resistances and reservations before he can, almost like a hypnotist, implant his own ideas. In that regard, Norton could not choose just anyone. There are certain people he understands are easier to seduce, entice, or tempt—ripe for the picking, as it were.

It is as if Norton has put his victim under his spell, but hypnotism is not quite the word for it—it is more of a psychological invasion or violation; as Poirot says, "It was something more insidious, more deadly. It was a marshalling of the forces of a human being to widen a breach instead of repairing it. It called on the best in a man and set it in alliance with the worse" (217). This suggests that Norton tactic is to take advantage of a victim's wish to do good and align it to aggressive impulses—which means that both Norton and his surrogate have found a way to secure innocence while practicing criminality. Another way is saying this is that Norton can take a victim's aggressive impulses and attach it to some manner of benevolent rationale.

Christie advances this idea not simply through Norton, but through her story of Hastings' daughter Judith and her love affair with the scientist for whom she works, Dr. John Franklin. It is this that make Judith a suspect in the death of Franklin's wife, Barbara. But Christie assigns more than a personal motive for Judith's interest in getting rid of Franklin's invalid wife; Judith has aligned herself with a philosophical justification for hastening the deaths of the old or the ailing. It is Judith who first articulates this philosophy, but eventually we learn this is also the view of Franklin as well, who tells Poirot: "Lots of people I'd like to kill" said Dr. Franklin cheerfully. "Don't believe my conscience would keep me awake at night afterwards. It's an idea of mine, you know, that about eighty percent of the human race ought to be eliminated. We'd get on much better without them" (60).

This ideology also makes the couple suspect in the death of Franklin's invalid wife Barbara. Judith's eugenic philosophy is one she believes to be a component of her affiliation with modern, progressive science; it is what she believes all the best people believe. The issue was likely on Christie's mind because she was writing this novel during the Second World War. Dr. Franklin here is cheerfully articulating an idea that, at the time of Christie's writing of the novel, had found its way from theory to practice. During the period, the German government was given permission to cause the deaths of those deemed disabled or otherwise undesirable, a practice that, as with Judith's theories, was accompanied by utopian ideations.

Here, the eugenic philosophy is established as a false good, and as a pretext for unjustifiable aggression against those deemed expendable within the context of utilitarian premise. Today, "effective altruism," as discussed by such philosophers as Will MacAskill and Toby Ord, is seeking to advance a similar idea of "the good"—that is, a perspective that toggles between valuing the individual and suggesting that the end justifies the means by introducing the concept of a general good for the future of humanity.

This perspective is not far from what Poirot does when he kills because Norton has killed so many others and will continue to kill so many more through insinuation if unstopped. Poirot's altruism has effectively stopped a killer. But perhaps he has stopped there. There is no suggestion that he has also killed Norton because Norton stands in the way of a good new future for humanity as a whole—there are none of Judith and Franklin's utopian ideations in the crime Poirot commits. Norton himself, however, on one level represents the kind of psychology that can turn up in the political sphere, and indeed may have been inspired by the notorious demagogue of the 1930s and 1940s and his production of "good Germans." In this regard, even as Christie has lifted the novel deliberately out of its historical context, a 1940s-layer seethes beneath its more contemporary setting.

This issue of disposable people is a running theme throughout the novel—it is germane especially because so many people at Styles are not at their best. As Elizabeth Cole, whose life has been broken by her sister's Norton-induced murder of her father, puts it: "That's the depressing part of places like this. Guest houses run by broken-down gentle people. They're full of failures—of people who have never got anywhere and never will get anywhere, of people—who have been defeated and broken by life, of people who are old and tired and finished" (85).

Franklin and Judith suggest that in a better world guest houses such as Styles would no longer be necessary, the guests having been discreetly but summarily removed from the land of the living. That Judith herself found a permissive rationale that eliminated any guilt or anxiety does bring her into exactly the zone that the murderer Norton usually must work to create in his targets to predispose them to murder.

Judith's strong, young modernity becomes a justification for dispensing with those who are deemed of little utility, although her sense of certainty about her status as a modern, progressive woman is here interestingly depicted as a weakness, leaving her vulnerable to influencers such as Norton. Judith is led to consider murdering Barbara when Norton suggests that she did not have the courage to turn theory into action. Barbara is deemed useless mainly because she is an obstacle to Judith's romance with Franklin; Judith's high-minded principles are fueled by her desire to eliminate a personal inconvenience. Norton immediately sees he can use her theories to goad her into action: "He played very cleverly on the theme of useless lives. It was an article of faith with Judith—and the fact that her secret desires were in accordance with it was a fact that she ignored patiently while Norton knew it to be an ally. He was very clever about it—taking himself the opposite point of view, gently ridiculing the idea that she would ever have the nerve to do such a decisive action" (221).

Just as he managed to enhance the self-esteem of Hastings by suggesting that getting rid of Allerton would be what a good, protective father should do, Norton subtly weakens Judith's self-esteem by insinuating that she does not have the courage to act on her beliefs. He then flatters her, stressing the nobility of her intentions by comparing her to the biblical Judith who was capable of heroically saving her city from Assyrian siege by beheading General Holofernes. In this way he reshapes Judith's homicidal impulses so that they appear noble.

Whether it is through lowering or raising Judith's self-esteem, Norton is putting Judith into a state of mind in which she is more likely to want to prove herself a heroine. The Shakespearean character of Iago is deployed to understand more clearly Norton's capacity to influence. Interestingly, in both of Christie's last-published books a Jacobean play (as *Othello* was written in the reign of King James I) plays a key role not just in the allusive frame of the text but in understanding the nature of the crime and the criminal. *Sleeping Murder* deploys John Webster's *The Duchess of Malfi*, but it is the play *Othello* that becomes a way to interpret Elizabeth Cole's sister Maggie, Hastings, and Judith. Hastings in particular quotes Iago's line about the "green eyed monster" to his daughter Judith, who is already been overwhelmed with a volley of quotations about jealousy, or what Heta Pyrhönen calls "envious desire" (200), in a way that appears to be not simply a happenstance of a crossword puzzle the guests are working on. Hastings is suggesting that Norton reaches into the dark side of his victims, who are misled and manipulated by what Samuel Taylor Coleridge described as the motiveless malignity of our modern Iago.

The other major reference that creates both a clue and a resonant psychological context is through the 1915 play that might have seemed passé in the 1940s, but by the 1970s is possibly pleasingly recherché and thereby refreshing. Christie was almost daring her reader to see her as outdated by putting in a reference that was old-fashioned even in the early 1940s, but later can be said to be so old as to become new again, much like the hippie Peacock in *Third Girl* looking like a Van Dyck portrait.

The play by the Irish playwright St. John Greer Ervine is called *John Ferguson*, whose title character contravenes his own moral code to become a murderer. This second literary reference refers not to the figure of Norton, but to his victims—the decent people who are driven to commit or consider committing an unthinkable crime. These two literary references also speak to the instability of the categories of innocence and guilt, in which those who are innocent shade into the category of the guilty, and those who are guilty can secure an innocence that protects them from punishment—for instance, as Franklin suggests, moral indignation or sanctimony can lead a murderer to feel innocent of any crime.

It is here that Christie deploys the African image of the Calabar or "ordeal" (59) bean to bring home this point. The poison from this bean kills Barbara Franklin, but we also learn that the people of Old Calabar in Africa decided guilt and innocence through a suspect's ability to signal innocence by surviving ingestion of the poisoned bean. The unreliability of the bean as an actual way to tell guilt from innocence also becomes an inspired metaphor for the way so many of the characters in *Curtain* also have an unstable and insecure relationship to innocence and guilt.

The issue here is the accountability of both Norton and his victims. One might conclude that although Norton is innocent of committing any crime, he is responsible for inspiring and inciting the act; the actual murderer has been pushed to the edge of sanity by the mastermind. On the other hand, the actual murderer, it is suggested, must nevertheless assume responsibility for motive, method, and opportunity.

Although Barbara Franklin was also inspired to murder, her attempt to murder her husband John Franklin is *not* a choice influenced by Stephen Norton. Barbara's death, which occurs when Hastings swerves the bookshelf around so that she herself takes the poison intended for her husband, is not a Norton Murder. Instead of being a crime inspired by X, the motive is Boyd Carrington, an old friend of Barbara's family, who turns up at Styles and rekindles Barbara's interest in him. Her desire to make herself more

12. No More Murders

eligible for Carrington is motivated in part by the desire of the heart but is also inspired by her ambition. The prospect of marriage to the wealthy Carrington is sufficient motive for Barbara to try to murder her husband—it is not as if everyone needs a Norton to push them over the edge.

This means we do have one character in the story whose homicidal ideations have not been provoked by X. Poirot in his posthumous letter to Hastings almost implies that the poisonous Calabar bean, through some mysterious agency of its own, has not acted to serve Barbara's purposes, but instead has acted in such a way as to kill the guilty wife and protect the innocent husband. Ruled out as well is the possibility that Norton could have somehow, out of a pang of conscience, influenced Poirot to kill him; Poirot's murder of Norton is more out of the logic of the Calabar bean than of murder by persuasion.

Norton does interfere with the plan of the Calabar bean by insinuating that what he has seen through his binoculars could implicate Franklin and Judith as murderers of Barbara, requiring Poirot to testify at the inquest in a way that will lift suspicion off the young couple. This is a good example of the way that, although this is a mystery about a serial killer, there are *no* serial murders in *Curtain*. Poirot is there because of five previous serial murders which have led him to Styles and Norton. There is one attempted murder in which Luttrell, somewhat comically, only manages to wing his wife; and there is one comedy of errors in which the murderess Mrs. Franklin ends up killing herself instead. It is the third murder of Norton by Hercule Poirot that is this novel's only true murder. This murder, however, is staged as a suicide, and to everyone but Poirot and Hastings this is what the world will believe. Similarly, Hastings' role in the death of Barbara Franklin is something only Poirot and Hastings know—the world will believe it was a suicide.

Poirot's actual assumption of the identity of X in *Curtain* can call to mind other times in which he has also formed an intimate bond with his prime suspect, such as his bond with Dr. Sheppard in *The Murder of Roger Ackroyd* or Henrietta in *The Hollow*, Mrs. Hubbard in *Murder on the Orient Express*, or Jacqueline de Bellefort in *Death on the Nile*. These four books, along with *And Then They Were None*, alluded to by mention of the mark of Cain, and *The ABC Murders*, explicitly mentioned in the book, are the major previous Poirot novels referenced in the novel.

Curtain clearly aspires to be in a superleague of memorable Poirot novels. Unlike more routine cases assayed by Poirot in mysteries such as *Death in the Air* or *Lord Edgware Dies*, the innovation here caps the implied sequence of Christie's truly memorable fictions the jewel in the crown in Christie's lineage of extraordinary criminals—Poirot himself is the murderer.

But unlike Norton, Poirot compares himself to a reluctant Hamlet, and, unlike Norton, Poirot owns his murder. This novel, like *Towards Zero*, did not begin with a murder, but set up the expectation of one, an expectation fulfilled in this case not by the criminal but by the detective.

Previously, when the murderer had been identified, Poirot might pass the execution of a murderer on to the authorities, or allow the murderer to take things into his own hands, but here Poirot faces Norton directly, confronts him with what he knows, tells him ahead of time that he is going to shoot him, does just that, and then arranges it to look like a suicide. Once again, hot chocolate plays a part, a cozy touch that also reminds us of the considerate way Poirot murders Norton by first putting him under the influence of sleeping pills. After confronting Norton and giving him the hot chocolate, he returns to his room to disguise himself as Norton, and, as such, shoots his double with characteristic fussy accuracy in the middle of his forehead. The disguise of Poirot when murdering Norton is the one episode that echoes *The Mysterious Affair at Styles*, which depicts a mix-up involving the disguise of a black beard used by the real murderer. The doubling through disguise of the murderer and his cousin is here replicated as the doubling through disguise of the murderer and the detective.

The doubling of one brother for another is here replicated as the doubling of the detective and the murderer. The murderer Norton becomes the victim—although, ironically, he has driven Poirot to kill him for the purposes of effective altruism, as if he has been caught in his own trap. Yet another message of this murder is that Hastings is made to realize that, although elderly, Poirot is still spry enough to execute this plan. Poirot has been pretending infirmity, fulfilling as if a performance of a stereotypical senescence, when in reality he is still at the top of his game. Hastings enables this senescent disguise, lamenting the way his life also has been reduced to "gray heads, gray hearts, gray dreams" (86).

But it is the oldest person at Styles who saves the day. That Poirot is the oldest detective in literary history speaks to the way Christie has deliberately and from the start made his old age his advantage, his superpower, his crowning glory. Once again, Christie is celebrating the value of the elderly here—that Poirot is in decline should rule him out, but it is a very old man who not only committed the crime, but it is also a very old man who prevented future crimes on the part of a very clever killer.

On one level, Norton is a unique sociopath, someone who murders by inciting people to commit other murders, and thus multiplies the effectiveness of murder by harming not just the victim but the person he also victimizes by maneuvering his target to take another's life. But on another level, the latent potential of everybody to murder is evident in the novel. Even Luttrell, the least suspicious person in the novel, shoots his wife, albeit in a gray "accidentally on purpose" area. His name, the most unusual in the novel, has a suggestion of the French lutte, or struggle, and indeed Luttrell does struggle with the meaning of his action after the fact, and is one example of the way everybody in *Curtain* is implicated in one death wish or another.

Hastings, like Dr. Sheppard, appears above suspicion; he not only wants to kill Allerton, but also he is almost persuaded by Norton to do so. By concentrating on the idea of what R.A. York calls "indirect persuasion to murder," she spotlights the latent potential to kill in anyone (165). And here, as is typical of Christie, there are continuities between murder and ordinary life, as shown, for example in how Norton, by interfering in the lives of others, is a malevolent version of Jane Austen's Emma, and Barbara Franklin a literalized version of Rosamund Vincy in *Middlemarch*, who is not only disappointed in her research-obsessed scientific spouse, but who also wants to murder him.

There are occasions when everybody has wished someone dead; if Norton's mind to murder, his demonic persuasion, can do the deed, how firm is the boundary between any latent idea and the manifest act? Norton is spectacularly, discernibly evil, and yet is also one of us. Norton comes close to a variation on *Murder on the Orient Express*—not "they all did it," but "we all did it" or "could have done it." Norton is a dangerous murderer; he is also ordinary, and it is that sense of the ordinary that is so much an ingredient in Christie's mysteries. Furthermore, as Norton influences his victims, the novelist herself is exercising an influence on the reader through sympathy and persuasion. Like Norton and his victims, a novelist operates on her readers by inference, suggestion, and readiness to be persuaded.

But that Poirot's only recourse was to take the law into his own hands can introduce the possibility that Poirot's last case is his first failure. One can find echoes of *Murder on the Orient Express* here, with Poirot acting—in the wake of the failure of the system to bring a murderer to justice—as detective, judge, and executioner. There are also echoes of *The Murder of Roger Ackroyd*, especially in our feeling tricked by the revelation that Poirot was the murderer of Norton. Readers had built such trust in Poirot over many years that there is a certain sense of betrayal that accompanies this revelation. This outcome is also a plot twist that must conclude Poirot's career, since he can never again be above suspicion—there is no going back to his previous identity as the trusted detective.

We can also see Poirot's last case as a triumph, in that he did stop a serial killer from continuing to ruin more lives. In a court of law, this would be deemed justifiable homicide—that is, a homicide justified if it prevents harm to innocent people. This is, logically, the right thing to do, especially in the context of solving the puzzle satisfactorily, but at the same time, the ending of this novel is a very emotional one—murder in Christie is never simply logical. Norton represents something toxic, something poisonous, and this is what gives Poirot a motive that goes deeper than reason.

Similarly, Christie concludes this novel with a depiction of a Poirot who is no longer the confident egotist he appeared to be in the early mysteries—instead, he confides in Hastings that he has doubts about everything he has done, including allowing himself to die through the refusal of his medication. It is Poirot's own wavering that brings ambiguity instead of clarity to the solution of the mystery and opens it to a variety of interpretations. In this regard, as R.A. York has noted, the conventions of the mystery genre compete with Christie's ingenuity, leading to a narrative that "overrides the distinction of genre fiction and literary" (York 165).

One example of Christie's ingenuity is the way Poirot's letter to Hastings permits Christie to draw us into the inner life of Poirot to make his guilty conscience central to the interpretation of the ending. Poirot's conscience is what differentiates him from Norton or even Judith. Norton and Judith will find justifications that allow murder in good conscience, free of Poirot's feelings of doubt and guilt. Poirot does entertain this idea—as he points out, a just cause permits violence, and becomes not a guilty deed, but an innocent one. Looking at it this way, Poirot's murder can be said to send him out in a blaze of glory, but Poirot does once again ask us to question the justice and morality, and once again does not resolve these issues with any clarity.

Poirot sacrifices his own peace of mind for the sake of hindering Norton, introducing doubt and self-doubt into his inner life in an unexpected way. He cannot be sure he has done the right thing. Poirot also allows himself to die, something that appears to be a consequence of his murder of Norton. In refusing medication and letting nature take its course, it is almost as if a penitential Poirot is leveling the death penalty against himself. Like the question of innocence or guilt, this is left ambiguous.

Christie has often been described as writing mysteries of crime and detection in which everything is satisfactorily resolved. This is not actually the case in any of her novels, which can often end in a deliberately untidy way, but here the crime and Poirot himself are especially complex, the mood at the end pensive and elegiac. The reader also is encouraged to move into a more contemplative frame of mind, especially as Poirot's old age is now absolutely in evidence in a way that has never been so before. His age and illness tell us that nature has taken its course and that it is time for him to go. His is a gentle death rather than a spectacular superhero one, which readers who have grown fond of Poirot would likely appreciate.

12. No More Murders

He has not been cruelly struck down while in peak condition—we see that his hair is truly gray, and that, while not as impaired as he has pretended to be, he nevertheless is now in the winter of his years. This is how life goes, and perhaps readers who have bonded with Poirot will understand that his death cannot as a result be considered a tragedy.

To bring Poirot back to Styles for his last case creates a sense of an unbroken psychological circle that contains all his investigations. But while the doubling of the setting of Styles creates a certain elegance, the actual narratives are more likely to mirror *The Murder of Roger Ackroyd* and *Murder on the Orient Express*. Poirot commits the same sort of vigilantist murder for which he has pardoned the composite criminal conspirators in *Murder on the Orient Express*, and for similar reasons—to facilitate extralegal justice in a situation the law cannot reach. The relation to *The Murder of Roger Ackroyd* is a bit more complicated. There, the narrator Sheppard is the one person we would never suspect of murder; by the time of *Curtain*, however, we are aware that Poirot has not played by the rules in earlier mysteries.

In *The Murder of Roger Ackroyd*, he persuades Dr. Sheppard to die by suicide. Poirot bends the rules in subsequent mysteries: in *The Hollow*, he rearranges the teacups so that Gerda will die by the poison she had meant for her friend Henrietta. In *Murder on the Orient Express*, Poirot can be said to be complicit in the collective murder of somebody who deserves death. Even if he had not shot anyone before *Curtain*, he had brought about the death of earlier criminals much as he does with Norton. In *Curtain*, he does it through overt action; in the other cases he has done so tacitly or with greater subtlety.

Poirot kills and dies; Hastings does not kill and lives. Poirot dies childless, but Hastings not only has children but also will remarry. Hastings, the cipher, the bland Sancho Panza to Poirot's rococo Don Quixote, is the ultimate survivor, and in *Curtain* Hastings almost becomes not just a Watson figure but a more modernist first-person writer, a narrator like Marlow or Nick Carraway, whose story addresses the moral flaws of someone he would have liked to present to his audience as uncomplicatedly heroic.

Hastings' marriage to Elizabeth Cole becomes the ultimate vehicle of what might be called Poirot's manipulative beneficence. Removing Captain Hastings from all further mysteries and saving him for last can be said to bring back the old days, the days that began with Styles, and had appeared to have ended for good. The series reader will have forgotten about Hastings or dismissed him as a relic of the past—that Christie no longer needed a Watson figure to explain Poirot. Christie has strategically held Hastings back as Poirot's original "Watson," whose reunion with Poirot allows him to contemplate their first case at Styles, setting up *Curtain* as an ending that can stand as a full circle. Christie has also this time made Hastings a suspect with his own narrative arc, a story that detaches from Poirot's. It is as if Christie had decided to save Hastings as another of the surprises she has arranged for this spectacular finale.

For there to be an effective final Poirot novel, however, the entire series of Poirot novels must be excellent, must have kept faith with its own original intentions, and must have confirmed Christie's sustained capacity for invention. Late novels such as *Third Girl* show Poirot in near-prime form, as indeed do many earlier novels from the 1940s and 1950s. *Curtain* then becomes become a topping completion of a long and Shakespearean oeuvre. It is as if in this novel Poirot has broken his staff and buried it certain fathoms in the earth, as did Prospero when he rang down his own curtain on the stage of his world in *The Tempest*. But perhaps the final word belongs to *Hamlet*, from which we can repurpose the line, "we will have no more marriages." Instead, we can say that, with this last Poirot novel, "we will have no more murders."

Chapter References

Christie, Agatha. *Curtain* (New York: Dodd, Mead, 1975).
Coleridge, Samuel Taylor. *Literary Remains*, Volume 2. Accessed March 10, 2024, Project Gutenberg, https://www.gutenberg.org/ebooks/8533.
Conan Doyle, Arthur. *The Adventure of the Empty House*. https://bakerstreet.fandom.com/wiki/Story_Text:_The_Adventure_of_the_Empty_House.
Curran, John. *Agatha Christie's Secret Notebooks: Fifty Years of Mystery in the Making* (London: HarperCollins, 2019).
MacAskill, Will. *Effective Altruism: How Doing Good Better Can Help You Make a Difference* (New York: Gotham, 2015).
Moretti, Franco. *Distant Reading* (London: Verso, 2013).
Ord, Toby. *The Precipice: Existential Risk and the Future of Humanity* (New York: Hachette, 2020).
Pyrhönen, Heta. *Mayhem and Murder: Narrative and Moral Issues in the Detective Story* (Toronto Studies in Semiotics and Communication) (Toronto: University of Toronto Press, Scholarly Publishing Division, 1999).
Rolls, Alastair. *Agatha Christie and New Directions in Reading Narrative Fiction* (New York: Routledge, 2022).
Shakespeare, William. *Hamlet*. https://www.folger.edu/explore/shakespeares-works/hamlet/read/3/1/.
York, R.A. *Agatha Christie: Power and Illusion* (New York: Palgrave Macmillan, 2007).

Bibliography

Aldridge, Mark. *Agatha Christie's Marple: Expert on Mysteries* (London: HarperCollins, 2024).
Aldridge, Mark. *Agatha Christie's Poirot: The Greatest Detective in The World* (London: HarperCollins, 2021).
Alewyn, Richard. "The Origin of the Detective Novel." In Glenn Most and William W. Stowe, eds., *The Poetics of Murder: Detective Fiction and Literary Theory* (New York: Harcourt Brace, 1983), 62-78.
Arnold, Jane. "Detecting Social History: Jews in the Works of Agatha Christie." *Jewish Social Studies*, vol. 49, no. 3/4, Summer-Autumn 1987, pp. 275-282.
Bargainnier, Earl F. *The Gentle Art of Murder: The Detective Fiction of Agatha Christie* (Bowling Green, OH: Popular Press, 1980).
Barnard, Robert. *A Talent to Deceive: An Appreciation of Agatha Christie* (New York: Dodd, Mead, 1980).
Baučekova, Silvia Rosivalova. "The Salt of the Earth or the Murderess: The Problem of Femininity in the Novels of Agatha Christie." *Prague Journal of English Studies*, vol. 10, no. 1, 2021, pp. 7-22.
Bayard, Pierre. *Who Killed Roger Ackroyd: The Mystery Behind the Agatha Christie Mystery* (New York: New Press, 2001).
Bernthal, J.C. *Agatha Christie: A Companion to the Mystery Fiction* (Jefferson: McFarland, 2022).
Bernthal, J.C. *Queering Agatha Christie: Revisiting the Golden Age of Detective Fiction* (London: Palgrave Macmillan, 2015).
Bernthal, J.C., ed. *The Ageless Agatha Christie: Essays on the Mysteries and the Legacy* (Jefferson: McFarland, 2016).
Bernthal, J.C., and Mary Anna Evans, eds. *The Bloomsbury Handbook to Agatha Christie* (London: Bloomsbury, 2022).
Birns, Margaret Boe. "Agatha Christie's Portrait of the Artist." *Clues: A Journal of Detection*, vol. 1, no. 2, 1980, pp. 31-34.
Birns, Nicholas, and Margaret Boe Birns. "Agatha Christie: Modern and Modernist," in Ronald G. Walker and June Frazer, eds., *The Cunning Craft: Original Essays on Detective Fiction* (Essays in Literature) (Macomb: Western Illinois University, 1990).
Birns, Nicholas, and Margaret Boe Birns. "Detective Fiction and the Prose of Everyday Life: Agatha Christie, Margery Allingham, Ngaio Marsh, and Gladys Mitchell in the 1950s," in Nick Bentley, Alice Ferrebe, and Nick Hubble, eds., *The 1950s: A Decade of Modern British Fiction* (London: Bloomsbury, 2018), pp. 205-234.
Cawelti, John G. "The New Mythology of Crime." *Boundary 2*, vol. 3, no. 2, 1975, pp. 324-57.
Clanton, Dan W., Jr. *God and the Little Grey Cells: Religion in Agatha Christie's Hercule Poirot Stories* (London: T.T. Clark/Bloomsbury, 2024).
Curran, John. *Agatha Christie: Murder in the Making: More Stories and Secrets from Her Archives* (London: HarperCollins, 2011).
Gildersleeve, Jessica. "Commemorating Forgetting: 1922 and Golden Age Detective Fiction."

Modernism/Modernity, December 15, 2022, https://modernismmodernity.org/forums/posts/gildersleeve-commemorating-forgetting-1922-golden-age-detective-fiction.

Gildersleeve, Jessica. "Nowadays: Trauma and Modernity in Agatha Christie's Late Poirot novels." *Clues: A Journal of Detection*, vol. 31, no. 1, 2016.

Gill, Gillian. *Agatha Christie: The Woman and Her Mysteries* (New York: The Free Press, 1990).

Green, Julius. *Agatha Christie: A Life in Theater* (London: HarperCollins, 2015).

Grella, George. "Murder and Manners: The Formal Detective Novel." *Novel: A Forum on Fiction*, vol. 4, no. 1, 1970, pp. 30–48.

Gulddal, Jesper. "'That deep underground savage instinct': Narratives of Sacrifice and Retribution in Agatha Christie's *Appointment with Death*." *Textual Practice*, vol. 34, no. 11, 2019, pp. 1803–1821.

Hoffman, Megan. *Gender and Representation in British "Golden Age" Crime Fiction* (London: Palgrave, 2016).

Knepper, Marty S. "Contemporary Cozy Mysteries, Agatha Christie and the 1990s: Six Steps Towards a Definition," in Phyllis M. Betz, ed., *Reading the Cozy Mystery: Critical Essays on an Underappreciated Subgenre* (Jefferson: McFarland, 2021).

Knight, Stephen. *Secrets of Crime Fiction Classics: Detecting the Delights of 21 Enduring Stories* (Jefferson, NC: McFarland, 2014).

Lassner, Phyllis. "The Mysterious New Empire: Agatha Christie's Colonial Murders," in Robin Hackett, Freda Hauser and Gay Wachman, eds., *At Home and Abroad in the Empire: British Women Write the 1930s* (Newark: University of Delaware Press, 2009), pp. 31–50.

Light, Alison. *Forever England: Femininity, Literature and Conservatism Between the Wars* (London: Routledge, 1991).

Makinen, Merja. "Agatha Christie (1890–1976)," in Charles J. Rzepka and Lee Horsley, eds., *A Companion to Crime Fiction* (Chichester: Blackwell, 2010), pp. 415–26.

Mills, Rebecca, and J.C. Bernthal. *Agatha Christie Goes to War* (New York: Routledge, 2019).

Most, Glenn W., and William W. Stowe, eds, *The Poetics of Murder: Detective Fiction and Literary Theory* (New York: Harcourt Brace, 1983).

Munt, Sally. *Murder by the Book? Feminism and the Crime Novel* (New York: Routledge, 1994).

Panek, LeRoy Lad. *Watteau's Shepherds: The Detective Novel in Britain 1914–1940* (Bowling Green, OH: Popular Press, 1979).

Plain, Gill. *Sacrificial Bodies: The Corporeal Anxieties of Agatha Christie* (London: Routledge, 2001).

Prideaux, Desirée, *Sleuthing Miss Marple: Gender, Genre, and Agency in Agatha Christie's Crime Fiction* (Liverpool: Liverpool University Press, 2022).

Priestman, Martin. *A Version of Pastoral, Detective Fiction and Literature: The Figure in the Carpet* (London: Palgrave Macmillan, 1990).

Pugh, Tison. *Understanding Agatha Christie* (Columbia: University of South Carolina Press, 2023).

Pyrhönen, Heta. *Mayhem and Murder: Narrative and Moral Issues in the Detective Story*. Toronto Studies in Semiotics and Communication (Toronto: University of Toronto Press, Scholarly Publishing Division, 1999).

Rezvin, I.I., and Julian Graffy. "Semiotic Analysis of Detective Novels: With Examples from the Novels of Agatha Christie." *New Literary History*, vol. 9, no. 2, 1978, pp. 385–388.

Riley, Dick, and Pam McAllister. *The Bedside, Bathtub & Armchair Companion to Agatha Christie* (New York: Workman, 1981).

Rolls, Alistair. *Agatha Christie and New Directions in Reading Narrative Fiction* (New York: Routledge, 2022).

Shaw, Marion, and Sabine Vanacker. *Reflecting on Miss Marple* (London: Routledge, 1991).

Slung, Michele. "Let's Hear it for Agatha Christie: A Feminist Appreciation," in Barbara A. Rader and Howard G. Zettler, eds., *The Sleuth and the Scholar* (Westport, CT: Greenwood, 1988), pp. 63–68.

Suh, Judy. "Rerouting Wartime Paranoia in Agatha Christie's *N or M?*" *Journal of Modern Literature*, vol. 46, no. 2, 2023, pp. 140–156.
Thompson, Laura. *Agatha Christie: An English Mystery* (London: Hodder Headline, 2007).
Worsley, Lucy. *Agatha Christie: An Elusive Woman* (London: Pegasus, 2022).
Yiannitsaros, Christopher. "Delicious Death: Criminal Cake in and Beyond Agatha Christie's *A Murder Is Announced.*" *Clues: A Journal of Detection*, vol. 39, no. 2, Fall 2021, pp. 107–118.
York, R.A. *Agatha Christie: Power and Illusion* (New York: Palgrave Macmillan, 2007).

Index

The ABC Murders 1, 9, 66, 70–85, 124, 136, 142, 201, 207, 244, 256
Africa 85, 90, 114, 181, 192, 197, 206
Akhnation 101–103
Aldridge, Mark 2, 37, 43, 45, 117, 160, 165, 173
Aleppo 55
Alewyn, Richard 56
Allingham, Margery 41, 71
America 56, 59, 61, 67, 90, 92, 129, 140, 158, 160, 173, 183, 197
And Then They Were None 108, 112, 121, 207
Anglicanism 93, 172, 191
Appointment with Death 101
archaeology 43, 104, 115, 172
architecture 180
Armbruster, Heidi 29
Arnold, Jane 28
art and artists 14, 39, 45, 133–38, 144, 149, 168, 180
At Bertram's Hotel 1, 16, 41, 132, 165–77, 182
Austen, Jane 112, 165, 209

Barnard, Robert 14, 107
Barzun, Jacques 276
Bayard, Pierre 5, 78, 29–31, 35
Belgium 11, 55, 161, 184, 199
Belgrade 56
Bennett, Arnold 188
Beresford, Tommy and Tuppence 86–91
Bernthal, J.C. 1–5, 9, 63
Betz, Phyllis M. 14, 166
The Bible 102–3, 173
The Body in the Library 14
Bolaño, Roberto 99
Booth, Wayne C. 21
Bright, Brittain 118
Brontë, Charlotte 165
Brooks, Peter 8
Byatt, A.S. 102
By The Pricking of My Thumbs 87–89, 91

Cards on the Table 123
Cat Among the Pigeons 196
Catton, Eleanor 17
Challis, Debbie 104
Chesterton, G.K. 13–4
children 13, 48, 83–4, 86, 107, 119, 133, 174–211
Christie, Agatha: autobiography 53, 111, 148; friendships 104; literary style 30; politics 197; sense of humor 10, 89; travels 55–6
Christie, Col. Archibald 103, 134
The Clocks 117, 196
close reading 2, 6–12, 16–127, 176, 196
coloniality and colonialism 22, 55, 103, 119, 188–9, 192, 197
Come, Tell Me How You Live 104–5
Conan Doyle, Arthur 21, 23–4, 42, 63
Conrad, Joseph 35
Cooper, James Fenimore 1
Cornwall 117, 193
country houses 66, 86, 131–2, 149, 199
Coward, Noël 140
cozy mystery 1, 14, 29, 167
criminality 44, 49, 51–2, 124, 181, 203
Crooked House 172
Cueva, Edmund P. 101
Curran, John 40, 102, 120, 128, 196
Curtain 1, 2, 15, 21, 119, 154, 184, 196–212

Death Comes at the End 1–2, 13, 101–15, 198, 202
Death on the Nile 103, 111, 141, 202, 207
Demoor, Marysa 11
Dickens, Charles 65
disguise 65, 95–6, 156, 160, 176, 190, 202, 208
distant reading 6, 196
Dostoyevsky, Fyodor 72
double bluff 38, 124
drugs 89, 186, 189–90

Index

Edwardian era 16, 46, 90, 132, 134, 140, 157, 166, 168–70, 174–7, 198–9
effective altruism 204
Egypt 2, 101–15, 202; under British colonial rule 103
Elephants Can Remember 164, 195–6, 198
Eliot, George 5, 13, 14, 152, 165
England 9–16, 22, 29, 38, 44, 57, 72–3, 86, 88, 90, 92, 94, 97–9, 111, 114, 132–4, 138–42, 158, 160, 162–3, 165–9, 179, 187–8, 192–4
espionage 83, 95, 191
European Union 90

Facebook 156
feminist presses 5
Flecker, James Elroy 133
Ford, Ford Madox 21
foreigners 90, 157, 192
France 55, 92–4
Freud, Sigmund 187
futurity 16, 30, 34, 43, 47, 68, 79, 93–4, 110, 114, 130, 143, 147, 166, 172, 176–7, 182, 194, 197–8, 204

Gaskell, Elizabeth 265
Germany 11, 90, 92–8, 114
Gildersleeve, Jessica 2, 91, 195
Gill, Gillian 4
Glanville, Stephen 104, 111
Gospodinov, Georgi 166
Grella, George 26
Guglielmi, Waltraud 104
Gulddal, Jesper 2, 7–8, 30, 60, 64, 101
Gunn, Battiscombe 102

Hallowe'en Party 87, 198
Hammett, Dashiell 89
Harrower, Elizabeth 187
Hastings, Capt. Arthur 21–3, 70–84, 197–209
Heaney, Seamus 129
Hercule Poirot's Christmas 66, 133
Hickory, Dickory Death 156, 197
historical memory 175
historical mystery 2, 101
The Hollow 1, 4, 13, 15, 107, 131–49, 152, 196, 198, 207, 211
Hope, Anthony 13
Hopkins, Gerard Manley 85
Hopkins, Lisa 104
Houellebecq, Michel 148
Humble, Nicola 4, 175
humdrum mystery 179

imperialism 56–8
injustice 49, 83, 123, 135

Instagram 156
Iraq and Mesopotamia 14, 44, 55, 58, 101, 103–4, 140
Ireland 27, 97, 137
irreverent reading 7

James, Henry 25, 131
Jews and Judaism 56, 58, 131, 149–40
Joyce, James 20
justice 11–12, 16, 17, 32, 35, 38, 48, 58, 60, 65–6, 83, 85, 118, 123, 135, 143–5, 173, 197, 201, 203, 209–11

Kermode, Sir Frank 5–6
Knepper, Marty S. 166
Knight, Stephen 6

law and lawyers 30, 64–6, 122, 172
lesbianism 9, 155, 159
Light, Alison 15, 177
Lockridge, Frances 89
Lockridge, Richard 89
London 41, 95, 131, 165–77, 183, 193–4
Lubbock, Percy 8

Macdonald, Ross 182
Maclaren-Ross, Julian 4
Macmillan, Harold (Earl of Stockton) 165
Makinen, Merja 4
Mallowan, Max 43–44, 58, 89, 103
The Man in the Brown Suit 22–3
Mann, Thomas 99
Mann, Klaus 99
Manning, Olivia 114
Marcus, Sharon 9
Marple, Miss Jane 14, 16, 30, 37–53, 86–92, 118–19, 151–77
Marx, Karl 142
Marx, Sina 102
Marxism 142
McNeill, Dougal 6
medicine and doctors 24, 48–9, 137, 198
Meredith, George 167
Middleton, Stanley 5
migrants 56, 152, 155–6, 158–9
modernism 20–1, 29, 66, 163, 167, 176, 186, 211
Monaghan, Elizabeth Michaelson 16
Montgomery, Gen. Bernard Law 114
Moretti, Franco 6
The Moving Finger 112
Mrs. McGinty's Dead 183
Murder at Hazelmoor 193
The Murder at the Vicarage 1, 9, 30, 37–53, 65, 77, 136, 172, 188
Murder in Mesopotamia 14, 43, 55, 58, 103, 140

A Murder Is Announced 1, 4, 9, 41, 52, 141, 151–64
Murder Is Easy 90–91
The Murder of Roger Ackroyd 1, 7, 9, 12, 19–35, 42, 46, 74, 207, 209, 211
Murder on the Links 21–23, 199
Murder on the Orient Express 1, 3, 7, 13, 15, 55–69, 70, 144, 207

N or M? 1, 86–99, 108, 196
narcissism 43, 123, 125
Nemesis 14, 47, 87, 165
Nesbit, E. 83
New Criticism 6
New Zealand 197
Ngai, Sianne 172
Nigeria 91
1920s 1, 8, 22–3, 89, 151
1930s 1, 55, 77
1940s 1, 13, 134, 142, 196, 197, 204, 206, 212
1950s 1, 4, 6, 134, 151, 157, 196, 212
1960s 1, 5, 40, 66, 88, 166, 172–5, 179–82, 188–9, 193, 196
1970s 1, 5, 197, 206

Oates, Joyce Carol 181
old age 22, 87, 174, 208, 210
Oliver, Ariadne 23, 87, 178–85, 189
An Overdose of Death 115, 196

The Pale Horse 7, 40
Palestine 102
Pamboukian, Sylvia A. 7–8
Partners in Crime 22, 86–9
Passenger to Frankfurt 12
Petrie, Sir William Flinders 104
Plain, Gill 2, 92
A Pocket Full of Rye 156
poetic justice 118
Poirot, Hercule 11–12, 15–35, 43–44, 55–64, 89–91, 106, 118–19, 121, 135–7, 140, 143–9, 158, 160, 179–209
Poland 157
police and policemen 52–3, 65, 67, 71, 76–7, 92, 119, 201
postcolonialism 192
Postern of Fate 86–91
postwar 9, 23, 56, 89, 137–8, 141, 168, 192, 197–8
Priestman, Martin 158
Proust, Marcel 20
psychiatry 44, 184–5, 194
Pugh, Tison 1, 4
puzzles 1, 7, 9–10, 12–13, 29, 38, 75, 77, 151–3, 155, 165, 173, 179, 188, 206, 210 252
Pyne, Parker 140
Pyrhönen, Heta 205

Queen, Ellery 71
Quin, Mr. 23

Rahman, Zia Haider 11
"The Regatta Mystery" 140
revenge 63, 66, 125, 189
Richardson, Samuel 27
Rolls, Alistair 2, 7–8, 30, 197–8
Rosenfeld, Colleen Ruth 8
Russian formalists 8

Sandbrook, Dominic 165
Satterthwaite, Mr. 23
Sayers, Dorothy L. 182
Schorer, Mark 8
Schulz, Kathryn 11
Scotland 126
The Secret Adversary 86–91
The Secret of Chimneys 191
serial killers 70–77, 81, 92, 200–2, 207, 209
serialization 173
The Seven Dials Mystery 13, 139
sexuality 63, 106
Shakespeare, William 28, 55, 94, 212
Sinuhe 106
Suh, Judy 97
surface reading 8–9
Swados, Harvey 5
Syria 55

Tey, Josephine 183
There Is a Tide 112
They Came to Baghdad 13, 43, 103
Third Girl 1, 76, 87–8, 112, 112, 136, 178–95, 198, 202, 206
Thompson, Laura 5, 104, 172
Tiglath-Pileser 151
Towards Zero 1, 4–5, 9, 13, 106, 115–30, 136, 144, 186, 201, 208
trauma 64, 72, 89, 156
Trollope, Anthony 1, 42
Türkiye 58

Van Dine, S.S. 101
Victorian Era 1, 5, 38, 40, 44, 46, 64, 88, 90, 104, 162, 174–5, 181, 187–8
Voždová, Maria 120

Waugh, Evelyn 131, 175
Webster, John 305
Wenamon 106
Westmacott, Mary 1, 4, 13–14, 23, 58, 180, 188; *Absent in the Spring* 58, *The Burden* 180; *Unfinished Portrait* 13
Wilkinson, Toby 197
Wilson, Edmund 176

Wilson, Harold (Lord Wilson of RIevalux) 165
Woolf, Virginia 77, 140, 163, 185
Woolley, Sir Leonard 43
World War I 174
World War II 86–99, 114, 132, 138
Worsley, Lucy 134, 179

xenophobia 70, 72, 90, 130, 160, 192
Yiannitsaros, Christopher 160
York, R.A. 4, 10, 209–10

www.ingramcontent.com/pod-product-compliance
Lightning Source LLC
Chambersburg PA
CBHW032041300426
44117CB00009B/1142